Globe-Trotting

Interesting Facts For Curious Minds

2011 Random Yet Amazing Trivia Discoveries about History, Science, Sports and Beyond

Fun Facts for Kids, Teens and Adults

The Curiosity Co.

Cover Design by Lordan Pinote

Interior Design by John Ruiz

Table of Contents

Table of Contents

Introduction

Did you know that Cleopatra spoke nine languages, or that there's a planet made entirely of diamonds?

How about finding out the longest English word in existence? Or being able to advise your friends that its actually illegal to chew gum, should they be visiting Singapore?

Imagine having a treasure trove of surprising, mind-blowing, and downright bizarre facts at your fingertips, ready to amaze friends and family. Whether you're looking to spark up some chit-chat, learn something new, or simply entertain yourself on a lazy afternoon, this book has you covered!

2011 Interesting Facts, spread out over 132 chapters and subsections. We designed it just so for you to read from cover to cover, reveling in all these curated, mind-blowing discoveries; Or you might just want to jump from the wild expanse of the animal kingdom, straight into another topic which catches your fancy! However way you wish to enjoy this book, you can be sure the journey through these 2011 pieces of knowledge will definitely be well worth your while!

Whilst flicking through these pages, you'll not only learn loads of cool facts across a variety of topics, from history to space to pop culture, you'll also find yourself equipped with endless conversation starters to impress those around you. This isn't just a book—it's your go-to guide for mental stimulation, fun, and even some family bonding time. So, what are you waiting for? Let's start our journey through the maze of fun facts!

P.S.

You'll notice those handy circles next to each fact as you read through the book. They're your personal space to mark the ones that truly capture your imagination! Feel free to tick them, color them, or personalize them in any way you like.

Echoes of the Past

Ancient Civilizations and Their Secrets

O **Mystery of the Pyramids:** The Great Pyramid of Giza were built over 4,500 years ago. It's made with enormous stone blocks and is perfectly aligned with the compass, pointing north, south, east, and west.

O **Mysterious Moai of Easter Island:** Easter Island's giant stone heads, called Moai, were created by the Rapa Nui people. No one knows how they moved these massive statues across the island without modern technology!

O **The Peruvian Nazca Lines:** The Nazca Lines are giant drawings in the ground in Peru. They look like animals and shapes and can only be seen in full from the sky as they're so enormous!

O **Secrets of Stonehenge:** Stonehenge is a circle of huge stones in England, built around 5,000 years ago. This is another mystery of how ancient people moved enormous stones around - some of these weigh as much as an elephant!

O **The Indus Valley's Plumbing:** The Indus Valley Civilization, who lived 4,500 years ago in parts of modern-day Pakistan and northern India, had awesome plumbing! Their bathrooms in their houses connected to a city sewer system.

O **Mysterious Machu Picchu:** Machu Picchu is an ancient city high in the Andes Mountains in South America. It was hidden from the world until it was rediscovered in 1911 - a real-life lost city in the clouds!

O **The Library of Alexandria:** The Library of Alexandria, built over 2,300 years ago in Egypt, housed up to 700,000 scrolls full of knowledge. People travelled from other empires to learn from the scrolls in this library.

O **Cave Paintings of Lascaux:** The Lascaux Caves in France contain an array of amazing paintings of animals, created by prehistoric people about 17,000 years ago. It's like an ancient art gallery!

O **The Hanging Gardens of Babylon:** The Hanging Gardens of Babylon were so amazing they were named one of the Seven Wonders of the Ancient World. They're the only ancient wonder where we don't know the exact location, but it's thought to be in Iraq, that's if they even existed at all!

O **Pompeii's Volcanic Fate:** The city of Pompeii was buried under ash when Mount Vesuvius erupted in AD 79. Everything was petrified by the ash, making it like a time capsule, showing us what life was like in ancient Rome.

O **The Rosetta Stone:** The Rosetta Stone bears inscriptions in different ancient languages and scripts, making it an excellent tool for translation! Found in 1799, it helped scientists read ancient Egyptian hieroglyphs.

O **Mysterious Mayan Calendar:** The Maya civilization, who lived in Central America, created a complex calendar system, with their "Long Count" calendar famously ending its cycle on December 21, 2012. The end of the calendar meant that many people thought the world might end!

o **The Terracotta Army:** China's first emperor, Qin Shi Huang, also known as Shi Huang Di, had thousands of clay soldiers buried with him to protect him in the afterlife. They're called the Terracotta Army and they're all life-sized!

o **The Elgin Marbles Controversy:** These ancient Greek sculptures were discovered in the Parthenon, a temple from Ancient Greek times. They're displayed in a museum in England, but people often argue about where they should be kept!

o **The Great Wall of China:** The Great Wall of China was built to protect ancient China from invaders. It spans over 13,000 miles and can be seen from space under the right conditions! (it would be even more certain if you had a set of binoculars with you)

Epic Battles and Brave Warriors

o **The Battle of Marathon:** Over 2,500 years ago, just 10,000 brave Athenians defeated a huge Persian army at Marathon, Greece. One messenger ran 26 miles non-stop to share the victory, and that's why we have marathon races today!

o **Spartan Stand at Thermopylae:** In 480 BC, a small force of 300 Spartans and their allies stood against thousands in a narrow mountain pass in Greece. Their unbelievable bravery didn't just become a story; it turned into legend and even inspired a movie centuries later!

o **Alexander the Great's Conquests:** By the time he was 30, Alexander the Great had conquered across the world, creating one of the biggest empires ever. He never lost a battle, thanks to his talent for strategic planning!

o **Hannibal Crosses the Alps:** Hannibal, a daring Carthaginian general, didn't just cross mountains with his army; he brought war elephants all the way over the snowy Alps to surprise Rome in a sneaky attack.

o **The Siege of Troy:** For many years, the Greeks tried to conquer the city of Troy. Their secret weapon? A giant wooden horse with soldiers hidden inside—it was the ultimate trick to win the city!

o **Joan of Arc's Leadership:** At just 19 years old, Joan of Arc wasn't just any girl—she led the French army to a huge victory and became a hero in France. What an amazing accomplishment!

o **The Battle of Hastings:** Back in 1066, William the Conqueror earned his name by beating King Harold at the Battle of Hastings, changing England forever and starting a whole new chapter with Norman kings.

o **Viking Warriors:** The Vikings weren't just fierce—they were bold explorers! They set sail from Scandinavia and even reached North America, where they found wild grapes and named it Vinland.

o **Samurai of Japan:** In ancient Japan, Samurai warriors were the ultimate fighters, living by a strict honor code called bushido and mastering the art of sword fighting. They were the real-life action heroes!

o **The Battle of Agincourt:** In 1415, a band of English archers, outnumbered and under pressure, pulled off an epic win against the French knights at Agincourt thanks to their trusty longbows!

- **The Battle of Waterloo:** In 1815, Napoleon, a famous French leader, met his match at Waterloo where British and Prussian soldiers teamed up to put an end to his rule, reshaping the future of Europe.

- **The Battle of Stalingrad:** One of the biggest and toughest battles of World War II happened in Stalingrad from 1942 to 1943. The Soviets turned the tide against Nazi Germany with a hard-fought victory that marked a huge turning point in the war.

- **Saladin's Chivalry:** During the old Crusade wars, Saladin wasn't just a fearless leader—he was also super chivalrous! He even sent his own doctors to help his enemy, King Richard the Lionheart, when he was sick!

- **Boudicca's Rebellion:** Boudicca was so fearless that she stood up to a giant empire! In 60AD she led a fierce rebellion against Rome, becoming a legendary hero in Britain.

- **The Battle of the Teutoburg Forest:** In a deep, dark forest in AD 9, Germanic tribes pulled off a huge surprise by ambushing and defeating three Roman legions. This victory put a stop to Rome's expansion plans into Germania.

- **The Vanishing Roanoke Colony:** In 1590, a whole colony, known as the Roanoke colony, disappeared without a trace! All they left behind was a mysterious word, "CROATOAN," carved into a tree. Where did they go?

History's Mysteries and Legends

- **The Curse of King Tutankhamun:** When explorers opened King Tut's tomb in 1922, some spooky things started happening. People who entered the tomb began to mysteriously die, sparking rumors of an ancient mummy's curse.

- **The Mystery of the Voynich Manuscript:** The Voynich Manuscript, written in an unknown script and filled with strange illustrations, has puzzled scholars for centuries. Despite many attempts, no one has been able to decipher it.

- **The Bermuda Triangle:** The Bermuda Triangle is a mysterious patch of ocean where ships and planes are rumored to have vanished without a trace. What's causing all these disappearances? It's a puzzle that still baffles scientists and adventurers today.

- **The Loch Ness Monster:** Deep in Scotland's Loch Ness lurks Nessie, a mysterious sea monster that people have tried to spot for years. Is she real or just a legendary tale? The mystery continues!

- **Stonehenge's Purpose:** Stonehenge is a giant circle of massive stones set up thousands of years ago, and we're still trying to figure out why. Was it a calendar, a place for rituals, or something else?

- **The Mystery of the Sphinx:** The Great Sphinx of Giza, a huge statue with the body of a lion and the head of a human, has puzzled people for ages. No one can say for certain who built it and why?

- **The Fate of the Ark of the Covenant:** The Ark of the Covenant, which was supposed to hold the Ten Commandments, just vanished one day. Some think it might be hidden in Ethiopia, but its true location still remains a mystery.

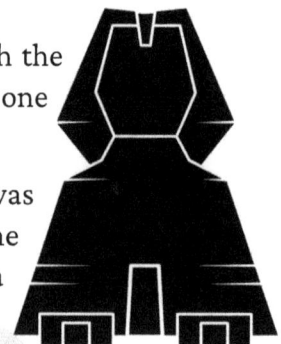

- **El Dorado, the City of Gold:** El Dorado, the famous city full of gold, has tempted adventurers for centuries with its promise of riches. Despite many expeditions, it has remained hidden.

- **The Dancing Plague of 1518:** In 1518, people in Strasbourg couldn't stop dancing, and some even danced till they dropped! What caused this bizarre dancing fever? No one knows!

- **The Green Children of Woolpit:** In the 12th century, it was recorded that two children with green skin appeared in Woolpit, England. They spoke an unknown language and claimed to be from a subterranean world. Their true origins remain a mystery.

- **The Oracle of Delphi:** The Oracle of Delphi was like the ancient world's fortune teller, giving mysterious advice that shaped many historical decisions. No one knows how she managed to make her predictions...

- **The Lost City of Z:** Explorer Percy Fawcett disappeared into the Amazon jungle searching for the "Lost City of Z," a legendary ancient city. He was never seen again...

- **The Taos Hum:** In Taos, New Mexico, some residents report hearing a low-frequency hum with no identifiable source. Scientists have investigated, but the origin of the sound remains a mystery.

- **The Antikythera Mechanism:** Discovered in an ancient shipwreck, the Antikythera Mechanism is over 2,000 years old and works like a very old computer. What was it used for? Maybe to track stars or calculate dates, but its true purpose is still unknown.

Incredible Inventions and Discoveries

- **The Wheel:** Over 5,000 years ago, people in Mesopotamia came up with an awesome idea—the wheel! First used for pottery, the evolution of the wheel made moving things easier and changed how we travel and work forever.

- **The Aeolipile:** Also known as Hero's engine, this ancient steam-powered device, invented by Hero of Alexandria around the 1st century CE, demonstrated the principle of jet propulsion. It consisted of a hollow sphere mounted on a pivot, with two nozzles emitting steam that caused the sphere to rotate.

- **Penicillin:** In 1928, Alexander Fleming spotted mold in a petri dish – this is when penicillin was discovered. This wonder drug has cured tons of bacterial infections, saving millions of lives.

- **The Light Bulb:** In 1879, Thomas Edison created the first practical light bulb that glowed long enough to light up our homes and streets, changing the way we live forever.

- **The Telephone:** In 1876, Alexander Graham Bell made it possible to chat across long distances with his invention of the telephone. Suddenly, everyone's voice could travel miles in seconds.

- **The Internet:** The internet, which began as a project by the U.S. Department of Defense in the 1960s, has become the backbone of modern communication. It connects billions of people worldwide.

- **Vaccination:** Thanks to Edward Jenner's smart thinking in 1796, we got vaccinations! By figuring out how cowpox could stop smallpox, he kicked off a way to beat lots of diseases and save countless lives.

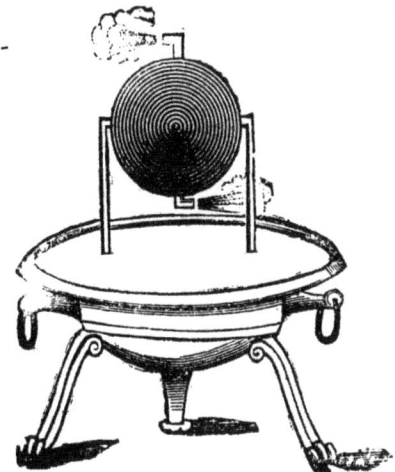

- **The Steam Engine:** James Watt harnessed the power of the steam engine in the 18th century, kick-starting the Industrial Revolution. Trains, factories, and machines got a big boost, and travel and manufacturing haven't been the same since.

- **The Compass:** The Chinese introduced the magnetic compass for navigation during the Song Dynasty, guiding sailors safely to new lands. It was a real game-changer for explorers everywhere.

- **Electricity:** The 19th century sparked a revolution with the harnessing of electricity, powering up homes, businesses, and eventually, the entire world with this dazzling force.

- **The Airplane:** In 1903, the Wright brothers achieved the first powered, controlled flight with their aircraft, the Wright Flyer, at Kitty Hawk, North Carolina. This momentous event marked the birth of modern aviation.

- **The Computer:** In 1945, the ENIAC (Electronic Numerical Integrator and Computer) became the world's first general-purpose computer, capable of performing complex calculations much faster than any human.

- **Radio:** Thanks to Guglielmo Marconi's genius in the late 1890s, the radio was born, letting us tune into music, news, and voices from far away, all without wires!

- **Plastic:** From toys to tech gadgets, plastic has shaped the modern world since its popularization in the 20th century. It's everywhere—keeping things light, affordable, and colorful.

- **The Refrigerator:** The refrigerator, evolved from the old-school icebox, keeps our food fresh and tasty, and its invention changed the way we cook and eat.

Moments That Changed the World

- **The Discovery of Fire:** When early humans sparked the first flame, fire not only cooked their food but also kept predators away and lit up the night. It was a game changer for human survival and comfort!

- **The Creation of the Constitution:** Back in 1787, the U.S. Constitution was created, a plan that would lead to modern democracy. This document laid down rules that not only shaped America but also inspired nations around the globe.

- **The Chernobyl Disaster:** In 1986, the Chernobyl nuclear disaster showed just how dangerous nuclear power could be. It led to super strict safety rules globally, and the deserted area around Chernobyl reminds us of its lasting impact.

- **The Building of the Panama Canal:** Completed in 1914, the Panama Canal links the Atlantic and Pacific oceans right through the middle of the 2 American continents! This massive waterway cut down sea voyages by thousands of miles and reshaped global trade.

- **The Invention of the Automobile:** In 1886, Karl Benz made the world more mobile. The first cars changed how people moved, turning distant dreams into drivable destinations and eventually transforming cities and how we live our lives.

- **The Introduction of the Smartphone:** The IBM Simon, released in 1994, is considered the world's first smartphone. It combined a mobile phone with a touchscreen, calendar, email, and fax machine!

- **The Cuban Missile Crisis:** The Cuban Missile Crisis in 1962 was a tense time for all, bringing the world to the brink of nuclear war. It showed just how high the stakes could be with nuclear weapons on the table.

- **The Signing of the Treaty of Versailles:** The Treaty of Versailles not only ended World War I in 1919 but also set the stage for World War II, showing how tough penalties can sometimes backfire, leading to even bigger problems.

- **The First Heart Transplant:** In 1967, Dr. Christiaan Barnard performed the world's first successful human heart transplant in South Africa. The patient lived for 18 days, marking a significant milestone in medical history.

- **The Invention of Paper:** Around 100 BC, China invented paper, revolutionizing how we share and store knowledge. Books, art, and eventually schools spread more widely thanks to this fantastic invention.

- **The Discovery of Insulin:** In 1921, a life-saving liquid called insulin was discovered, turning diabetes from a fatal disease into a manageable condition. Thanks to this discovery, millions of lives have been saved.

- **The First Use of Anesthesia:** In 1846, the first successful use of Anesthesia made surgery painless, transforming it from a nightmare into a lifesaving procedure.

- **The Apollo-Soyuz Test Project:** In 1975, the Cold War thawed a bit when American and Soviet astronauts shook hands in space! The Apollo-Soyuz Test Project opened the door for countries to work together high above planet Earth.

- **The Fall of Apartheid:** In 1994, apartheid in South Africa ended with the election of Nelson Mandela as president. The new laws dismantled the system of racial segregation and promoted equality for all citizens.

- **The Launch of Sputnik:** In 1957, the Soviet Union launched Sputnik, the first satellite to orbit Earth. This kicked off the space race, leading to incredible advances in science and technology and even putting humans on the Moon!

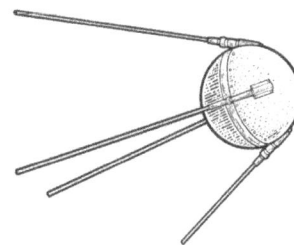

Remarkable Rulers and Their Reigns

- **Cleopatra's Multilingual Mastery:** Cleopatra, the last Pharaoh of Egypt, was known for her intelligence and charm. She reportedly spoke nine languages, allowing her to communicate with various cultures across her empire.

- **Charlemagne's Educational Reform:** Charlemagne, known as Charles the Great, believed everyone should get the chance to learn and read. He set up schools all across his empire, making sure learning wasn't just for the rich and powerful.

- **Elizabeth I's Pirate Ties:** Queen Elizabeth I had a secret weapon against Spain—pirates! Well, kind of. She supported sea captains like Sir Francis Drake, privateers who had permission to disrupt Spanish ships, helping make England richer and strengthen its navy.

- **Genghis Khan's Postal System:** Genghis Khan created a hugely impressive postal system across the vast Mongol Empire, helping him keep tabs on his enormous realm and ensuring everyone stayed connected.

o **Napoleon's Love for Mathematics:** Napoleon Bonaparte wasn't just a military genius; he was also a math whiz. His love for numbers helped him plan his battles carefully, which is why he won so many of them!

o **Emperor Justinian's Architectural Triumphs:** Justinian I loved big, bold buildings. He ordered the construction of the Hagia Sophia in what's now Istanbul, a giant church that's been standing strong for almost 1,500 years and is still one of the world's architectural wonders.

o **Wu Zetian's Promotion of Buddhism:** Empress Wu Zetian spread Buddhism far and wide across China, making her reign a time of great spiritual and cultural growth.

o **Louis XIV's Ballet Passion:** King Louis XIV of France loved ballet so much that he performed in many dances himself and helped turn ballet into a hugely popular activity in France.

o **Meiji's Cultural Transformation:** Emperor Meiji of Japan loved mixing Western styles with Japanese traditions, upgrading everything from trains to schools during his reign. Some may argue he was sort of forced into it, but the Emperor was the driving force for modernization during his time on the throne.

o **Ashoka's Edicts:** Emperor Ashoka had his laws inspired by Buddhist teachings, promoting kindness and moral behavior, carved on giant stones all over his empire so he could inspire everyone around him.

o **Suleiman's Architectural Marvels:** Sultan Suleiman I was passionate about architecture and commissioned lots of amazing buildings, including the stunning Suleymaniye Mosque in Istanbul, which is still an amazing sight today.

o **Cyrus the Great's Charter of Human Rights:** Over 2,500 years ago, Cyrus the Great wrote a charter that said people should be free and not slaves, which was a revolutionary way of thinking at the time!

o **Peter the Great's European Tour:** Peter the Great of Russia went on a tour across Europe to learn shipbuilding and science. He used his new knowledge to modernize Russia and even started a brand-new city - St. Petersburg!

o **Mansa Musa's Economic Impact:** Mansa Musa, the king of Mali, was so rich that during his famous trip to Mecca, he spent so much gold that he boosted the economies of entire regions!

o **Queen Victoria's Love of Technology:** Queen Victoria loved technology. She was one of the first monarchs to get her photograph taken and often travelled by train.

And that's a wrap on our history section! We've explored some fascinating moments in the sands of time, from the iconic architecture commissioned by emperors across the world to the strategic genius of rulers. We've unravelled past secrets and revealed stories that have had lasting impacts on our current day life.

Our next stop takes us into the exciting realm of scientific discoveries and the laws of the universe! Be prepared for mind-blowing experiments, life-altering discoveries and find out who was behind them. Step into another chapter filled with amazing facts, unbelievable data and stories all about science. Let's go!

Eureka! World of Science

Breakthroughs and Brainstorms

O **Einstein's Theory of Relativity:** In 1905, Albert Einstein showed that time can stretch and bend, especially if you're moving really fast, like in a spaceship! This changed how we think about the universe.

O **Marie Curie's Amazing Elements:** Marie Curie was a pioneer in the study of radioactivity. She discovered the elements polonium and radium, and her research laid the foundation for cancer treatment and nuclear energy.

O **The Human Genome Map:** Scientists finished a giant puzzle in 2003 called the Human Genome Project, which mapped out all the genes in our DNA, helping us understand what makes us who we are.

O **The Expanding Universe:** Edwin Hubble discovered that the universe is expanding, meaning galaxies are moving away from each other. This led to the Big Bang theory, explaining the universe's origin.

O **CRISPR Gene Editing:** CRISPR is a ground-breaking technology that allows scientists to edit genes with precision. This innovation has the potential to cure genetic diseases, modify crops, and even bring extinct species back to life.

O **Pasteurization Saves the Day:** Louis Pasteur discovered how to keep milk and juice safe to drink by heating them to kill germs. This process, called pasteurization, makes our food much safer.

O **The Mysterious Higgs Boson:** In 2012, scientists found the Higgs boson, a tiny particle that helps give everything mass. It's like finding a missing puzzle piece in how the universe works.

O **The Double Helix of DNA:** In 1953, scientists James Watson and Francis Crick figured out that DNA looks like a twisted ladder. This helped us understand how living things grow and change.

O **The Moving Continents:** The theory of plate tectonics showed that the Earth's continents move around on giant plates. This explains why we have earthquakes and volcanoes! You may have heard of Pangea, the supercontinent, but before it existed its predecessor called Rodinia, which existed about 1.1 billion years ago. All of these continents broke up and reassembled due to.. you guessed it.. plate tectonics!

O **The First Microscope:** In the 1600s, Anton van Leeuwenhoek built a microscope that could see tiny things like bacteria, opening up a whole new world of tiny living creatures.

O **The Development of the Electric Motor:** In 1821, Michael Faraday discovered the principles behind the electric motor by demonstrating how a magnetic field can produce a continuous circular motion. This breakthrough laid the groundwork for modern electric power.

O **The Invention of X-Rays:** In 1895, Wilhelm Roentgen discovered X-rays, allowing us to see inside our bodies without surgery. X-rays are still used today to check bones and teeth.

O **Newton's Laws of Motion:** Isaac Newton came up with three laws of motion that explain how things move. His ideas help us understand everything from falling apples to launching rockets.

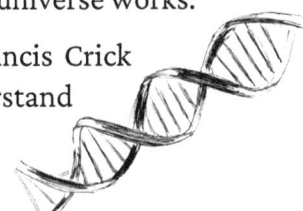

○ **The Discovery of Gravitational Waves:** Albert Einstein predicted gravitational waves, ripples in space-time caused by accelerating massive objects like merging black holes. They were first detected in 2015, confirming his theory.

○ **The First Solar Panel:** In 1954, Bell Labs created the first solar panel that turned sunlight into electricity, leading the way for the renewable energy we have today that helps power our homes and gadgets.

Fascinating Phenomena

○ **Auroras: Nature's Light Show:** Auroras, also known as the Northern and Southern Lights, are colorful displays in the sky caused by charged particles from the sun interacting with Earth's atmosphere.

○ **The Butterfly Effect:** The Butterfly Effect is the idea that tiny changes, like a butterfly flapping its wings, can lead to big differences, such as a tiny flutter causing a storm on the other side of the world a few days later!

○ **Bioluminescent Glow:** Some creatures, like fireflies and deep-sea fish, can glow in the dark! This is known as bioluminescence, a natural chemical reaction that creates light.

○ **The Strange Phenomenon of Ball Lightning:** Ball lightning is a rare and mysterious phenomenon where glowing orbs of light appear during thunderstorms. Scientists still don't yet know how they form.

○ **The Great Red Spot on Jupiter:** Jupiter's Great Red Spot is a huge storm that's been going on for over 300 years. It's so big that three Earths could fit inside it!

○ **The Sahara Desert's Snowfall:** You may think of the desert as hot and dry, but it has snowed in the Sahara Desert before! In 2018, the sand dunes had a dusting of snow, creating a beautiful winter wonderland.

○ **The Mystery of Dark Matter:** Dark matter makes up about 27% of the universe, but it can't be seen or touched. Scientists know it's there because of the way it affects galaxies' movements.

○ **Animals and Magnetic Fields:** Some animals, like birds and sea turtles, use Earth's magnetic field to travel long distances. It's like having a built-in compass!

○ **The Super Long Wave:** There's a wave in Brazil called the Pororoca that travels up the Amazon River for miles. Surfers love to ride this massive wave that can last for over half an hour!

○ **The Singing Sand Dunes:** In some deserts, sand dunes can "sing" or "boom" when the sand grains slide down the slope. The sound is caused by vibrations as the sand moves around.

○ **The Giant's Causeway:** The Giant's Causeway in Northern Ireland is made up of thousands of hexagonal basalt columns, formed by ancient volcanic activity.

○ **The Star-Nosed Mole's Super Nose:** The star-nosed mole has a unique nose with 22 tentacle-like appendages. It uses this amazing organ to detect prey in complete darkness.

o **The Great Barrier Reef's Size:** Australia's Great Barrier Reef is the largest coral reef in the world, covering over 1,400 miles. It's home to countless marine species and is even visible from space, specifically the International Space Station!

o **The Fibonacci Sequence in Nature:** The Fibonacci sequence, where each number is the sum of the two preceding ones, often appears in nature. You can find it in the arrangement of leaves, flower petals, and even the spiral of seashells.

o **The Mystery of the Sailing Stones:** In Death Valley, California, rocks mysteriously move across the desert floor, leaving long trails behind them. This phenomenon, called the sailing stones, happens due to a rare combination of ice, wind, and sunlight.

Mind-Blowing Experiments

o **The Double-Slit Experiment:** The double-slit experiment showed that light can act like both a wave and a particle. This mind-boggling discovery is a key concept in quantum physics.

o **The Miller-Urey Experiment:** In 1953, scientists recreated early Earth's conditions in a lab, creating amino acids—the building blocks of life. This experiment helped us understand how life might have started.

o **The Marshmallow Test:** In the 1960s, scientists gave children a marshmallow and told them they could eat it or wait for another. It tested self-control and has influenced how we think about delayed gratification.

o **The Stanford Prison Experiment:** In 1971, researchers turned a university basement into a fake prison to study behavior. It showed how quickly people can adopt roles of authority and submission.

o **The LHC and Particle Smashers:** The Large Hadron Collider (LHC) in Switzerland is the world's largest particle collider. It smashes particles together at high speeds to discover fundamental particles like the Higgs boson.

o **Pavlov's Dogs and Classical Conditioning:** Ivan Pavlov trained dogs to salivate when they hear a bell, showing how animals can learn to associate sounds with food. This experiment laid the foundation for behavioral psychology.

o **The Stanford Memory Experiment:** Elizabeth Loftus conducted experiments showing how memories can be influenced by misinformation, revealing that our memories can be surprisingly unreliable.

o **The Asch Conformity Experiment:** In the 1950s, Solomon Asch showed that people are likely to conform to group opinions, even if they know the group is wrong, revealing the power of social pressure.

o **The Zimbardo Time Paradox Experiment:** Psychologist Philip Zimbardo explored how our perceptions of time affect our behavior, helping us understand why some people focus on the past while others look to the future.

o **The Harlow Monkey Experiments:** In the 1950s, Harry Harlow's experiments with rhesus monkeys demonstrated the importance of love and affection in early childhood development.

o **The Bobo Doll Experiment:** Albert Bandura's Bobo doll experiment showed that children can imitate aggressive behavior they observe in adults, highlighting the impact of role models.

O **The Copenhagen Interpretation of Quantum Mechanics:** This interpretation suggests that particles can exist in multiple states until they're observed. It was tested with experiments like Schrödinger's cat, a thought experiment that's still debated today.

O **The Pitch Drop Experiment:** The pitch drop experiment, started in 1927, demonstrates that pitch, a tar-like substance, flows very slowly. Only nine drops have fallen since it began, proving that some liquids flow slower than we think.

O **The Milgram Obedience Experiment:** In the 1960s, psychologist Stanley Milgram conducted an experiment to see how far people would go to obey authority. Participants thought they were delivering electric shocks to others, but they were actually fake and the people being shocked were actors!

O **The Blue Brain Project:** Initiated in 2005, the Blue Brain Project aims to create a digital reconstruction of the human brain. This project seeks to unlock the mysteries of the brain and understand how we think and learn.

Wonders of the Natural World

O **Salar de Uyuni's Reflective Salt Flats:** Salar de Uyuni in Bolivia is the world's largest salt flat. In the rainy season, it reflects the sky like a giant mirror, creating a breathtaking optical illusion.

O **The Bioluminescent Bays:** Mosquito Bay in Puerto Rico is famous for its bioluminescent (glowing) waters. Tiny organisms called dinoflagellates light up when disturbed, making the water glow bright blue at night.

O **The Catatumbo Lightning:** Lake Maracaibo in Venezuela has powerful storms that produce nearly continuous lightning flashes for up to 297 nights a year. It's known as the place with the most frequent lightning.

O **The Giant Sequoias of California:** The giant sequoias in California's Sequoia National Park are among the largest and oldest living trees on Earth, reaching heights of over 300 feet and ages of more than 3,000 years.

O **The Dead Sea's Unique Properties:** The Dead Sea, between Jordan and Israel, is one of the saltiest bodies of water in the world. Its high salt content makes it easy for people to float effortlessly.

O **Mount Roraima's Tabletop Mountain:** Mount Roraima is a giant tabletop mountain located at the border of Venezuela, Brazil, and Guyana, is often covered by clouds. Its captivating landscape inspired the fictional setting in Arthur Conan Doyle's novel, *The Lost World*

O **Pamukkale's Travertine Terraces:** Pamukkale in Turkey features stunning white travertine (a type of stone) terraces filled with mineral-rich thermal waters. These natural hot springs have been used for relaxation and healing for centuries.

O **The Great Blue Hole of Belize:** The Great Blue Hole is a giant underwater sinkhole off the coast of Belize. It's about 1,000 feet across and over 400 feet deep, attracting divers from around the world.

O **Victoria Falls' Smoke that Thunders:** Victoria Falls, on the border of Zambia and Zimbabwe, is one of the largest and most famous waterfalls in the world. Locals call it "Mosi-oa-Tunya," which means "The Smoke that Thunders."

O **The Salar de Atacama's Pink Flamingos:** The Salar de Atacama in Chile is home to large populations of flamingos that thrive in its salty lagoons. Despite having these lagoons, the Atacama Desert is one of the driest places on Earth.

O **The Fairy Chimneys of Cappadocia:** Cappadocia in Turkey is known for its unique rock formations called "fairy chimneys," created by volcanic eruptions and erosion. People have carved homes and churches into these rocks for centuries.

O **The Marble Caves of Patagonia:** The Marble Caves, located in Chile's Patagonia region, feature stunning blue and white marble formations shaped by waves over thousands of years. They're only accessible by boat.

O **The Crooked Forest of Poland:** The Crooked Forest in Poland is a grove of pine trees with unusual curved trunks, all bending in the same direction. The reason for their strange shape remains a mystery.

O **The Spotted Lake of British Columbia:** Spotted Lake in Canada has natural spots of different colors, created by high concentrations of minerals. In summer, the water evaporates, revealing colorful mineral deposits.

O **The Eye of the Sahara:** The Eye of the Sahara, also known as the Richat Structure, is a circular geological formation in the Sahara Desert. It's so large it can be seen from space, but its origin is still debated.

Tech That Transformed Tomorrow

O **The Rise of Artificial Intelligence:** Artificial Intelligence (AI) is changing our daily lives, making tasks easier and more efficient. It's the brain behind helpful tools like Siri and smart cars that drive themselves.

O **The Invention of 3D Printing:** Imagine creating a toy or a medical implant layer by layer from a digital design. That's what 3D printing does, and it's even being used to make parts for space missions!

O **The Development of GPS Technology:** GPS, or the Global Positioning System, is what guides us when we're navigating new places. From your phone's map app to guiding airplanes and ships, it uses satellites to show the way.

O **The Invention of the Internet of Things:** The Internet of Things (IoT) connects everyday items to the internet, allowing them to talk to each other. It's the technology behind smart homes and wearable devices that make life more convenient.

O **The Creation of Smart Cities:** Smart cities use technology to make urban life better, like managing resources efficiently and improving quality of life. Think about how data and sensors help reduce traffic jams and save energy.

O **The Launch of Reusable Rockets:** SpaceX has developed rockets that return to Earth safely after launching into space, cutting down the cost of space travel and paving the way for more discoveries.

O **The Rise of Quantum Computing:** Quantum computers process data in ways regular computers can't, using qubits. They have the potential to solve complex problems much faster, opening doors to new possibilities.

- **The Development of Wearable Tech:** Wearable devices like fitness trackers and smartwatches keep us informed about our health and help us stay connected wherever we are. These gadgets keep getting better and smarter.

- **The Advancement of Biotechnology:** Biotechnology harnesses living organisms to create innovative products for health, agriculture, and industry. It's the science behind advancements like genetically modified crops and gene-editing tools like CRISPR.

- **The Evolution of Virtual Reality:** Virtual Reality (VR) immerses us in digital worlds, creating experiences that feel incredibly real. It's not just for gaming; VR is also used in education and astronaut training!

- **The Growth of Renewable Energy:** Solar and wind power are leading a shift in how we produce electricity, helping to cut down on carbon emissions and fight climate change.

- **The Introduction of Digital Currency:** Digital currencies like Bitcoin use blockchain technology to operate independently of central banks, offering a new way to think about money and transactions.

- **The Revolution of Electric Vehicles:** Electric vehicles (EVs) run on electricity instead of gasoline, helping to reduce pollution and our reliance on fossil fuels. Companies like Tesla are at the forefront of EV technology.

- **The Impact of Social Media:** Social media connects us with people worldwide, making it easy to share information instantly. It has transformed how we communicate, do business, and even how politics work.

- **The Rise of Cloud Computing:** Cloud computing lets us store and access data over the internet rather than on our personal computers. This has revolutionized business operations and online collaboration.

Unbelievable Theories

- **The Theory of Quantum Entanglement:** Imagine two particles so deeply connected that what happens to one instantly affects the other, even if they are light-years apart. This is quantum entanglement, a mind-boggling idea at the heart of quantum physics.

- **The Multiverse Theory:** What if our universe is just one of countless others, each with its own rules? That's the multiverse theory, a fascinating concept suggesting parallel universes that could redefine how we see reality.

- **Heisenberg's Uncertainty Principle:** In the quirky realm of quantum mechanics, Heisenberg's uncertainty principle tells us that you can't know a particle's exact position and momentum at the same time. It highlights the inherent unpredictability of the quantum world.

- **The Simulation Hypothesis:** Ever feel like life might be a video game? The simulation hypothesis suggests our reality could be a super-advanced computer simulation, challenging everything we think we know about existence.

- **String Theory:** Think of the universe's tiniest building blocks as vibrating strings. String theory proposes this idea, aiming to unify all forces of nature into one grand framework.

- **The Theory of Evolution:** Charles Darwin introduced the theory of evolution, explaining how species evolve over time through natural selection. It's the story of how diverse life on Earth came to be.

- **The Law of Conservation of Energy:** This fundamental law states that energy can't be created or destroyed, only transformed. It's a guiding principle of how energy works throughout the universe.

- **The Big Bang Theory:** The Big Bang theory tells us how the universe started from a tiny, dense point and has been expanding ever since, explaining the origins of galaxies, stars, and planets.

- **Fermat's Last Theorem:** A mathematical puzzle unsolved for over 350 years, Fermat's Last Theorem claims there are no whole number solutions to the equation $xn+yn=znx^n + y^n = z^nxn+yn=zn$ when nnn is greater than 2.

- **Gödel's Incompleteness Theorems:** Kurt Gödel revealed that in any sufficiently complex mathematical system, some statements can't be proven true or false, highlighting the limits of logic and mathematics.

- **The Gaia Hypothesis:** The Gaia hypothesis views Earth as a self-regulating system, with living and non-living parts working together to maintain life-friendly conditions, like one giant organism.

- **Panspermia Theory:** The panspermia theory suggests that life on Earth may have originated from microscopic life forms that traveled through space on comets, creating life wherever they landed!

- **Time Dilation:** Time dilation, a part of Einstein's theory of relativity, tells us that time moves slower the faster you travel. For astronauts moving at near-light speeds, a short trip might mean coming back to a world that has aged years!

- **The Big Freeze:** The Big Freeze theory predicts the ultimate fate of the universe, suggesting it will expand forever, growing colder and emptier until it's too cold for life to exist. It's a chilly end to everything as we know it!

- **Antimatter:** Antimatter is like matter's mirror image, with opposite charges. When matter and antimatter meet, they annihilate each other in a burst of energy. This fascinating substance could potentially power futuristic spacecraft!

As we finish our exploration of the fantastic world of science, we've explored the microscopic realm of atoms and molecules, unlocked the mysteries of quantum mechanics, and marveled at the mind-bending theories that challenge our understanding of reality.

And the adventure continues! Our next chapter takes us from the laboratories into the vibrant arena of sports and athletic achievements. Prepare to be inspired by the awesome stories of athletes who defied the odds, broke records, and pushed their limits. We'll explore unforgettable moments, jaw-dropping records and the awe-inspiring dedication that drives athletes to greatness.

So, lace up your shoes and get ready to jump into this wonderful world, where passion, perseverance, and skill collide to create moments of magic. Let's go!

The Ball's in Your Court

Amazing Feats of Endurance

O **The Longest Tennis Match:** The longest tennis match ever lasted 11 hours and 5 minutes! It took place over three days at Wimbledon 2010. John Isner eventually defeated Nicolas Mahut 70-68 in the fifth set.

O **The Barkley Marathons Challenge:** The Barkley Marathon is a 100-mile race through the Tennessee mountains that only 20 runners have completed since it began in 1986! The course changes every year, making it a true test of endurance and navigation.

O **Ross Edgley's Great British Swim:** Ross Edgley became the first person to swim around the whole of Great Britain's mainland in 2018. He swam over 1,780 miles in 157 days, braving the cold waters and dangerous tides.

O **The Antarctic Ice Marathon:** The Antarctic Ice Marathon is held at the bottom of the world, where temperatures can reach a chilly -20 degrees Celsius! Runners brave these icy conditions to race on the continent's snowy terrain.

O **Dean Karnazes' 50 Marathons in 50 Days:** Ultra-marathon runner Dean Karnazes ran 50 marathons in 50 states in 50 consecutive days. This incredible achievement showcased exceptional stamina and highlighted the possibilities of human endurance.

O **How Far can One Go on a Single Breath:** Free diver Herbert Nitsch set the record for the deepest free dive, reaching a depth of 831 feet (253 meters) on a single breath! He's often called "The Deepest Man on Earth."

O **Jasmin Paris Wins the Spine Race:** In 2019, Jasmin Paris won the Montane Spine Race, a 268-mile race along the Pennine Way in the UK, and she even set a new course record! Not only that, she did this while expressing breast milk for her baby at aid stations.

O **The Longest Bicycle Race:** The Trans-Siberian Extreme is one of the longest bike races in the world, spanning 5,700 miles across Russia. Cyclists endure varying terrains and climates, from the Urals to the Siberian tundra.

O **The Marathon des Sables:** The Marathon des Sables is a six-day, 156-mile ultramarathon across the Sahara Desert, where participants must carry their supplies. It's often dubbed the toughest footrace on Earth.

O **Sarah Thomas' Four-Way English Channel Swim:** In 2019, Sarah Thomas became the first person to swim across the English Channel four times non-stop. She swam for over 54 hours, covering around 134 miles.

O **The Endless Run of Yiannis Kouros:** Yiannis Kouros is known as the "Running God" for his ultramarathon achievements. He holds world records for distances beyond the marathon, including running 188.28 miles (303 kilometers) in 24 hours.

- **Longest Solo Journey on Foot:** George Meegan walked 19,019 miles from the southern tip of South America to the northern tip of Alaska between 1977 and 1983. His journey took six years and set a world record for the longest unbroken walk!

- **Farthest Distance Swum in 24 Hours:** Pablo Fernandez holds the record for the farthest distance swum in open water in 24 hours, covering 147.88 miles (238 kilometers) in 2021 in Miami, Florida.

- **Crossing the Gobi Desert on Foot:** Rob Lilwall and Leon McCarron crossed the 1,000-mile Gobi Desert on foot, enduring extreme temperatures and treacherous terrain. Their journey highlighted the sheer willpower of human endurance.

- **The 100-Mile Ultra Run Record:** Aleksandr Sorokin set a new record for the 100-mile ultramarathon distance, finishing in 10 hours, 51 minutes, and 39 seconds in Tel Aviv in 2022.

Incredible Comebacks

- **Tiger Woods' Return to Glory:** After years of injuries and personal struggles, Tiger Woods made an incredible comeback by winning the 2019 Masters Tournament, his first major victory in 11 years.

- **Monica Seles' Triumph After Tragedy:** Monica Seles returned to tennis in 1995 after being stabbed during a match in 1993. She won her first tournament back and later claimed the Australian Open title in 1996.

- **Leicester City's Premier League Win:** In 2016, Leicester City Football Club made a historic comeback by winning the English Premier League after starting the season as 5000-1 underdogs.

- **Kerri Strug's Vault for Gold:** In the 1996 Olympics, gymnast Kerri Strug secured gold for Team USA with a heroic vault performance on an injured ankle, showcasing grit and determination.

- **Michael Jordan's NBA Return:** Michael Jordan returned to basketball in 1995 after a brief retirement and led the Chicago Bulls to three consecutive NBA championships, cementing his legacy as one of the greatest athletes ever.

- **Ben Hogan's Recovery from a Crash:** Golfer Ben Hogan survived a near-fatal car accident in 1949. He returned to win six more major championships, including the 1950 U.S. Open.

- **Bethany Hamilton's Surfing Return:** After losing her arm in a shark attack in 2003, surfer Bethany Hamilton made an incredible comeback, winning her first national title just two years later.

- **Niki Lauda's F1 Comeback:** Formula 1 driver Niki Lauda survived a horrific crash in 1976. He made a miraculous recovery to race again just 40 days later and went on to win two more world championships.

- **Liverpool's Champions League Miracle:** In 2005, Liverpool FC staged a stunning comeback in the UEFA Champions League final, overcoming a 3-0 deficit against AC Milan to win the match on penalties. Some may argue Manchester United's 1999 Champions League final against Bayern Munich, where they won 2-1 scoring both goals in the 91st and 93rd minute of the match should warrant a place in our facts. We reckon that most of you would have already known about this feat from Manchester United, so we included the Liverpool one instead!

- **Andre Agassi's Return to Tennis:** Andre Agassi battled through personal and professional struggles to make a comeback in tennis, winning five Grand Slam titles from 1999 to 2003 and regaining the world No. 1 ranking.

- **George Foreman's Boxing Comeback:** At age 45, George Foreman became the oldest heavyweight champion in boxing history by defeating Michael Moorer in 1994, 20 years after losing his title to Muhammad Ali.

- **The Boston Red Sox's 2004 Comeback:** The Boston Red Sox overcame a 3-0 series deficit to defeat the New York Yankees in the 2004 ALCS, 86 years after they won their last World Series title!

- **The Comeback of Monica Puig:** Monica Puig made history at the 2016 Rio Olympic Tennis competition by winning Puerto Rico's first ever gold medal!

- **Alex Zanardi's Racing Return:** After losing both legs in a crash, racing driver Alex Zanardi made an inspiring comeback, winning Paralympic gold medals in handcycling and returning to professional motorsports.

- **Serena Williams' Maternity Comeback:** After giving birth in 2017, Serena Williams returned to tennis and reached four Grand Slam finals, showing her resilience and dedication to the sport.

Legends of the Game

- **Pele's Soccer Legacy:** Pele is often regarded as the greatest soccer player of all time, scoring over 1,280 goals and winning three World Cups with Brazil.

- **Babe Ruth's Baseball Stardom:** Babe Ruth, known as the "Sultan of Swat," was a legendary baseball player whose hitting prowess and larger-than-life personality helped popularize the sport in the 1920s.

- **Muhammad Ali's Boxing Brilliance:** Muhammad Ali was not just a boxing champion but also a cultural icon. His charisma, skill, and activism made him one of the most famous athletes in history.

- **Michael Jordan's Basketball Dominance:** Michael Jordan is widely considered the greatest basketball player ever, leading the Chicago Bulls to six NBA championships and becoming a global icon in the process.

- **Usain Bolt's Speed Records:** Usain Bolt, the "Fastest Man Alive," won eight Olympic gold medals and set world records in the 100m and 200m sprints, leaving his mark on athletics.

- **Serena Williams' Tennis Greatness:** Serena Williams has won 23 Grand Slam singles titles, the most in the Open Era, and is celebrated for her powerful play and influence on women's sports.

- **Wayne Gretzky's Hockey Mastery:** Wayne Gretzky, known as "The Great One," holds numerous NHL records, including most career goals and assists. He revolutionized hockey with his incredible vision and skill.

- **Jackie Robinson's Historic Breakthrough:** Jackie Robinson broke baseball's color barrier in 1947, becoming the first African American to play in Major League Baseball. His courage and talent paved the way for future generations.

- **Martina Navratilova's Tennis Dominance:** Martina Navratilova is one of the greatest female tennis players, with a record 167 singles titles and 59 Grand Slam titles across singles, doubles, and mixed doubles.

- **Lionel Messi's Soccer Magic:** Lionel Messi has dazzled fans worldwide with his extraordinary dribbling, vision, and goal-scoring ability. He's won numerous awards, including multiple Ballon d'Or titles.

- **Billie Jean King's Advocacy and Tennis Skill:** Billie Jean King was a trailblazer for women's sports and gender equality. She won 39 Grand Slam titles and famously defeated Bobby Riggs in the "Battle of the Sexes."

- **Tom Brady's Football Excellence:** Tom Brady is considered one of the greatest quarterbacks in NFL history, winning seven Super Bowl titles and numerous MVP awards over his illustrious career.

- **Nadia Comăneci's Perfect 10:** At the 1976 Montreal Olympics, gymnast Nadia Comăneci became the first person to score a perfect 10, capturing the world's attention with her flawless routines and grace.

- **Roger Federer's Tennis Mastery:** Roger Federer is celebrated for his elegant style and sportsmanship. He holds 20 Grand Slam singles titles, showcasing his longevity and dominance in the sport.

- **Jesse Owens' Olympic Triumph:** Jesse Owens won four gold medals at the 1936 Berlin Olympics, defying racial barriers and delivering a powerful message of equality and excellence.

Record-Breaking Moments

- **Wilt Chamberlain's 100-Point Game:** On March 2, 1962, NBA legend Wilt Chamberlain scored 100 points in a single game, setting a record that still stands today and showcasing his incredible talent.

- **Michael Phelps' 8 Gold Medals:** Swimmer Michael Phelps made history at the 2008 Beijing Olympics by winning eight gold medals, the most ever in a single Games, breaking Mark Spitz's record.

- **Roger Bannister's 4-Minute Mile:** On May 6, 1954, Roger Bannister became the first person to run a mile in under four minutes, a feat once thought impossible. His record-breaking time was 3:59.4.

- **Florence Griffith-Joyner's Speed:** Florence Griffith-Joyner, known as "Flo-Jo," set the women's 100m and 200m world records in 1988, with times of 10.49 and 21.34 seconds. Her records still stand today.

- **Rafael Nadal's French Open Dominance:** Rafael Nadal has won the French Open 14 times, a record for any Grand Slam tournament, demonstrating his unparalleled mastery on clay courts.

- **Tony Hawk's Legendary 900:** In 1999, Tony Hawk became the first skateboarder to land a 900-degree spin at the X Games, cementing his place in skateboarding history.

- **Simone Biles' Gymnastics Greatness:** Simone Biles has won 25 World Championship medals, making her the most decorated gymnast in history. Her incredible skills have been an inspiration for others in the sport.

- **Kipchoge's Sub-2-Hour Marathon:** Eliud Kipchoge became the first person to run a marathon in under two hours, clocking 1:59:40 in a special event in Vienna in 2019, though not officially recognized as a world record.

- **The Longest Home Run:** Mickey Mantle hit the longest home run in history, estimated at 643 feet, at Griffith Stadium in Washington, D.C., on April 17, 1953. His legendary power left fans in awe.

- **Jack Nicklaus' Major Wins:** Jack Nicklaus holds the record for the most major golf championships, with 18 victories. His career spanned three decades, earning him the nickname "The Golden Bear."

- **Barry Bonds' Home Run Record:** Barry Bonds set the MLB single-season home run record with 73 homers in 2001 and holds the career record with 762, cementing his place in baseball history.

- **Martina Hingis' Youngest No. 1:** Martina Hingis became the youngest world No. 1 tennis player in 1997 at 16 years old. Her impressive career includes five Grand Slam singles titles.

- **Wilt Chamberlain's Double-Double:** Wilt Chamberlain set a record for the most consecutive double-doubles in the NBA, achieving 227 straight from 1964 to 1967, showcasing his dominance on the court.

- **Paula Radcliffe's Marathon Record:** Paula Radcliffe set the women's marathon world record in 2003 with a time of 2:15:25, a record that stood for 16 years, demonstrating her incredible endurance.

- **Longest Field Goal in NFL History:** On September 26, 2021, Justin Tucker kicked a 66-yard field goal for the Baltimore Ravens, setting the record for the longest field goal in NFL history. We shall see if it can be broken!

- **Klay Thompson's 37-Point Quarter:** On January 23, 2015, Klay Thompson of the Golden State Warriors scored an incredible 37 points in a single quarter against the Sacramento Kings, setting an NBA record for most points scored in a quarter.

Unbelievable Underdogs

- **The Kenyan Hockey Team's Heroic Journey:** In 1971, the Kenyan national field hockey team stunned the world by reaching the semifinals of the Barcelona Hockey World Cup. Despite limited resources and being relatively unknown, they played with heart and skill, putting Kenyan hockey on the global map.

- **Buster Douglas' Knockout of Tyson:** In 1990, James "Buster" Douglas shocked the world by defeating the undefeated heavyweight champion Mike Tyson, despite being a 42-1 underdog.

- **The Miracle on Ice:** The U.S. men's ice hockey team, made up of amateurs, defeated the Soviet Union's professional team in the 1980 Winter Olympics, pulling off one of the biggest upsets in sports history.

- **Greece's Euro 2004 Victory:** Greece defied the odds to win the UEFA European Championship in 2004, defeating several top teams along the way and securing their first major international title.

- **Emma Raducanu's US Open Victory:** In 2021, Emma Raducanu became the first qualifier in history to win a Grand Slam, triumphing at the US Open without dropping a set. Her victory inspired countless young athletes.

- **The Cleveland Cavaliers' Comeback:** The Cleveland Cavaliers overcame a 3-1 deficit in the 2016 NBA Finals against the Golden State Warriors, winning the title and securing their first championship in franchise history.

O **The Mighty Ducks' Championship:** In 2003, the Anaheim Mighty Ducks reached the Stanley Cup Finals despite being considered underdogs, showcasing determination and teamwork against stronger opponents.

O **Rulon Gardner's Olympic Wrestling Win:** Rulon Gardner defeated three-time Olympic champion Aleksandr Karelin in the 2000 Olympics, ending Karelin's 13-year undefeated streak in Greco-Roman wrestling.

O **North Carolina State's NCAA Victory:** In 1983, North Carolina State University pulled off a remarkable upset by defeating the University of Houston in the NCAA championship game, capturing the hearts of fans nationwide.

O **The New York Giants' Super Bowl Upset:** In Super Bowl XLII, the New York Giants defeated the undefeated New England Patriots, delivering a stunning upset and claiming the NFL championship.

O **The Oakland Athletics' Moneyball Season:** The 2002 Oakland Athletics, using a data-driven approach known as Moneyball, reached the playoffs despite having one of the lowest budgets in Major League Baseball.

O **The Jamaican Bobsled Team:** Jamaica's bobsled team made its Olympic debut in 1988, capturing the world's attention with their determination and inspiring the hit movie "Cool Runnings."

O **The Miracle Mets of 1969:** The New York Mets won the World Series in 1969, defying expectations and earning the nickname "Miracle Mets" for their unlikely championship run.

O **Andy Ruiz Jr.'s Heavyweight Victory:** In 2019, Andy Ruiz Jr. defeated the heavily favored Anthony Joshua to become the heavyweight boxing champion, shocking fans and proving that anything is possible.

O **The San Francisco Giants' 2010 World Series Win:** In 2010, the San Francisco Giants defied the odds to win their first World Series in over 50 years, triumphing over the Texas Rangers in a stunning underdog victory.

Unforgettable Olympics

O **This Time it's a Guy's Perfect 10:** Alexander Dityatin (Soviet Union) was the first man to score a perfect 10, achieved on the vault in the 1980 Moscow Olympics. He also won a record-breaking eight medals in these games.

O **The Dream Team's Dominance:** The 1992 U.S. Olympic basketball team, known as the "Dream Team," featured NBA legends like Michael Jordan and Magic Johnson, dominating opponents and winning gold.

O **Cathy Freeman's Golden Moment:** Cathy Freeman won the 400m race at the 2000 Sydney Olympics, becoming a symbol of reconciliation for Australia and inspiring the nation.

O **Allyson Felix's Longevity:** Allyson Felix is the most decorated female track and field Olympian, with 11 medals over five Olympic Games, demonstrating her consistency and talent.

O **Abebe Bikila's Barefoot Marathon:** Abebe Bikila won the marathon at the 1960 Rome Olympics while running barefoot, becoming the first Ethiopian to win a gold medal.

o **Bob Beamon's Long Jump:** Bob Beamon shattered the long jump world record at the 1968 Mexico City Olympics, leaping 8.90 meters and setting a mark that stood for 23 years.

o **Eric the Eel's Unlikely Swim:** At the 2000 Sydney Olympics, swimmer Eric Moussambani from Equatorial Guinea captured hearts by completing his race despite limited training and experience.

o **Wilma Rudolph's Triple Gold:** Wilma Rudolph overcame polio to win three gold medals at the 1960 Rome Olympics, inspiring generations of athletes with her perseverance and talent.

o **Derek Redmond's Finish with Help:** In the 1992 Barcelona Olympics, British sprinter Derek Redmond tore his hamstring during the 400m. Determined to finish, he was helped across the finish line by his father, creating an emotional Olympic moment.

o **Usain Bolt's Lightning Bolt Pose:** Usain Bolt became famous for his "Lightning Bolt" pose at the Olympics, celebrating his victories with a signature gesture that captured the world's attention and became iconic in sports history.

o **Michael Johnson's Golden Shoes:** American sprinter Michael Johnson won gold in both the 200m and 400m at the 1996 Atlanta Olympics, setting a world record in gold-colored shoes, marking one of the most stylish victories ever.

o **Simone Manuel's Historic Win:** In 2016, Simone Manuel became the first African American woman to win an individual Olympic swimming gold, claiming victory in the 100m freestyle and making history in the process.

o **Tommie Smith and John Carlos' Protest:** In 1968, American sprinters Tommie Smith and John Carlos raised their fists in a Black Power salute on the podium to protest racial injustice, creating a powerful and enduring symbol of activism.

o **Eddie the Eagle's Daring Jump:** British ski jumper Eddie "The Eagle" Edwards captured hearts at the 1988 Calgary Olympics despite finishing last. His perseverance and cheerful spirit made him a beloved figure in Olympic history.

o **Nawal El Moutawakel's Ground-breaking Gold:** In 1984, Nawal El Moutawakel became the first Moroccan and the first Muslim woman from an Islamic nation to win an Olympic gold medal. She triumphed in the inaugural women's 400m hurdles event, inspiring women worldwide.

As we reach the end of this segment, we've celebrated some of the most incredible feats in sports history, from record-breaking moments that pushed the boundaries of human potential to the inspiring stories of underdogs who defied the odds. We've marveled at legendary athletes who redefined greatness and relived unforgettable Olympic moments that united nations and inspired generations. These stories of perseverance, skill, and heart remind us that sports are not just games but powerful stories of human triumph and spirit.

But our journey of discovery doesn't stop here! Now, prepare to blast off into the infinite unknown of space. Get ready to explore the mysteries of the cosmos, where stars are born, galaxies collide, and black holes bend the fabric of reality. In the next chapter, we'll journey through the solar system, unlock the secrets of distant planets, and discover the ground-breaking missions that have expanded our understanding of the universe. So fasten your seatbelts and get ready for an out-of-this-world exploration in the next chapter!

The Intergalactic Guide

Astronaut Adventures

O **Longest Spacewalk:** Astronauts Jim Voss and Susan Helms performed the longest spacewalk in history, lasting 8 hours and 56 minutes, in 2001. They repaired the International Space Station's robotic arm.

O **First Human in Space:** Yuri Gagarin, a Soviet cosmonaut, became the first human to travel into space on April 12, 1961, aboard Vostok 1, orbiting Earth for 108 minutes.

O **Space Food Innovation:** In space, food is packaged to prevent crumbs. Astronauts eat tortillas instead of bread, enjoying meals like shrimp cocktail and thermostabilized beef stew.

O **The First Space Selfie:** Buzz Aldrin took the first space selfie during the Gemini 12 mission in 1966, capturing himself with the Earth in the background.

O **Women in Space:** Valentina Tereshkova became the first woman in space in 1963. Since then, over 60 women have followed in her footsteps, exploring the cosmos.

O **Longest Space Flight:** Russian cosmonaut Valeri Polyakov holds the record for the longest single spaceflight, spending 437 days aboard the Mir space station from 1994 to 1995.

O **Sleeping in Space:** Astronauts sleep in sleeping bags attached to walls to prevent floating. They experience sunrises and sunsets every 90 minutes while orbiting Earth.

O **Space Station Recycling:** The International Space Station recycles 93% of its water, including sweat and urine, to sustain astronauts. Water is precious in space!

O **First American Woman in Space:** Sally Ride became the first American woman in space in 1983, breaking barriers and inspiring future generations of female astronauts.

O **Space Fashion: Spacesuits:** Spacesuits are super high-tech! They protect astronauts from extreme temperatures and radiation. Each suit costs about $12 million to build.

O **Astronaut Exercise Routine:** Astronauts exercise for two hours daily in space to counteract muscle and bone loss due to microgravity, using treadmills, bikes, and resistance machines.

O **First Space Station Resident:** Russian cosmonaut Sergei Krikalev was aboard the Mir space station for 10 months in 1991, marking the longest continuous stay on a space station at that time.

O **Astronauts' Fun in Space:** Astronauts play games like weightless ping pong using water droplets and enjoy floating somersaults to unwind during their missions.

O **Chris Hadfield's Guitar Performance in Space:** Canadian astronaut Chris Hadfield became famous for his rendition of David Bowie's *Space Oddity* while aboard the International Space Station. It was the first music video recorded in space!

O **Astronaut Twins Study:** NASA studied twin astronauts, Scott and Mark Kelly, to understand space's effects on the human body. Scott spent a year in space, while Mark stayed on Earth.

Fantastic Flight: Space Missions

○ **Apollo 11's Moon Landing:** In 1969, Apollo 11 successfully landed humans on the Moon for the first time. Neil Armstrong and Buzz Aldrin walked on the lunar surface while Michael Collins orbited above.

○ **Voyager 1's Interstellar Journey:** Launched in 1977, Voyager 1 is the first spacecraft to enter interstellar space, carrying a Golden Record with sounds and images from Earth.

○ **Mars Rover Perseverance:** Launched in 2020, the Perseverance rover explores Mars, searching for signs of ancient life and collecting rock samples for future return to Earth.

○ **Hubble Space Telescope:** Launched in 1990, the Hubble Space Telescope has captured stunning images of distant galaxies, stars, and nebulae, transforming our understanding of the universe.

○ **International Space Station:** The International Space Station (ISS) is a collaborative space lab orbiting Earth. It's home to astronauts from different countries, conducting experiments in microgravity.

○ **New Horizons' Pluto Flyby:** NASA's New Horizons spacecraft provided the first close-up images of Pluto during its flyby in 2015, revealing mountains, plains, and possible ice volcanoes.

○ **Cassini's Saturn Exploration:** The Cassini spacecraft orbited Saturn for 13 years, studying its rings and moons. In 2017, it made a dramatic plunge into Saturn's atmosphere, ending its mission.

○ **Galileo's Jupiter Mission:** The Galileo spacecraft studied Jupiter and its moons from 1995 to 2003, discovering evidence of an ocean beneath Europa's (the sixth-closest moon to Jupiter) icy surface.

○ **Rosetta's Comet Rendezvous:** The European Space Agency's Rosetta spacecraft orbited Comet 67P, and its lander, Philae, made history by landing on a comet's surface in 2014.

○ **Juno's Mission to Jupiter:** Juno has been studying Jupiter since 2016, revealing information about its atmosphere, magnetic field, and deep interior.

○ **Pioneer 10's Journey:** Pioneer 10 was the first spacecraft to travel through the asteroid belt and make a flyby of Jupiter, paving the way for future outer planet exploration.

○ **Challenger's Tragic Launch:** The Space Shuttle Challenger tragically exploded shortly after launch in 1986, reminding us of the risks and bravery involved in space exploration.

○ **Lunar Reconnaissance Orbiter:** Launched in 2009, the Lunar Reconnaissance Orbiter maps the Moon's surface in detail, aiding future lunar missions and discoveries.

○ **Kepler's Exoplanet Discovery:** The Kepler Space Telescope discovered thousands of exoplanets, expanding our understanding of potentially habitable worlds beyond our solar system.

○ **InSight's Mars Mission:** NASA's InSight lander, which arrived on Mars in 2018, studies the planet's interior structure, detecting marsquakes and providing valuable data on Mars' seismic activity and geological history.

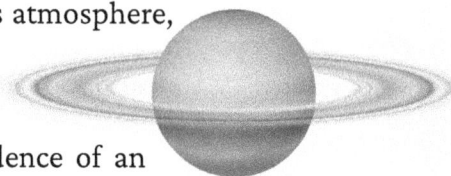

Galactic Mysteries and Wonders

O **The Great Attractor:** The Great Attractor is a gravitational anomaly pulling galaxies, including the Milky Way, toward it. Its mysterious nature is hidden behind the Milky Way's dense galactic plane.

O **The Fermi Paradox:** With billions of stars, why haven't we found aliens? The Fermi Paradox wonders why, in such a vast universe, we've yet to detect other civilizations.

O **The Missing Matter Mystery:** Scientists know the universe's mass, but half of the normal matter is missing. It might be hidden in huge, unseen clouds between galaxies.

O **The Mystery of 'Oumuamua:** In 2017, an oddly-shaped object from another solar system passed through ours. Some scientists even wondered if it might be an alien spacecraft.

O **Black Holes' Mysterious Pull:** Black holes are regions of space with gravity so strong that nothing, not even light, can escape. They warp space-time and remain some of the universe's most intriguing objects.

O **The Moon Is Drifting Away:** The Moon is moving away from Earth at 3.8 centimeters per year. In billions of years, this will affect solar eclipses and Earth's rotation.

O **The Supermassive Black Hole:** At the center of our galaxy lies a supermassive black hole called Sagittarius A*, which has a mass equivalent to four million suns. It's a powerhouse of gravitational energy.

O **The Mystery of Dark Energy:** Dark energy makes up about 68% of the universe, driving its accelerated expansion. Despite its abundance, scientists know very little about this mysterious force.

O **The Pillars of Creation:** The Pillars of Creation are stunning cosmic structures within the Eagle Nebula, where new stars are forming. They were famously photographed by the Hubble Space Telescope.

O **Quasars' Distant Glow:** Quasars are the brightest and most energetic objects in the universe, powered by supermassive black holes at the centers of distant galaxies, shining brightly across the cosmos.

O **Galactic Lunch:** Larger galaxies sometimes "eat" smaller ones by pulling them in with gravity. The Milky Way has absorbed several smaller galaxies over billions of years.

O **The Andromeda-Milky Way Collision:** The Andromeda Galaxy is on a collision course with the Milky Way, expected to merge in about 4.5 billion years, forming a giant elliptical galaxy.

O **The Cosmic Microwave Background:** The cosmic microwave background is the afterglow of the Big Bang, a faint radiation filling the universe, providing a snapshot of the universe's early conditions.

O **The Oort Cloud's Icy Visitors:** The Oort Cloud is a theoretical shell of icy bodies surrounding the solar system. It's believed to be the source of long-period comets that occasionally visit the inner solar system.

O **The Drake Equation:** The Drake Equation estimates the number of intelligent civilizations in our galaxy, considering factors like star formation rates and the likelihood of planets supporting life.

- **The Mystery of Fast Radio Bursts:** Fast radio bursts are intense, milliseconds-long bursts of radio waves from distant galaxies. Their origins are still unknown, sparking curiosity and speculation among astronomers.

- **The Cosmic Cold Spot:** The Cold Spot is an unusually large and cold area of the cosmic microwave background. Its existence challenges our understanding of the universe's uniformity and origins.

Marvels of the Milky Way

- **The Milky Way's Spiral Arms:** The Milky Way is a barred spiral galaxy with four main arms. Our solar system is located in the Orion Arm, a smaller, partial arm of the Milky Way.

- **Venus: The Hottest Planet:** Despite being farther from the Sun, Venus is the hottest planet in our solar system due to its thick, heat-trapping atmosphere.

- **Stellar Nurseries:** The Milky Way is home to vast regions of gas and dust where new stars are born. These "stellar nurseries" include the famous Orion Nebula, visible to the naked eye.

- **The Solar System's Location:** Our solar system is located about 27,000 light-years from the Milky Way's center. This enormous distance is only about two-thirds of the way from the center!

- **The Galactic Habitable Zone:** The Galactic Habitable Zone is an area in the Milky Way where conditions might be right for life. It's not too close to the center, avoiding harmful radiation, but not too far out either.

- **Star Clusters:** The Milky Way contains many star clusters, including globular clusters, which are tight groups of old stars, and open clusters, which are looser groups of young stars.

- **Interstellar Medium:** The space between stars in the Milky Way is filled with the interstellar medium, composed of gas, dust, and cosmic rays, playing a crucial role in star formation.

- **Earth's Atmosphere Reaches Beyond the Moon:** The exosphere, Earth's outermost atmospheric layer, extends about 600,000 miles, reaching beyond the Moon's orbit.

- **The Halo of the Milky Way:** The Milky Way has a halo, a spherical region of stars, gas, and dark matter surrounding the galactic disk. This halo contains some of the oldest stars in our galaxy.

- **The Milky Way's Rotation:** The Milky Way rotates, with stars and other objects orbiting the galactic center. Our solar system travels at about 514,000 miles per hour as it orbits the center of the galaxy.

- **The Sagittarius Stream:** The Sagittarius Stream is a vast, looping structure of stars that wraps around the Milky Way, believed to be remnants of a smaller galaxy that was absorbed by our own.

- **Stars Are Constantly Being Born:** The Milky Way creates about seven new stars every year. These stars form in giant clouds of gas and dust called nebulae.

- **Billions of Planets:** Scientists estimate that the Milky Way has billions of planets, including many that could potentially support life. We've only just started exploring these distant worlds.

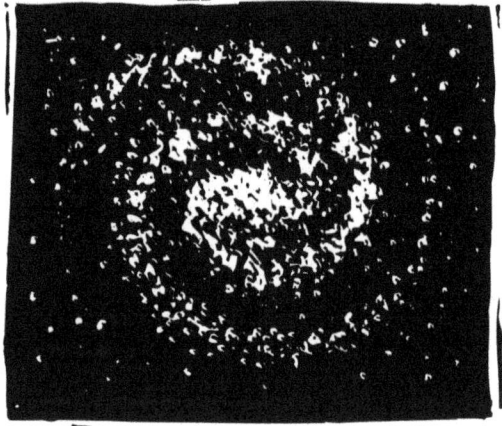

- **Gamma-Rays:** The Milky Way has enormous gamma-ray bubbles extending above and below its center. These structures, known as Fermi Bubbles, may result from past galactic events like supermassive black hole activity.

- **Exoplanet Discoveries:** The Milky Way is home to countless exoplanets. Missions like Kepler and TESS have identified thousands of these distant worlds, some of which may lie in their star's habitable zone.

- **The Milky Way's Size:** If you could travel at the speed of light, it would take you about 100,000 years to cross the Milky Way from one side to the other!

- **Cosmic Recycling:** When stars die, they release gas and dust into space, which helps form new stars and planets. The Milky Way is constantly recycling its material!

Phenomena Beyond Our Planet

- **Supernova Explosions:** Supernovae are massive stellar explosions marking the end of a star's life cycle. These blasts create elements like gold and silver!

- **Pulsars:** Pulsars are highly magnetized, rotating neutron stars that emit beams of electromagnetic radiation. They serve as precise cosmic lighthouses, aiding in navigation and study of the cosmos.

- **Solar Flares:** Solar flares are intense bursts of radiation from the Sun's surface, capable of disrupting communications on Earth and creating spectacular auroras.

- **Exoplanet Atmospheres:** Some exoplanets have atmospheres with exotic conditions, such as 4,000-degree temperatures and glass rain!

- **Cosmic Rays:** Cosmic rays are high-energy particles from space that constantly bombard Earth. They originate from sources like supernova, black holes, and even the Sun.

- **Gravitational Lensing:** Gravitational lensing occurs when a massive object, like a galaxy cluster, bends light from objects behind it, magnifying and distorting their appearance.

- **Gamma-Ray Bursts:** Gamma-ray bursts are the most powerful explosions in the universe, emitting intense radiation for short periods.

- **Neutron Stars:** Neutron stars are incredibly dense remnants of supernova explosions. A sugar-cube-sized amount of neutron star material would weigh a billion tons on Earth.

- **The Aurora of Jupiter:** Jupiter has auroras, just like Earth, but they are much more intense. These light shows are caused by the planet's strong magnetic field interacting with particles from the Sun.

- **The Solar Wind:** The solar wind is a stream of charged particles released from the Sun's atmosphere. It creates phenomena like auroras on Earth.

- **Rogue Planets:** Rogue planets are planets that don't orbit a star. These lonely worlds drift through space, and some might even have conditions suitable for life despite their isolation.

- **Cosmic Voids:** Cosmic voids are vast, empty regions of space between galaxy clusters. They make up a significant portion of the universe's structure, showing how spread out everything is!

- **Planetary Nebula:** Planetary nebula are clouds of gas and dust ejected by dying stars. They create beautiful, colorful shells around the remains.

- **Black Hole Jets:** Some black holes shoot out jets of particles at nearly the speed of light. These jets can extend for thousands of light-years, influencing the formation of galaxies around them.

- **Spaghettification:** In a black hole's intense gravitational field, objects are stretched into long, thin shapes in a process known as "spaghettification." This would happen to anything that gets too close.

Uncharted Worlds and New Frontiers

- **Proxima Centauri b: A Nearby Planet:** Proxima Centauri b is the closest planet outside our solar system. It orbits the star Proxima Centauri and might have conditions that allow liquid water, just like Earth.

- **Trappist-1's Seven Earth-like Planets:** The TRAPPIST-1 system has seven planets similar in size to Earth. Three of them could have the right conditions for life, making it a key target for future exploration.

- **Kepler-452b: Earth's Cousin:** Kepler-452b is an exoplanet often called "Earth's cousin." It's located 1,400 light-years away and shares many characteristics with our planet, making it fascinating to scientists.

- **Titan's Methane Seas:** Saturn's moon Titan has lakes made of liquid methane instead of water. These strange seas make Titan one of the most interesting moons in our solar system.

- **The Mystery of Planet Nine:** Scientists believe there might be a ninth planet in our solar system, far beyond Neptune. This could explain the strange orbits of distant objects in the Kuiper Belt.

- **Enceladus' Icy Geysers:** Enceladus, another moon of Saturn, has geysers that shoot ice and water vapor into space. These plumes suggest a subsurface ocean, sparking interest in its potential for life.

- **Mars' Dry Riverbeds:** Mars once had flowing rivers and lakes, as shown by dry riverbeds and lake beds on its surface. Scientists study these features to understand Mars' wet past.

- **WASP-12b: A Dying Planet:** WASP-12b is a planet so close to its star that it's being slowly eaten away. This "hot Jupiter" helps scientists learn about how planets can change over time.

- **Gliese 581c: A Potential New World:** Gliese 581c is a planet 20 light-years away, located in its star's habitable zone. Scientists are curious about whether it might support life.

- **Kepler-186f: An Earth-Size Planet:** Kepler-186f was the first Earth-sized planet found in a star's habitable zone, showing that there might be many Earth-like planets in the galaxy.

- **Ganymede's Hidden Ocean:** Jupiter's moon Ganymede has an ocean hidden beneath its icy surface. This ocean may contain more water than all of Earth's oceans combined!

- **The James Webb Space Telescope:** Launched in 2021, the James Webb Space Telescope is designed to explore the universe's first galaxies, study the formation of stars and planets, and search for signs of life on distant worlds.

O **The Diamond Planet:** 55 Cancri e is a planet that might have a surface made of diamond due to its carbon-rich makeup, making it a sparkling jewel in space.

O **Io's Active Volcanoes:** Jupiter's moon Io is the most volcanic place in the solar system, with hundreds of active volcanoes that spew lava fountains miles high.

O **Haumea's Strange Shape:** Haumea is a dwarf planet with a unique egg-like shape because it spins so fast. Its day lasts only four hours, making it quite a whirlwind!

As we come to the end of our cosmic journey, we've explored new worlds, unlocked secrets of our solar system, and learned about the exciting discoveries that continue to expand our understanding of the universe.

Next, get ready to dive into the extraordinary world of human anatomy, where every organ and system has a story to tell. Let's explore the ins and outs of the human body and what make us who we are. Off we go!

Fellowship of the Five Senses

Amazing Anatomy

O **Your Skin: The Body's Largest Organ:** Your skin is the largest organ of your body, covering about 22 square feet and weighing roughly 8 pounds. It protects you from germs, helps regulate body temperature, and enables touch.

O **Your Tongue: A Muscle Powerhouse:** Your tongue is the only muscle in your body that's attached at just one end. It's made up of eight different muscles, giving it the flexibility and strength it needs.

O **The Stomach's New Lining:** Your stomach gets a new lining every few days to prevent it from digesting itself. The acidic environment is so strong that the cells must constantly renew.

O **The Amazing Power of the Human Eye:** Your eyes can distinguish about 10 million different colors, and the irises of our eyes are all unique, with more than 256 distinguishable features. You can call them your "visual fingerprints!"

O **Your Brain's Neurons:** Your brain contains about 86 billion neurons, which send signals to different parts of your body at speeds of up to 268 miles per hour!

O **The Nose Knows:** The human nose can detect over a trillion different scents, making it super powerful and essential for memory and emotion.

O **Tiny Bones with Big Jobs:** The smallest bones in your body are the ossicles in your middle ear. These tiny bones are essential for hearing and are smaller than a penny!

O **The Power of Fingernails:** Fingernails grow about 3.5 millimeters per month, which means you grow about 1.5 inches of nail each year. Your fingernails are made of the same protein as your hair - keratin.

O **Your Liver's Superpowers:** Your liver performs over 500 vital functions, including detoxifying chemicals, metabolizing drugs, and producing bile for digestion. It's the only organ that can regenerate itself!

O **Bones Are Stronger Than Concrete:** Your bones are four times stronger than concrete. Despite being incredibly strong, they're also lightweight, allowing your skeleton to support your body.

O **The Longest Muscle:** The longest muscle in your body is the sartorius, which runs from your hip to your knee. It helps you cross your legs, making it essential for sitting and squatting.

O **Your Blood's Busy Journey:** If all the blood vessels in your body were laid end to end, they would stretch far enough to circle the Earth more than twice!

- **Amazing Alveoli:** Your lungs contain about 480 million alveoli, tiny air sacs where oxygen enters your blood. If stretched out, your alveoli would cover a tennis court!

- **The Mighty Muscles of Your Jaw:** The masseter muscle in your jaw is one of the strongest muscles in your body. It can exert a force of up to 200 pounds!

- **Red Blood Cell Replacement:** Your body produces about 2 million red blood cells every second to replace the ones that wear out. These cells carry oxygen through your body, keeping you energized.

- **Sweat Glands Galore:** You have 2 to 4 million sweat glands spread across your body. They help regulate your body temperature by releasing sweat when you're hot.

- **The Spiral of Your DNA:** If all the DNA in your body were uncoiled, it would stretch far enough to reach Pluto and back!

- **The Stretchy Esophagus:** Your esophagus, the tube that carries food from your throat to your stomach, is about 10 inches long and can stretch to fit large pieces of food as you swallow.

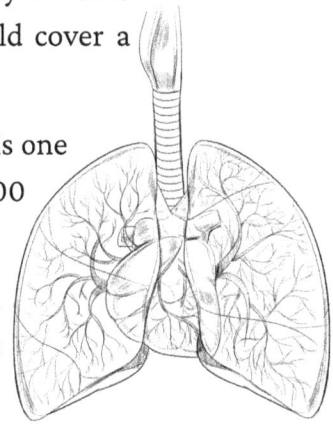

Bizarre Bodily Functions

- **Hiccups: A Mystery of the Body:** Hiccups are caused by sudden, involuntary contractions of the diaphragm. Scientists aren't sure why we hiccup, but they're usually harmless and go away on their own.

- **The Purpose of Ear Popping:** Your ears pop when you experience a change in altitude because you are adjusting the pressure in your middle ear to match the outside environment. This helps maintain balance and hearing clarity.

- **Saliva Pools:** You produce about 25,000 quarts of saliva in a lifetime—enough to fill two swimming pools! Saliva is crucial for digestion and oral health.

- **Why We Get Goosebumps:** Goosebumps occur when tiny muscles at the base of hair follicles contract, making your hair stand on end. This reflex dates back to when humans had more body hair and needed warmth or to appear larger when threatened.

- **The Purpose of Earwax:** Earwax helps protect your ears by trapping dust and dirt, preventing them from reaching your eardrum. It also has antibacterial properties.

- **The Reason for Blushing:** Blushing happens when adrenaline causes blood vessels in your face to widen, increasing blood flow. It's a response to emotions like embarrassment, excitement, or stress.

- **Why We Yawn:** Yawning is contagious, but its exact purpose is still unknown. Some scientists think yawning helps cool your brain, while others believe it's a way to increase oxygen intake.

O **Photic Sneeze Reflex:** About 10-35% of people sneeze when exposed to bright light, a phenomenon known as the photic sneeze reflex. It's inherited, and scientists are still studying why it happens.

O **The Click of Your Joints:** When you crack your knuckles, you're creating bubbles of gas that form and pop in the fluid around your joints. Contrary to popular belief, this doesn't cause arthritis.

O **The Strange Taste of Crying:** Tears contain different substances depending on why you're crying. Emotional tears, for example, contain more stress hormones than tears caused by something like cutting an onion.

O **Why We Get "Pins and Needles":** The tingling sensation of "pins and needles" happens when nerves are compressed, cutting off signals. When the pressure is relieved, the nerves "wake up," causing the prickly feeling.

O **The Science of Burping:** Burping is your body's way of releasing excess air from your stomach. This air can be swallowed while eating or drinking, especially if you're consuming something carbonated.

O **We're all Taller in The Morning:** You are actually approximately 1 centimeter taller when you just wake up as compared to the time when you go to bed. Reason? Gravity! The cartilage in your spine experiences less compression while you are lying down, hence the reason for your extra height!

O **Sleepwalking: A Nighttime Mystery:** Sleepwalking occurs during deep sleep and can involve simple actions like walking around the house, or more complex behaviors like driving a car, all without waking up!

O **The Belly Button:** Some people have "outie" belly buttons instead of "innies" due to the way their umbilical cords heal after birth. This harmless difference is simply part of what makes you unique!

O **The Sound of Your Stomach Growling:** Your stomach growls when it's empty because it's moving air and fluid through your intestines. This process is part of digestion and can happen even when you're not hungry.

Incredible Human Machines

O **The Brain's Processing Speed:** The human brain processes information at an astonishing speed—up to 120 meters per second. That's faster than the speed of the fastest Formula 1 car!

O **The Brain's Electrical Power:** Your brain generates about 20 watts of electricity, enough to power a small light bulb. It uses this energy to process information and control your body's functions.

O **The Immune System's Defense:** Your immune system is like an army inside your body, constantly fighting off harmful invaders like bacteria, viruses, and parasites to keep you healthy.

O **Avascular Wonder: The Cornea:** The cornea lacks blood vessels, so that means it is the only organ in our body to not receive oxygen the regular way. It gets the oxygen it needs direct from the air!

o **The Flexibility of Muscle:** Your muscles are incredibly flexible, allowing you to perform a wide range of movements. The human body has over 600 muscles, from tiny ones in your eyes to large ones in your legs.

o **The Precision of the Eye:** Your eyes work like cameras, focusing light on the retina to create images. They can adjust to see clearly in different lighting conditions and can focus on about 50 different objects every second.

o **The Complexity of the Digestive System:** Your digestive system is a complex machine that processes food, absorbs nutrients, and eliminates waste. It's about 30 feet long and includes organs like the stomach, intestines, and liver.

o **The Power of the Respiratory System:** Your respiratory system supplies oxygen to your blood and removes carbon dioxide. The average person breathes about 20,000 times a day!

o **The Coordination of the Skeletal System:** Your skeletal system provides structure, protects your organs, and works with your muscles to make you move. It's also constantly renewing and repairing itself.

o **The Efficiency of the Circulatory System:** Your circulatory system, composed of your heart, blood, and blood vessels, works efficiently to deliver oxygen and nutrients to every cell in your body, keeping you alive and energized.

o **Never-ending Hair Growth:** Human hair grows at an average rate of 0.5 inches per month. A single hair has a lifespan of 3 to 7 years before falling out and being replaced by a new one.

o **The Precision of the Endocrine System:** Your endocrine system releases hormones that regulate various functions, including growth, metabolism, and mood. This system is vital for maintaining balance in your body.

o **Your Kidneys: Nature's Filters:** Your kidneys filter about 50 gallons of blood every day, removing waste and extra water to make urine. They're vital for keeping your blood clean and your body in balance.

o **The Adaptability of the Nervous System:** Your nervous system is incredibly adaptable, capable of changing itself in response to new experiences and learning. This allows you to recover from injuries and learn new skills.

o **The Strength of Your Core:** Your core muscles, including those in your abdomen and back, provide stability and support for nearly every movement you make!

Marvels of the Mind

o **The Brain's Memory Capacity:** Your brain has a huge capacity for storing memories. It can hold around 2.5 petabytes of information, which is equivalent to about 3 million hours of TV shows!

o **The Power of Dreams:** Dreams allow you to process emotions, memories, and experiences while you sleep. Most people have about 4 to 6 dreams per night.

o **The Speed of Thought:** Your brain processes information incredibly fast, with signals moving between neurons at speeds of up to 268 miles per hour!

o **The Mystery of Déjà Vu:** Déjà vu is the feeling that you've experienced something before, even though it's new. Scientists believe it might be caused by the brain misfiring, creating a false sense of familiarity.

o **The Power of Focus:** The brain has an incredible ability to focus on a single task, filtering out distractions. This concentration allows you to complete complex tasks, like solving math problems or reading a book.

o **The Power of Imagination:** The brain can't always distinguish between real and imagined experiences. This is why imagining something vividly can sometimes trigger the same emotional and physical responses as actually experiencing it.

o **The Brain's Ability to Learn Languages:** Your brain is particularly good at learning languages, especially when you're young. The left hemisphere is where most language processing occurs.

o **The Brain's Energy Demand:** Although the brain makes up only about 2% of your body weight, it uses around 20% of your body's total energy, mainly for maintaining electrical charges in neurons and processing information.

o **The Role of the Subconscious:** Most of what your brain does happens subconsciously. For example, your heart rate, breathing, and digestion are all controlled without you even thinking about it.

o **The Importance of Sleep:** Sleep is essential for the brain to function properly. During sleep, your brain consolidates memories, clears out toxins, and prepares for the next day, which is why it's so important!

o **The Brain's Creative Power:** The right hemisphere of your brain is associated with creativity and imagination. It's the part of your brain that helps you come up with new ideas and think outside the box.

o **The Brain's Emotional Center:** The amygdala, a small almond-shaped structure in your brain, is responsible for processing emotions like fear, anger, and pleasure. It plays a key role in your emotional responses.

o **The Brain's Control of Movement:** The motor cortex, located in the frontal lobe of your brain, controls voluntary movements. It sends signals to your muscles, allowing you to perform actions like walking, writing, and speaking.

o **The Science of Decision-Making:** Your brain's prefrontal cortex is responsible for decision-making, weighing options, and considering consequences. This area is essential for making complex choices in daily life.

O **The Impact of Music on the Brain:** Listening to music activates multiple areas of the brain, including those responsible for emotion, memory, and movement. Music can improve mood, reduce stress, and enhance cognitive performance.

Mysteries of Medicine

O **The Placebo Effect:** The placebo effect occurs when a patient experiences real improvements in their condition after receiving a treatment that has no therapeutic value, simply because they believe it will work!

O **The Mystery of the Gut-Brain Connection:** Scientists are discovering that your gut and brain communicate through a complex network of nerves, hormones, and even gut bacteria, influencing everything from mood to immune response.

O **The Human Body's Natural Painkillers:** Endorphins are natural chemicals produced by your brain that help reduce pain and boost feelings of pleasure. They're often released during exercise, creating a "runner's high."

O **The Mystery of Phantom Limb Pain:** Phantom limb pain occurs when amputees feel pain in a limb that's no longer there. It's a mysterious condition that scientists believe is related to how the brain processes pain signals.

O **The "Nocebo" Effect:** The opposite of the placebo effect, the "nocebo" effect occurs when negative expectations lead to worsening symptoms. Understanding how and why this happens remains a challenge in medicine.

O **Laughing for Health:** Laughter has been shown to have real health benefits, like improving moods and boosting the immune system. Yet, the exact reasons why laughter is so good for us are still being studied.

O **The Science of Organ Transplants:** The first successful organ transplant was a kidney transplant in 1954. Since then, organ transplants have saved countless lives!

O **The Power of Stem Cells:** Stem cells are special cells that can develop into many different cell types. They're being studied for their potential to treat a wide range of diseases and injuries.

O **The Body's Healing Process:** When you get a cut, your body immediately begins to heal itself. Blood clots form to stop the bleeding, and cells called fibroblasts start to repair the damaged tissue.

O **The Mystery of Chronic Pain:** Chronic pain is pain that persists for months or even years, often without a clear cause. Scientists are still trying to understand why some people experience chronic pain and how to treat it effectively.

O **The Power of Vaccines:** Vaccines work by stimulating your immune system to recognize and fight off specific viruses or bacteria. They've been instrumental in eradicating diseases like smallpox and controlling others like polio.

o **The Complexity of the Human Microbiome:** Your body is home to trillions of microorganisms, collectively known as the microbiome. These tiny organisms play a crucial role in digestion, immunity, and overall health.

o **The Mystery of Autoimmune Diseases:** Autoimmune diseases occur when the immune system mistakenly attacks the body's own cells. Conditions like lupus, rheumatoid arthritis, and type 1 diabetes are examples, and their exact causes are still not fully understood.

o **The Power of Antibiotics:** Antibiotics are drugs that fight bacterial infections, saving millions of lives since their discovery. However, overuse has led to antibiotic resistance, making it a growing concern in medicine.

o **The Future of Genetic Medicine:** Advancements in genetic medicine are paving the way for potential cures for genetic disorders. Scientists are exploring how to edit genes to prevent and treat diseases.

Strength and Stamina

o **The Endurance of Your Muscles:** Your muscles are designed for endurance. They're made up of different types of fibers, some of which are built for short bursts of power, while others are designed for sustained activity.

o **The Stamina of the Human Body:** The human body is capable of incredible feats of endurance. Ultramarathon runners, for example, can run for hours or even days without stopping, thanks to their highly trained muscles and cardiovascular systems.

o **The Power of the Mind:** Mental strength is just as important as physical strength. The brain's ability to focus, persevere, and stay motivated can make a significant difference in athletic performance and overall well-being.

o **The Role of Oxygen in Endurance:** Oxygen is crucial for endurance. During exercise, your muscles use oxygen to produce energy. The more efficiently your body delivers oxygen to your muscles, the longer you can sustain physical activity.

o **The Power of Hydration:** Staying hydrated is essential for maintaining strength and stamina. Water helps regulate your body temperature, lubricate joints, and transport nutrients, all of which are crucial for peak physical performance.

o **The Power of Protein:** Protein is essential for building and repairing muscles. After exercise, your body uses protein to rebuild muscle fibers, making them stronger and more resilient.

o **The Endurance of the Heart:** Your heart is built for endurance. It can keep pumping blood throughout your body for decades, even under the stress of physical activity, without getting tired.

O **The Power of Carbohydrates:** Carbohydrates are the body's primary source of energy during exercise. They're stored in your muscles and liver as glycogen, which your body can quickly convert into energy when needed.

O **The Strength of the Lungs:** Your lungs are incredibly strong and efficient at delivering oxygen to your blood. With training, you can increase your lung capacity, allowing you to take in more oxygen and improve your endurance. Think of the divers who dive great depths without an oxygen tank!

O **The Power of the Mind-Body Connection:** The mind-body connection plays a crucial role in strength and stamina. Techniques like visualization, meditation, and deep breathing can help enhance physical performance by calming the mind and focusing the body.

O **Endurance of Sherpas in High Altitudes:** Sherpas, native to the Himalayan region, have extraordinary endurance at high altitudes. Their bodies are adapted to low oxygen levels, allowing them to climb Mount Everest multiple times and with a lot more ease!

O **Muscle Memory:** Your muscles have a remarkable ability to "remember" past training. Even after a long break, your body can regain strength and skills more quickly thanks to this muscle memory.

O **The Power of the Diaphragm:** The diaphragm, a dome-shaped muscle under your lungs, plays a key role in breathing. It contracts and flattens when you inhale, allowing your lungs to fill with air.

O **Bone Density and Strength:** Your bones are constantly renewing themselves, and weight-bearing exercises like running and lifting weights can increase their density, making them stronger and more resistant to fractures.

O **Grip Strength:** Grip strength is a key indicator of overall muscular strength and endurance. Studies show it is correlated with longer life expectancy and lower risks of cardiovascular disease.

In this segment, we've explored the mysteries of our bodily functions, marveled at the strength and stamina our bodies possess, and discovered just how finely tuned our internal machines truly are. Each fact has revealed just how amazing and complex our bodies can be, inspiring us to appreciate the extraordinary systems working silently within us every day.

Next, we venture into the world of inventions— where human creativity, curiosity, and ingenuity come together to shape our world. So, let's turn the page and dive in, where every idea, big or small, has the power to change the world! Let's go!

The Tinkerers' Toolbox

Brilliant Breakthroughs

O **The First Artificial Heart:** The first successful implantation of a total artificial heart took place in 1982. Today, artificial hearts are used as a bridge to heart transplants, keeping patients alive until a donor is found.

O **The Invention of the Thermos**: The Thermos, invented in 1892 by Sir James Dewar, was originally designed to keep chemicals at a stable temperature for experiments. It was later adapted for everyday use to keep drinks hot or cold.

O **Velcro's Sticky Inspiration:** Velcro was invented in 1941 by Swiss engineer George de Mestral. He got the idea after noticing how burrs stuck to his clothes during a hike, showcasing a natural hook and loop system.

O **The Invention of the Transistor:** In 1947, the invention of the transistor at Bell Labs revolutionized electronics, enabling the development of smaller, more efficient devices like radios, computers, and smartphones.

O **The First Cloned Mammal:** In 1996, scientists in Scotland successfully cloned a sheep named Dolly using a technique called somatic cell nuclear transfer. This breakthrough opened new possibilities in genetics.

O **Bluetooth's Viking Roots:** Bluetooth technology, invented in 1994, was named after a Viking king, Harald "Bluetooth" Gormsson, known for uniting Denmark and Norway. The technology was designed to unite communication devices.

O **The Invention of the MRI Machine:** The development of Magnetic Resonance Imaging (MRI) in the 1970s by Raymond Damadian allowed doctors to see detailed images of organs and tissues inside the human body without surgery.

O **The Creation of the World's First Vaccine for COVID-19:** In 2020, multiple COVID-19 vaccines were developed in record time, using mRNA technology. This breakthrough helped to lessen the impact of the pandemic and saved millions of lives.

O **The Discovery of the Neutron:** In 1932, James Chadwick discovered the neutron, a particle in the atomic nucleus with no electric charge. This discovery was crucial for the development of nuclear energy and atomic theory.

O **The Invention of the Laser:** In 1960, Theodore Maiman built the first laser, a device that emits a concentrated beam of light. Lasers are now used in everything from surgery to telecommunications!

O **Wireless Pacemakers: Heart Health without Surgery:** Wireless pacemakers, introduced in the 2010s, are tiny devices that regulate heartbeats without requiring invasive surgery. They're implanted directly into the heart through a catheter.

- **The Discovery of Vitamins:** In the early 20th century, scientists discovered vitamins—essential nutrients that our bodies need to function properly. This led to the prevention and treatment of diseases like scurvy and rickets.

- **The Invention of the Jet Engine:** In the 1930s, Frank Whittle and Hans von Ohain developed the jet engine, making air travel faster and more efficient. This laid the foundation of the aviation we know today.

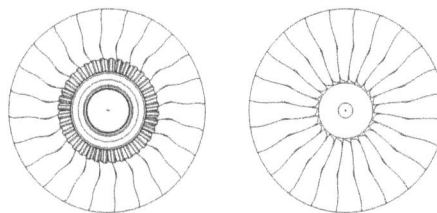

- **The Creation of the First Artificial Intelligence (AI) Program:** In 1951, Christopher Strachey wrote the first successful AI program—a checkers-playing software. This laid the groundwork for the field of artificial intelligence, which continues to advance today.

- **The Invention of the Electric Light:** In 1800, Humphry Davy invented the first electric light, known as the electric arc lamp. Although it was too bright and impractical for home use, Davy's breakthrough paved the way for future developments.

Gadgets That Changed the Playing Field

- **The Microwave Oven:** In 1945, Percy Spencer discovered that microwaves could cook food when a chocolate bar melted in his pocket during a radar experiment. This led to the invention of the microwave oven!

- **The Sony Walkman:** Released in 1979, the Sony Walkman was the first portable cassette player, allowing people to listen to music on the go. It changed the way we listen to music and shaped modern music consumption.

- **The iPhone:** In 2007, Apple introduced the iPhone, a revolutionary device that combined a phone, music player, and internet browser in one. It set the standard for smartphones and has been dominant ever since.

- **The E-Reader:** The first E Ink e-reader, the Sony Reader was created utilizing E Ink, and that marked the beginning of the modern e-reader era. It was lightweight, book-sized, and offered a more comfortable reading experience.

- **The Game Boy:** Released by Nintendo in 1989, the Game Boy was the first portable handheld gaming console to gain worldwide popularity. It made video games accessible anywhere for the first time.

- **The Personal Computer:** The first personal computer, the Altair 8800, was introduced in 1975. It inspired the development of the modern PC, becoming a staple in homes and offices around the world.

- **The Fitbit:** The Fitbit, first released in 2009, popularized the idea of wearable fitness trackers, allowing people to monitor their physical activity, sleep, and health metrics.

- **The Smartwatch:** The first smartwatch, the Pebble, was launched in 2013, offering notifications, fitness tracking, and apps on your wrist. It led to the development of other smart devices like the Apple Watch.

- **The Swiss Army Knife:** The Swiss Army Knife, invented in 1891, became famous for combining multiple tools in one gadget. It's still used today for its compact design and versatility.

- **The Electric Toothbrush:** The first electric toothbrush was developed in Switzerland in 1954. It was designed to help patients with limited motor skills maintain oral hygiene, but it soon became popular worldwide.

- **The Smart Thermostat:** Nest Labs introduced the first smart thermostat in 2011, allowing users to control their home's temperature remotely and learn their habits to save energy.

- **The Answering Machine:** The answering machine, invented in 1935 by Willy Mller, revolutionized communication by allowing people to leave voice messages when someone wasn't available to take a call. This gadget was the start of modern voicemail systems.

- **The Disposable Camera:** Introduced by Fujifilm in 1986, the disposable camera made photography more accessible and convenient. Since people didn't need expensive equipment, this contributed to the rise of casual photography.

- **The Electric Kettle:** The first electric kettle, invented in 1922, allowed water to be boiled much faster than on a stovetop. This gadget has since become a kitchen staple.

Inventors and Their Ingenuity

- **Nikola Tesla's Vision of Wireless Power:** Nikola Tesla dreamed of transmitting electricity wirelessly across the globe. Although he didn't fully realize this vision, his inventions, like the Tesla coil, were the beginnings of modern wireless technology.

- **Leonardo da Vinci's Inventions Ahead of Their Time:** Leonardo da Vinci designed flying machines, tanks, and even a robot centuries before they became reality. His notebooks revealed a mind far ahead of its time.

- **Hedy Lamarr: The Inventor of Wi-Fi's Foundation:** Hollywood actress Hedy Lamarr co-invented frequency hopping, a technology designed to prevent enemy detection of Allied torpedoes during World War II. This innovation became the foundation for Wi-Fi and Bluetooth.

- **Tim Berners-Lee and the World Wide Web:** In 1989, Tim Berners-Lee invented the World Wide Web, revolutionizing how information is shared and accessed. His invention turned the internet into a global communication tool.

- **George Washington Carver's Agricultural Innovations:** George Washington Carver developed hundreds of products using peanuts, sweet potatoes, and other crops. His work helped improve agriculture and promoted sustainable farming practices.

- **Grace Hopper: The Queen of Code:** Grace Hopper, a computer scientist, invented the first compiler, which translates written language into computer code. Her work laid the foundation for modern programming languages.

- **The Accidental Chocolate Chip Cookie:** Ruth Wakefield invented the chocolate chip cookie by accident in 1938 while trying to create a new kind of cookie for her inn's guests. Her recipe became an American classic.

- **Windshield Wipers: A Woman's Invention:** Mary Anderson invented the windshield wiper in 1903. It was initially met with much skepticism from automobile manufacturers. Luckily the wipers became standard equipment for cars in the end!

- **Elon Musk's Visionary Ventures:** Elon Musk, founder of companies like SpaceX and Tesla, has pushed the boundaries of space exploration, electric vehicles, and renewable energy, aiming to change the future of humanity.

- **Steve Jobs: Tech Visionary:** Steve Jobs, co-founder of Apple Inc., revolutionized personal computing, smartphones, and digital media. His innovative spirit and vision changed the way the world interacts with technology.

- **Margaret E. Knight: The Lady Edison:** Margaret E. Knight invented the machine that produced flat-bottomed paper bags in 1871. She held over 20 patents and was known as "the lady Edison" for her fantastic inventions.

- **Philo Farnsworth: The Father of Television:** At just 21 years old, Philo Farnsworth invented the first fully functional electronic television in 1927. His invention changed media and entertainment consumption forever.

- **Otis Boykin's Innovations in Electronics:** Otis Boykin, an African-American inventor, created over 25 electronic devices, including a control unit for pacemakers and components for IBM computers. His work has had a lasting impact on medicine and computing.

- **Elijah McCoy: The Real McCoy:** Elijah McCoy, an African-Canadian inventor, developed an automatic lubricator for steam engines in 1872, which was so effective that it inspired the phrase "the real McCoy," referring to his high-quality invention.

- **Jacques Cousteau: The Pioneer of Scuba Diving:** Jacques Cousteau co-invented the Aqua-Lung in 1943, a device that allowed divers to breathe underwater. His invention led to the popularization of scuba diving.

- **Lonnie Johnson: The Super Soaker:** Lonnie Johnson, an engineer who worked for NASA on the Galileo mission to Jupiter and the Cassini mission to Saturn, is best known for his invention of the Super Soaker water gun in 1989. Johnson's invention stemmed from his work on a heat pump that used water instead of Freon. While experimenting with a prototype in his bathroom, he noticed a powerful stream of water shooting across the room, sparking the idea for the Super Soaker.

- **Elisha Otis and the Safety Elevator:** In 1853, Elisha Otis invented the safety elevator, which would stop if the lifting rope broke. His invention made tall buildings and skyscrapers possible by improving elevator safety.

Revolutionary Rethinks

- **The Self-Driving Car:** Self-driving car technology, led by companies like Tesla and Google, is transforming transportation by making autonomous vehicles a reality, with the potential to reduce accidents and reshape cities.

- **Bubble Wrap's Bumpy Beginning:** Bubble wrap was originally invented as textured wallpaper. When it failed as decor, its inventors discovered its potential as packing material.

- **The Shift from Typewriters to Keyboards:** The typewriter, first invented in 1868, paved the way for modern computer keyboards. The layout we use today, known as QWERTY, was designed to prevent keys from jamming on early machines.

- **Reinventing Agriculture with Vertical Farming:** Vertical farming rethinks traditional agriculture by growing crops in stacked layers, often in urban environments. This innovation reduces the need for large plots of land and conserves water.

- **The Reimagining of Paper with E-Paper:** E-paper technology, used in devices like most of the current E-readers, mimics the appearance of ink on paper while being digital. This innovation provides a reading experience close to traditional books but happens to be more convenient.

- **From Coal to Clean Energy:** The shift from coal-powered energy to renewable sources like wind, solar, and hydroelectric power represents a revolutionary rethink in how we generate electricity, aiming for a sustainable future.

- **The Reinvention of Education with Online Learning:** The rise of online learning platforms has changed education dramatically, making it accessible to millions around the world. This rethink has allowed for flexible, personalized learning experiences.

- **Home Entertainment with Streaming Services:** The rise of streaming services like Netflix and Hulu in the 2000s revolutionized home entertainment by allowing on-demand access to vast libraries of movies, TV shows, and original content.

- **The Popularization of Concrete:** The ancient Romans developed their own concrete over 2,000 years ago, revolutionizing construction. Their secret formula allowed them to build enduring structures like the Colosseum and aqueducts, many of which still stand today.

o **The Stethoscope:** In 1816, René Laennec invented the stethoscope, transforming medicine by giving doctors a way to listen to internal sounds in the body, improving diagnosis for heart and lung conditions.

o **The Evolution of Money to Cryptocurrency:** Cryptocurrency, like Bitcoin, represents a rethink of money itself, using decentralized technology to create a new form of digital currency that operates outside traditional banking systems.

o **The Reinvention of Communication with Instant Messaging:** Instant messaging services, like AOL Instant Messenger launched in 1997, transformed personal communication by allowing real-time exchanges over the internet, laying the groundwork for modern social media messaging apps.

o **The Evolution of Cinematography with CGI:** Computer-generated imagery (CGI) transformed filmmaking by enabling the creation of realistic images that were previously impossible to achieve with practical effects alone. This technology rethought the possibilities of film.

o **QR Codes:** First introduced in 1994 by a Japanese company, QR codes revolutionized how we access information, allowing people to instantly link to websites, menus, or apps by scanning a code with their smartphones.

o **The Transition from Landlines to Mobile Phones:** The shift from landline telephones to mobile phones, starting with the first commercially available mobile phone by Motorola in 1983, revolutionized communication by making it accessible anywhere.

o **The Rethinking of Travel with the Electric Scooter:** The introduction of electric scooters, particularly with the rise of shared scooter services in the late 2010s, offers a convenient, eco-friendly alternative to cars and public transport for short trips.

Tech Triumphs

o **The First Email:** The first email was sent in 1971 by Ray Tomlinson. He chose the "@" symbol to connect the user and the machine, creating a system that changed global communication forever.

o **The Apollo Guidance Computer:** The Apollo Guidance Computer (AGC) was a key component of NASA's Apollo missions, enabling the first successful manned moon landing in 1969. It was one of the earliest digital computers used in space.

o **Wi-Fi: Wireless Freedom:** Wi-Fi technology, developed in the late 1990s, liberated computers from Ethernet cables, enabling wireless internet access and transforming our lives online.

o **Fiber Optics: Light-Speed Data:** Fiber optic technology uses thin strands of glass or plastic to transmit data as light pulses, allowing for high-speed internet in many areas of the world.

o **Bluetooth Connectivity:** Bluetooth, introduced in 1999, allows devices to communicate wirelessly over short distances. It's now used in everything from wireless headphones to smart home devices.

o **The First Laptop:** The Osborne 1, released in 1981, was the first commercially successful portable computer. Weighing 24 pounds, it marked the beginning of the laptop era!

o **The Rise of the Smart Home:** Smart home technology, like Amazon's Alexa and Google Home, allows users to control lights, thermostats, and appliances with their voice. This has revolutionized how we run our homes.

o **The Birth of the CD-ROM:** Introduced in 1982 by Sony and Philips, the CD-ROM (Compact Disc Read-Only Memory) became a groundbreaking data storage medium. It allowed for the storage of large amounts of data at the time, but has since become almost obsolete.

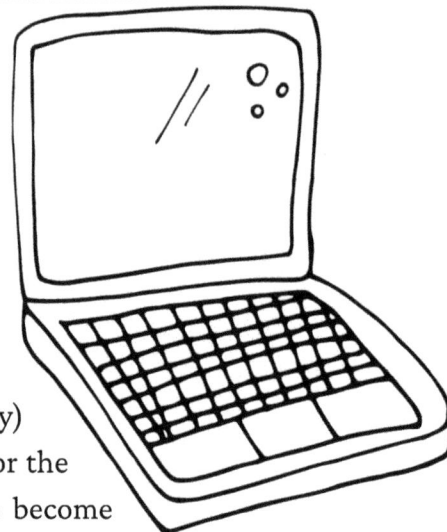

o **The Invention of the Touchscreen:** Touchscreen technology, first demonstrated by E.A. Johnson in 1965 and later refined for consumer devices, changed how we interact with gadgets, making it possible to use our devices with just a finger tap.

o **The Success of USB-C:** Introduced in 2014, USB-C became a universal standard for charging and data transfer across devices, offering faster speeds and a reversible connector, making it much easier for us to charge our gadgets!

o **The Rise of Mobile Payments:** Mobile payment systems like Apple Pay, launched in 2014, reshaped how we shop by allowing users to pay with their smartphones – making spending even more convenient!

o **The Development of Digital Assistants:** Digital assistants like Siri, launched by Apple in 2011, redefined user interaction with technology by allowing voice commands to perform tasks.

o **The Evolution of Video Conferencing:** The introduction of video conferencing technology, particularly with the rise of platforms like Zoom during the 2020 pandemic, transformed how people communicate, allowing for virtual meetings, classes, and social gatherings across the globe.

o **The Impact of 5G Technology:** The rollout of 5G technology, starting in 2019, significantly improved mobile network speeds and connectivity, making way for advancements in smart cities, autonomous vehicles, and the Internet of Things (IoT).

o **The Development of the Microprocessor:** In 1971, Intel introduced the first commercially available microprocessor, the Intel 4004. This tiny chip integrated the processing power of a computer onto a single chip, leading to the inventions of our smaller gadgets, like mobile phones.

Weird and Wacky Creations

o **The Pet Rock:** In 1975, Gary Dahl invented the Pet Rock, a smooth stone sold as a "pet" that came in a cardboard box with breathing holes and straw bedding. It became a wildly popular novelty item.

- **The Hula Hoop Craze:** The Hula Hoop, introduced by Wham-O in 1958, became a global sensation. People worldwide were mesmerized by the challenge of spinning it around their waists.

- **The Umbrella Tie:** The umbrella tie, invented in the 1980s, is a quirky combination of an umbrella and a necktie. While it didn't become a fashion staple, it certainly caught people's attention for its oddness!

- **The Flowbee Haircutter:** Invented in 1986, the Flowbee is a vacuum cleaner attachment designed to cut hair. Though unusual, it developed a surprising following and is still available today for DIY haircuts.

- **The Snuggie: A Blanket with Sleeves:** The Snuggie, a blanket with sleeves, became a viral sensation in 2008. Its bizarre yet practical design allowed users to stay warm while keeping their hands free for activities.

- **The Walking Bicycle:** The Walking Bicycle, invented in Japan, is a cross between a scooter and a treadmill. Riders walk on a treadmill-like surface to power the bike!

- **The Y2K Survival Kit:** In the late 1990s, as fears of the Y2K bug spread, companies sold Y2K survival kits containing everything from bottled water to canned food, playing on the anxiety surrounding the new millennium.

- **The Motorized Ice Cream Cone:** Invented in the 1980s, the motorized ice cream cone spins the ice cream for you, so you don't have to rotate the cone yourself—perfect for the laziest of snackers!

- **The Doggles: Sunglasses for Dogs:** Doggles are sunglasses designed specifically for dogs, protecting their eyes from UV light, dust, and wind. While it may seem wacky, some dog owners swear by them for their pets' outdoor adventures.

- **The Alarm Clock That Runs Away:** The Clocky alarm clock, invented in 2005, jumps off your nightstand and runs around the room, forcing you to get out of bed to turn it off. It's perfect for heavy sleepers who struggle to wake up.

- **The Selfie Toaster:** The Selfie Toaster allows you to toast your own face onto bread. Launched in 2014, it lets you start your day with a unique breakfast experience—literally eating a picture of yourself!

- **The Baby Mop:** The Baby Mop, a onesie with mop-like fringes on the bottom, claims to let your baby clean the floor as they crawl, giving you a tiny helper around the home!

- **The Hamster Wheel Standing Desk:** This standing desk, shaped like a giant hamster wheel, allows you to walk while you work. It's a more bizarre take on the treadmill desks that are popular today.

O **The Pizza Scissors:** Pizza scissors combine a spatula and a pair of scissors to allow for easy slicing and serving of pizza in one motion. This kitchen gadget claims to save time and washing up!

O **The Phone Fingers:** Phone Fingers are finger covers that prevent smudges on your smartphone screen. Though practical, their odd appearance makes them one of the more unusual tech accessories out there.

And there we have it-the end of our journey through some of the most revolutionary and sometimes strange inventions in history! From ground-breaking technologies that transformed our daily lives to quirky gadgets that brought unexpected joy, each invention has a story to tell.

Next up, we enter the vibrant scenes of film and pop culture. We'll explore the magic of the silver screen, the rise of iconic characters, and the cultural phenomena that have shaped generations. So, grab some popcorn and let's dive into the lights, camera, and action!

The Reel Red Carpet

Blockbuster Moments

O **The Highest-Grossing Film:** *Avatar* (2009), directed by James Cameron, holds the title of the highest-grossing film of all time, with over $2.9 billion in global box office earnings.

O **Psycho's Toilet Scene:** Alfred Hitchcock's "Psycho" (1960) was the first American film to show a flushing toilet on screen, which was considered shocking at the time.

O **The Birth of the Summer Blockbuster:** *Jaws* (1975), directed by Steven Spielberg, is widely considered the first summer blockbuster. Its massive success changed Hollywood's release strategies, making summer the prime season for big-budget films.

O **The Longest-Running Film Franchise:** *James Bond* is the longest-running film franchise in history, with 25 official films since *Dr. No* in 1962. The character has been portrayed by seven different actors.

O **The First Film to Win 11 Oscars:** *Ben-Hur* (1959) was the first film to win 11 Academy Awards, including Best Picture. This record was later tied by *Titanic* (1997) and *The Lord of the Rings: The Return of the King* (2003).

O **The First Full-Length Animated Film:** Walt Disney's *Snow White and the Seven Dwarfs* (1937) was the first full-length animated feature film. Its enormous success paved the way for future animated films.

O **The Most Expensive Film Ever Made:** *Star Wars: The Force Awakens* (2015) holds the record for the most expensive film ever made, with a budget estimated at $447 million.

O **The First Movie to Reach $1 Billion:** *Titanic* (1997) was the first film to reach $1 billion in global box office revenue, setting a new standard for success.

O **The Fastest Movie to $1 Billion:** *Avengers: Endgame* (2019) became the fastest movie to gross $1 billion worldwide, achieving the milestone in just five days.

O **The Longest Film Ever Made:** The experimental Swedish film *Logistics* (2012) holds the record for the longest movie ever made, running for 857 hours (35 days and 17 hours).

O **The First Movie to Use CGI:** *Westworld* (1973) was the first feature film to use CGI (computer-generated imagery), showcasing a pixelated robot's point of view, marking the beginning of digital effects in cinema.

O **The Most Successful Independent Film:** *Paranormal Activity* (2007), made on a budget of just $15,000, grossed over $193 million worldwide, making it one of the most profitable films ever produced.

O **The Oldest Film Still in Existence:** *Roundhay Garden Scene* (1888), filmed by Louis Le Prince, is the oldest surviving motion picture, showing a brief scene of people walking in a garden.

o **The First Movie with Sound:** *The Jazz Singer* (1927) was the first feature-length movie with synchronized sound, marking the beginning of the "talkies" and the end of the silent film era.

o **The Longest-Running Film in Theaters:** *The Rocky Horror Picture Show* (1975) holds the record for the longest theatrical run, still being shown in cinemas today, largely due to its cult following and midnight screenings.

o **The First 3D Film:** The first feature-length 3D film was *Bwana Devil* (1952), an adventure that led to a brief boom in 3D movies during the 1950s.

Cinematic Secrets

o **The Fake Snow in *The Wizard of Oz*:** The snow used in the famous poppy field scene in *The Wizard of Oz* (1939) was actually made from asbestos, a substance later found to be hazardous to health.

o **The Iconic Roar in *Jurassic Park*:** The terrifying T. rex roar in *Jurassic Park* (1993) was created by mixing sounds from a baby elephant, a tiger, and an alligator, among other animals.

o **The Hidden Starbucks Cup in *Game of Thrones*:** During a scene in *Game of Thrones* season 8, episode 4, a Starbucks coffee cup accidentally appeared on a table. The error became an instant internet sensation.

o **Alfred Hitchcock's Cameos:** Alfred Hitchcock made cameo appearances in 39 of his 52 surviving films, often placing himself in the background as a subtle Easter egg for his audience.

o **The Use of Chocolate Syrup in *Psycho*:** In Alfred Hitchcock's *Psycho* (1960), the blood in the iconic shower scene was actually chocolate syrup. Since the film was in black and white, the syrup's color didn't matter, and its consistency looked convincing.

o **The Script for *The Empire Strikes Back* Was Kept Secret:** To prevent leaks, only a few people knew the true script for *The Empire Strikes Back* (1980). Even the actor who played Darth Vader was unaware of the iconic "I am your father" twist until the premiere.

o **The Hidden Meaning in *The Shining*:** Many believe that Stanley Kubrick's *The Shining* (1980) is filled with hidden messages, including theories that the film is Kubrick's confession to faking the Apollo moon landing. Kubrick never confirmed these theories.

o **The Real-Language in *The Lord of the Rings*:** J.R.R. Tolkien invented entire languages, including Elvish, for *The Lord of the Rings* series. The movies' actors had to learn these languages for their roles, adding authenticity to the films.

o **The Dueling Directors of *Star Wars*:** George Lucas originally wanted Steven Spielberg to direct *Return of the Jedi* (1983), but Spielberg couldn't take the job due to a dispute between Lucas and the Directors Guild of America.

- **The Burning of *Gone with the Wind*:** The burning of Atlanta scene in *Gone with the Wind* (1939) was so massive that it required the destruction of old sets from previous films, including the giant gates from *King Kong* (1933).

- **The *E.T.* and *Poltergeist* Connection:** *E.T.* and *Poltergeist* were filmed simultaneously on adjacent lots. Some even believe that Steven Spielberg, who produced *Poltergeist*, directed parts of the film, although it's officially credited to Tobe Hooper.

- **The Mistaken Identity in *Three Men and a Baby*:** There's an urban legend that *Three Men and a Baby* (1987) shows a ghost in the background. It's actually a cardboard cutout of Ted Danson's character, but the myth persists.

- **The Secret Code in *The Matrix*:** The iconic green code in *The Matrix* (1999) is made up of sushi recipes from a cookbook belonging to the movie's production designer. The code has since become a symbol of digital worlds.

- **The Improvised Line in *Jaws*:** The famous line "You're gonna need a bigger boat" in *Jaws* (1975) was ad-libbed by actor Roy Scheider. It became one of the most iconic quotes in film history.

- **The Real Food in *Willy Wonka & the Chocolate Factory*:** Many of the edible set pieces in *Willy Wonka & the Chocolate Factory* (1971) were actually made of real food, allowing the child actors to eat their way through scenes.

Icons and Idols

- **Marilyn Monroe's Famous Dress:** Marilyn Monroe's iconic white dress from *The Seven Year Itch* (1955) was sold at auction for $4.6 million in 2011. The image of her standing over the subway grate remains a cultural icon.

- **Elvis Presley's Graceland:** Elvis Presley's Graceland mansion in Memphis, Tennessee, is the second most-visited house in the United States, after the White House. It attracts over 600,000 visitors each year.

- **James Dean's Lasting Legacy:** James Dean only made three films before his untimely death in 1955, yet he remains a symbol of youthful rebellion and Hollywood tragedy. His persona continues to influence pop culture today.

- **The Beatles' Ed Sullivan Show Appearance:** The Beatles' appearance on *The Ed Sullivan Show* in 1964 had an audience of 73 million viewers, solidifying their status as pop culture icons.

- **Michael Jackson's Moonwalk:** Michael Jackson debuted his signature moonwalk during a performance of "Billie Jean" on the Motown 25 television special in 1983. The move became one of the most famous dance steps in history.

- **Audrey Hepburn's *Breakfast at Tiffany's* Look:** Audrey Hepburn's black dress and pearl necklace from *Breakfast at Tiffany's* (1961) became one of the most iconic fashion moments in film history, influencing style for decades.

- **Bruce Lee's Impact on Martial Arts:** Bruce Lee is credited with bringing martial arts to mainstream Western cinema. His films, like *Enter the Dragon* (1973), made him a global icon and changed the way martial arts were portrayed in movies.

- **Mickey Mouse's Hollywood Star:** Mickey Mouse was the first animated character to receive a star on the Hollywood Walk of Fame, awarded in 1978 for his cultural impact.

- **The Rolling Stones' Tongue Logo:** The Rolling Stones' tongue and lips logo, designed by John Pasche in 1970, is one of the most recognizable symbols in rock music. It represents the rebellious spirit of the band.

- **Madonna's Reinventions:** Madonna has been dubbed the "Queen of Reinvention" for her ability to adapt and evolve her image and music throughout her career, from the "Material Girl" to the "Queen of Pop."

- **Oprah Winfrey's Media Empire:** Oprah Winfrey's talk show, *The Oprah Winfrey Show*, which ran from 1986 to 2011, made her one of the most influential media figures in history. She is also the first African American billionaire.

- **Bob Marley's Global Influence:** Bob Marley, through his music and messages of peace and unity, became a global icon for reggae music. His legacy continues to inspire social change and cultural pride worldwide.

- **Charlie Chaplin's Iconic Tramp:** Charlie Chaplin's "Tramp" character, with his bowler hat, cane, and mustache, became one of the most enduring symbols of early cinema, representing resilience and humor in the face of hardship.

- **Lucille Ball: The Queen of Comedy:** Lucille Ball's role in *I Love Lucy* made her the first woman to run a major television studio, Desilu Productions. She remains an icon of comedy and television history.

- **Muhammad Ali's Cultural Impact:** Muhammad Ali was not only a boxing champion but also a cultural icon known for his activism, charisma, and poetic trash-talking. His influence extended far beyond sports.

- **David Bowie's Ziggy Stardust:** David Bowie's alter ego, Ziggy Stardust, became a symbol of glam rock and artistic freedom in the 1970s. Bowie's ability to constantly reinvent himself made him a lasting cultural figure.

Music and Mayhem

- **The Beatles' Rooftop Concert:** The Beatles' final public performance was a surprise rooftop concert on January 30, 1969, atop Apple Corps headquarters in London. The impromptu show was famously shut down by the police.

- **The Birth of MTV:** MTV launched on August 1, 1981, with the music video for "Video Killed the Radio Star" by The Buggles. This moment marked the beginning of a new era in music and television.

O **Woodstock's Unforeseen Chaos:** The 1969 Woodstock Festival was expected to attract 50,000 people, but over 400,000 showed up, leading to massive traffic jams, food shortages, and a legendary three-day celebration of music and peace.

O **Nirvana's *Nevermind* Revolution:** Nirvana's album *Nevermind* (1991), featuring the hit "Smells Like Teen Spirit," unexpectedly knocked Michael Jackson's *Dangerous* off the top of the charts, ushering in the grunge era and transforming rock music.

O **The Milli Vanilli Lip-Sync Scandal:** In 1990, pop duo Milli Vanilli was exposed for lip-syncing their songs, leading to the revocation of their Grammy Award.

O **The Day the Music Died:** On February 3, 1959, rock and roll stars Buddy Holly, Ritchie Valens, and J.P. "The Big Bopper" Richardson died in a plane crash. This tragic event was later dubbed "The Day the Music Died."

O **The Rolling Stones' Altamont Free Concert Disaster:** The Rolling Stones' 1969 Altamont Free Concert, intended to be a "Woodstock West," ended in violence and tragedy, with a fan being killed by the Hells Angels who were hired as security.

O **The Rise of Hip-Hop:** The birth of hip-hop is often traced back to a 1973 party in the Bronx, where DJ Kool Herc used two turntables to extend the instrumental breaks, creating the foundation for a new genre.

O **The Breakup of The Beatles:** The Beatles officially broke up in 1970, but the seeds were planted earlier due to creative differences, business disputes, and personal tensions. Their split marked the end of an era in music.

O **Madonna's Controversial *Like a Prayer*:** Madonna's 1989 music video for "Like a Prayer" sparked outrage for its provocative imagery, including religious symbols. Despite the controversy, it became one of her most iconic hits.

O **The Who's Drum Destruction:** The Who's drummer Keith Moon was known for his explosive performances, often culminating in the destruction of his drum kit on stage.

O **The Birth of MTV Unplugged:** MTV Unplugged, launched in 1989, became famous for showcasing artists in stripped-down, acoustic performances. Nirvana's 1993 Unplugged session is one of the most celebrated in the series' history.

O **Freddie Mercury's Legacy:** Freddie Mercury, lead singer of Queen, is remembered as one of the greatest rock performers. His 1985 Live Aid performance is considered one of the best live shows in history.

O **The Infamous Led Zeppelin Hotel Incident:** Led Zeppelin's wild reputation includes the infamous incident at the Edgewater Inn in Seattle, where they supposedly caught a fish from their hotel room and played pranks with it—though the details remain murky.

o **Prince's Name Change:** In 1993, Prince changed his name to an unpronounceable symbol as a protest against his record label, leading to his moniker "The Artist Formerly Known as Prince." He later reclaimed his name in 2000.

Pop Culture Phenomena

o **The Harry Potter Craze:** J.K. Rowling's *Harry Potter* series, first published in 1997, became a global phenomenon, leading to blockbuster movies, theme parks, and a dedicated fanbase known as "Potterheads."

o **The Pokémon Explosion:** The Pokémon franchise, launched in 1996, quickly became one of the most successful video game series of all time, spawning TV shows, movies, trading cards, and the mobile game *Pokémon GO*.

o **The Star Wars Fandom:** *Star Wars*, created by George Lucas in 1977, developed one of the most devoted fanbases in history. The franchise's influence extends across movies, TV shows, toys, books, and conventions. -This is The Way-.

o **The Marvel Cinematic Universe:** The Marvel Cinematic Universe (MCU), launched with *Iron Man* in 2008, has become the highest-grossing film franchise ever, captivating audiences with interconnected superhero stories across dozens of films.

o **The Beatles' Beatlemania:** In the 1960s, Beatlemania swept the world, with The Beatles becoming a cultural phenomenon that transcended music. Their influence on fashion, art, and social movements is still felt today.

o **The Rise of K-Pop:** K-pop, led by groups like BTS and BLACKPINK, has grown into a global sensation. With millions of fans worldwide, it has defined pop culture through music, fashion, and social media.

o **The Twilight Fandom:** *Twilight*, a series by Stephenie Meyer, ignited a vampire craze in the mid-2000s. The books and movies generated massive fan followings and led to a revival of supernatural romance in pop culture.

o **The Impact of *Game of Thrones*:** HBO's *Game of Thrones* (2011-2019) became a cultural sensation, sparking debates, theories, and a worldwide fanbase. Its controversial ending remains a hot topic of discussion.

o **The Evolution of *The Simpsons*:** *The Simpsons*, first aired in 1989, is the longest-running animated TV show in history. Its satirical take on American life has made it a staple of pop culture for over three decades.

- **The LEGO Revolution:** LEGO, founded in 1932, has evolved from simple building blocks into a global brand, including movies, video games, and theme parks, making it one of the most beloved toys of all time.

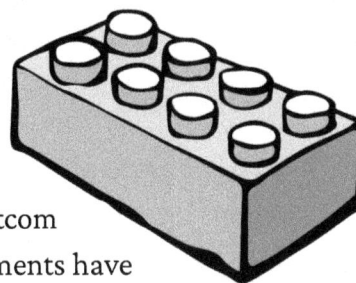

- **The Impact of *Friends*:** *Friends* (1994-2004) became a defining sitcom of the 1990s and early 2000s. Its characters, catchphrases, and moments have left an indelible mark on pop culture, with reruns still popular today.

- **The *Meme* Culture Explosion:** Internet memes, which began as simple images with captions, have grown into a vital part of online communication and pop culture, influencing everything from humor to political discussion.

- **The Influence of Disney:** Disney, founded by Walt Disney in 1923, has become synonymous with family entertainment. From classic animated films to theme parks, its impact on global pop culture is unparalleled.

- **The Viral *Gangnam Style*:** In 2012, South Korean artist PSY's "Gangnam Style" became the first YouTube video to reach one billion views, introducing K-pop to a global audience and sparking a viral dance craze.

- **The Influence of Reality TV:** Shows like *Survivor*, *The Real World*, and *Keeping Up with the Kardashians* revolutionized television, turning everyday people into celebrities and changing the landscape of entertainment.

Top Trends

- **The Selfie Boom:** The word "selfie" was named the Oxford Dictionaries Word of the Year in 2013. With the rise of social media, selfies influenced fashion, photography, and self-expression.

- **The Fidget Spinner Craze:** Fidget spinners became a massive trend in 2017, marketed as stress-relief toys. Though short-lived, the craze saw millions of spinners sold worldwide.

- **The Viral *Ice Bucket Challenge*:** In 2014, the ALS Ice Bucket Challenge became a global trend, raising over $220 million for ALS research. Participants dumped ice water on themselves and challenged others to do the same.

- **The Evolution of Emojis:** Emojis, originally created in Japan in the late 1990s, have become a universal language of digital communication. Today, there are over 3,500 emojis representing everything from emotions to objects.

- **The Beanie Babies Bubble:** In the 1990s, Beanie Babies became a collectible craze, with some toys selling for thousands of dollars. The bubble eventually burst, but the craze remains a symbol of 90s culture.

- **The YOLO Movement:** The phrase "You Only Live Once" (YOLO) became popular in the early 2010s, driven by the song "The Motto" by Drake. YOLO encouraged a carefree, live-in-the-moment lifestyle.

O **The Birth of the Hashtag:** The hashtag, first used on Twitter in 2007, revolutionized social media by creating a way to categorize and search for content. It has since become an essential tool for online conversations.

O **The Avocado Toast Influence:** Avocado toast became a symbol of millennial culture in the 2010s, representing trends in health, wellness, and social media-friendly food. It even sparked debates about financial priorities.

O **The Popularity of Escape Rooms:** Escape rooms, where participants solve puzzles to "escape" a themed room, became a global entertainment trend in the 2010s. This has since expanded into virtual and augmented reality formats.

O **The Trend of Unboxing Videos:** Unboxing videos, where creators open and review products on camera, became a massive trend on YouTube. This turned ordinary tasks into entertainment and marketing gold.

O **The Influence of TikTok Challenges:** TikTok challenges, where users participate in viral trends like dances or pranks, have shaped modern pop culture, launching songs, products, and even social movements into the spotlight.

O **The Craze of Instant Pot Cooking:** The Instant Pot, a multi-cooker that gained popularity in the 2010s, inspired a cult following. The appliance revolutionized home cooking, leading to countless recipes and even dedicated cookbooks.

O **Plant-Based Diets:** Plant-based eating has become a global trend, with more people turning to vegetarian and vegan diets for health, environmental, and ethical reasons. Plant-based food products are booming, from burgers to milk alternatives.

O **The Growth of Thrift Shopping:** Thrift shopping became a trend in the 2010s, driven by sustainability concerns and the rise of vintage fashion. It popularized the idea of "second-hand first" as a way to shop responsibly.

O **The Meme Stock Craze:** In 2021, "meme stocks" like GameStop and AMC surged in value due to coordinated efforts by retail investors on Reddit. This event highlighted the power of online communities in the financial markets.

With this curtain call, we've explored blockbuster moments that broke records to the icons and idols who shaped generations. We've also seen the trends, secrets, and phenomena that have left lasting marks on society.

Now, our next adventure awaits in the animal kingdom! Get ready to meet extraordinary creatures, uncover their unique abilities, and learn about the diverse ecosystems they call home. Let's embark on this wild journey together!

The Language of The Wild

Amazing Animal Abilities

O **The Mantis Shrimp's Super Punch:** The mantis shrimp can punch with the force of a bullet, moving its claws so fast that they create tiny bubbles of superheated water, capable of stunning or killing prey instantly.

O **The Gecko's Sticky Feet:** Geckos can climb walls and even walk on ceilings thanks to millions of tiny hairs on their feet which create a molecular bond with surfaces, allowing them to stick effortlessly.

O **The Super Hearing of Moths:** Some moths can detect the ultrasonic calls of bats, their natural predators, from over 100 feet away. This incredible hearing ability helps them evade being eaten.

O **The Speedy Cheetah:** Cheetahs are the fastest land animals, capable of reaching speeds up to 70 miles per hour in short bursts. They can accelerate from 0 to 60 mph in just a few seconds!

O **The Electric Eel's Shock:** Electric eels can generate electric shocks up to 600 volts, enough to stun prey or deter predators. They use this ability to navigate, communicate, and hunt in murky waters.

O **The Regenerating Axolotl:** The axolotl, a type of salamander, can regenerate entire limbs, spinal cords, and even parts of its heart and brain. Scientists are studying them to unlock the secrets of regrowth.

O **The Bombardier Beetle's Explosive Defense:** The bombardier beetle can spray a boiling chemical mixture from its abdomen to deter predators. This explosive defense system is both highly effective and fascinatingly complex.

O **The Arctic Tern's Long Migration:** The Arctic tern has the longest migration of any bird, traveling a 44,000 mile round-trip each year from its breeding grounds in the Arctic to its wintering grounds in Antarctica.

O **The Resilient Tardigrade:** Tardigrades, also known as water bears, can survive extreme conditions, including temperatures close to absolute zero, radiation, and even the vacuum of space. They're nearly indestructible!

O **The Lyrebird's Mimicry Mastery:** The lyrebird, a native of Australia, is renowned for its exceptional ability to mimic a vast array of sounds, including other bird calls, human-made noises like chainsaws and car alarms, and even music. Also they don't just parrot sounds they hear; the birds often improvise and rearrange them, creating unique musical compositions. It's like they have their own avian jazz band going on!

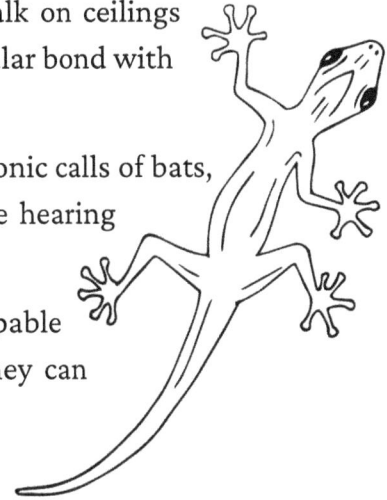

- **The Archerfish's Accurate Spit:** The archerfish can spit a jet of water with pinpoint accuracy to knock insects off of overhanging branches and into the water, where it can then eat them. Juvenile archerfish need to practice their spitting skills to become accurate hunters. They gradually learn to compensate for the refraction of light and adjust the power of their spit.

- **The Immortal Jellyfish:** The Turritopsis dohrnii, known as the "immortal jellyfish," can revert its cells to an earlier stage of life when injured or threatened, essentially starting its life cycle over again.

- **The Basilisk Lizard's Water-Walking:** The basilisk lizard, often called the "Jesus Christ lizard," can run across water on its hind legs, thanks to its speed, light weight, and specially adapted feet.

- **The Echolocation of Bats:** Bats use echolocation to navigate and hunt in complete darkness. They emit high-pitched sounds that bounce off objects, allowing them to "see" their surroundings through sound.

- **The Strong Bite of the Saltwater Crocodile:** The saltwater crocodile has the strongest bite of any living animal, with a force of 3,700 pounds per square inch (psi). This helps them easily crush the bones of their prey.

Fierce and Fearless Beasts

- **The Mighty Lion:** Lions, known as the "king of the jungle," are formidable predators with a roar that can be heard up to five miles away. A lion's bite is powerful enough to crush bones.

- **Crows Hold Grudges:** Crows remember human faces and hold grudges, especially if they perceive a person as a threat. They can even pass this information to other crows.

- **The Ferocious Honey Badger:** The honey badger is known for its fearlessness. It can fend off predators like lions and cobras and even break into beehives for honey despite getting stung repeatedly.

- **The Ruthless Komodo Dragon:** Komodo dragons are the largest lizards on Earth and can take down prey as large as deer with their powerful jaws and venomous saliva, which causes their prey to go into shock.

- **The Powerful Grizzly Bear:** Grizzly bears are one of the most powerful predators on land, capable of killing prey with a single swipe of their massive paws. They can also run up to 35 miles per hour.

- **The Aggressive Hippopotamus:** Despite their rotund appearance, hippos are extremely aggressive and territorial. They are responsible for more human deaths in Africa than any other large animal, thanks to their sharp teeth and powerful jaws.

- **The Stealthy Bengal Tiger:** Bengal tigers are expert hunters, using their striped coats as camouflage to blend into the dense forests of India. They can take down prey more than twice their size with a single powerful leap.

o **The Venomous King Cobra:** The king cobra is the world's longest venomous snake, reaching up to 18 feet in length. Its venom is so potent that a single bite can kill an elephant within hours.

o **The Deadly Great White Shark:** Great white sharks are apex predators of the ocean, known for their incredible speed and razor-sharp teeth. They can sense a drop of blood in 25 gallons of water from three miles away.

o **The Fierce African Buffalo:** African buffalo are known for their unpredictable nature and fearsome horns. They have been known to charge at and even kill lions, earning them the nickname "Black Death."

o **The Ferocious Tasmanian Devil:** Tasmanian devils have the strongest bite force relative to their size of any mammal. They can eat entire carcasses, including bones and fur, making them efficient scavengers.

o **The Formidable Polar Bear:** Polar bears are the largest land carnivores, with males weighing up to 1,600 pounds. They rely on their strength and keen sense of smell to hunt seals in the Arctic.

o **The Cunning Wolf Pack:** Wolves are highly social animals that hunt in packs, using coordinated strategies to take down large prey like elk and moose. Their teamwork and communication are key to their success.

o **The Deadly Box Jellyfish:** The box jellyfish, found in the waters of the Indo-Pacific, has venom so potent that it can kill a human within minutes. It's considered one of the most dangerous animals in the ocean.

o **The Territorial African Elephant:** African elephants, the largest land animals, are also highly protective of their herds. When threatened, they can charge at speeds of up to 25 miles per hour, using their massive tusks as weapons.

o **The Ruthless Harpy Eagle:** The harpy eagle, found in the rainforests of Central and South America, is one of the world's most powerful birds of prey. It can snatch monkeys and sloths from trees with its razor-sharp talons.

Hidden Habitats

o **Cave Ecosystems:** Deep within caves, ecosystems thrive in total darkness. These unique habitats support species like blind fish, albino crabs, and glow-in-the-dark fungi, all adapted to life without sunlight.

o **The Mariana Trench:** The Mariana Trench, located in the western Pacific Ocean, is the deepest part of the world's oceans. It's over 36,000 feet deep, with mysterious creatures that thrive in total darkness and crushing pressure.

o **The Congo Basin:** The Congo Basin is the world's second-largest rainforest and contains some of the most diverse wildlife on the planet, including gorillas, elephants, and hundreds of bird species.

o **The Okavango Delta:** The Okavango Delta in Botswana is a vast inland delta where the Okavango River spreads out into a maze of lagoons, channels, and islands, creating a rich habitat for hippos, crocodiles, and a variety of bird species.

o **The Caves of Borneo:** Borneo's caves are home to millions of bats and swiftlets, whose nests are harvested for bird's nest soup. The caves also house unique ecosystems and ancient human paintings.

o **The Madagascar Forests:** Madagascar's forests are a hidden world of biodiversity, with 90% of its wildlife found nowhere else on Earth, including lemurs, chameleons, and the mysterious fossa.

o **The Namib Desert:** The Namib Desert is home to some of the most resilient creatures, including the fog-basking beetle, which survives by collecting water droplets from the morning mist.

o **The Grand Prismatic Spring:** In Yellowstone National Park, the Grand Prismatic Spring is the largest hot spring in the U.S. Its vivid rainbow colors, caused by heat-loving bacteria, make it look like something from another planet.

o **The Black Forest:** Germany's Black Forest is a dense, dark woodland that has inspired many myths and fairy tales. It's home to a rich variety of wildlife, including deer, wild boar, and the elusive lynx.

o **The Galápagos Islands:** The Galápagos Islands are famous for their unique wildlife, including giant tortoises, marine iguanas, and blue-footed boobies. The isolation of these islands has led to the evolution of species found nowhere else.

o **The Siberian Taiga:** The Siberian Taiga is the world's largest forest, stretching across Russia. It's a remote and harsh environment, home to hardy species like the Siberian tiger, brown bear, and reindeer.

o **The Scottish Highlands:** The Scottish Highlands are a rugged region of mountains, lochs, and moorlands. This dramatic landscape is home to red deer, golden eagles, and Scotland's famous Highland cattle.

o **The Atacama Desert:** The Atacama Desert in Chile is the driest place on Earth. Despite its arid conditions, it supports life, including cacti, flamingos, and tiny, resilient creatures like the Atacama rat.

o **The Sundarbans Mangrove Forest:** The Sundarbans, spanning India and Bangladesh, is the largest mangrove forest in the world. It's a crucial habitat for the endangered Bengal tiger and supports a diverse array of aquatic and bird species.

o **The Great Rift Valley:** The Great Rift Valley in East Africa is a massive geological and ecological region. It's home to numerous lakes, volcanoes, and unique wildlife like flamingos, hippos, and some of the oldest known human fossils.

Incredible Animal Adventures

O **The Epic Journey of the Monarch Butterfly:** Monarch butterflies migrate up to 3,000 miles from North America to central Mexico each year, where they cluster together by the millions in dense forests to survive the winter.

O **The Great Wildebeest Migration:** Every year, over 1.5 million wildebeest, accompanied by hundreds of thousands of zebras and gazelles, embark on a 1,000-mile journey across the Serengeti and Masai Mara in search of fresh grazing grounds.

O **The Emperor Penguins' Winter Trek:** Emperor penguins march up to 70 miles across the Antarctic ice to reach their breeding grounds. Males then incubate the eggs on their feet for two months in freezing temperatures while the females hunt for food.

O **The Salmon's Upstream Battle:** Pacific salmon make an extraordinary journey from the ocean back to the freshwater streams where they were born. They swim upstream, often leaping up waterfalls, to spawn the next generation.

O **The Marathon Moths:** Bogong moths in Australia undertake an incredible journey of over 600 miles each year to escape the summer heat. They migrate to the cool caves of the Australian Alps, where they rest until winter.

O **The Loggerhead Sea Turtle's Oceanic Voyage:** Loggerhead sea turtles undertake a transatlantic journey from their nesting beaches in Japan to feeding grounds off the coast of California, covering more than 7,500 miles.

O **The Caribou's Cold Migration:** Caribou, also known as reindeer, migrate up to 3,000 miles annually across the Arctic tundra in one of the longest land migrations of any mammal, enduring harsh conditions and predators.

O **The African Elephant's Search for Water:** During dry seasons, African elephants embark on long treks across the savanna in search of water. Their ability to remember locations of water sources is crucial for the survival of their herds.

O **The Adélie Penguins' Ice Escape:** Adélie penguins travel over 8,000 miles each year, navigating the treacherous ice floes of Antarctica. Their journey includes dodging leopard seals and killer whales as they hunt for krill.

O **The Elephant Orphans of Tsavo:** At the Tsavo National Park in Kenya, orphaned baby elephants are raised by conservationists. These elephants are eventually released back into the wild after learning how to survive on their own.

O **The Honeybee's Dance for Directions:** Honeybees perform a "waggle dance" to communicate the location of food sources to their hive mates. This intricate dance involves precise movements that indicate direction and distance.

o **The Great Bat Exodus:** Each evening, millions of bats emerge from Bracken Cave in Texas, creating one of the largest bat exoduses in the world. They fly out in massive swarms to hunt insects, providing a crucial ecological service.

o **The Polar Bear's Icy Swim:** Polar bears are powerful swimmers, capable of covering more than 60 miles in one stretch. They use their large, webbed paws to paddle through the icy waters of the Arctic in search of seals.

o **The Snow Leopard's Stealthy Descent:** Snow leopards, known as "ghosts of the mountains," navigate steep, rocky terrain in the Himalayas with ease. They use their long tails for balance and thick, spotted coat for camouflage as they silently stalk their prey.

o **The Humpback Whale's Singing Journey:** Humpback whales migrate up to 5,000 miles between their feeding grounds in polar waters and their breeding grounds in tropical seas. Males sing complex songs to attract mates during this journey.

Masters of Camouflage

o **The Octopus's Instant Disguise:** Octopuses can change the color, pattern, and even texture of their skin in seconds to blend into their surroundings, making them nearly invisible to predators and prey alike.

o **The Leaf-Tailed Gecko's Perfect Disguise:** The phantastic leaf-tailed gecko from Madagascar looks exactly like a dead leaf, complete with ragged edges and spots. This amazing camouflage helps it avoid predators in the forest.

o **The Arctic Fox's Seasonal Coat:** The Arctic fox changes its fur color with the seasons—white in winter to blend in with snow and brown or gray in summer to match the tundra's rocks and plants.

o **The Cuttlefish's Shape-Shifting:** Cuttlefish are masters of disguise, capable of changing not only their color but also their texture to mimic their surroundings. They use this ability to ambush prey and evade predators.

o **The Stick Insect's Leafy Look:** Stick insects can resemble twigs, branches, or leaves, making them nearly impossible to spot among the foliage. Some species even sway gently to mimic the movement of leaves in the wind.

o **The Frogfish's Luring Lure:** The frogfish are masters of disguise, capable of disguising themselves to look like rocks, sponges or algae. Yet they have another trick up their sleeve: Their dorsal fin spine resembles a small worm or generally enticing bait, and they use this "bait" to lure unsuspecting prey near them.

o **The *Mimic Octopus's* Versatile Disguise:** The mimic octopus can impersonate various marine animals, such as lionfish, flatfish, and sea snakes, by changing its shape, color, and behavior. This trick helps it avoid predators.

O **The Chameleon's Color Changes:** Chameleons are famous for their ability to change color. While this is often used for communication or temperature regulation, it's also an effective camouflage technique to avoid predators.

O **The Pygmy Seahorse's Coral Camouflage:** Pygmy seahorses are tiny and perfectly match the color and texture of the coral they live on. This camouflage makes them nearly invisible to predators and researchers alike.

O **The Dead Leaf Mantis's Deception:** The dead leaf mantis, as its name suggests, looks remarkably like a dried-up leaf. This disguise allows it to blend into the forest floor while waiting to ambush unsuspecting prey.

O **The Stonefish's Deadly Disguise:** The stonefish is the world's most venomous fish and looks like a rock on the ocean floor. This camouflage helps it ambush prey while remaining hidden from potential threats.

O **The Owl Butterfly's Eye Spots:** The owl butterfly has large eye spots on its wings that resemble the eyes of an owl. When threatened, it opens its wings to scare away predators with this clever illusion.

O **The Gaboon Viper's Leafy Pattern:** The Gaboon viper has one of the most effective camouflage patterns in the snake world. Its leaf-like markings allow it to disappear into the forest floor while waiting to ambush prey.

O **The Leafy Sea Dragon's Plant-Like Appearance:** The leafy sea dragon looks like a floating piece of seaweed, with appendages that mimic leaves and fronds. This camouflage helps it hide from predators in kelp beds and seagrass meadows.

O **The Horned Lizard's Sand Blending:** Horned lizards can change their color to match the desert sand they live in. They can also stay completely still to avoid detection by predators, making them true masters of camouflage.

Wild and Wacky Creatures

O **The Axolotl's Eternal Youth:** The axolotl, a type of salamander, never undergoes metamorphosis like other amphibians. It retains its juvenile features throughout its life, including its adorable external gills, giving it a permanently youthful appearance.

O **Octopus Hearts:** Octopuses have three hearts. Two pump blood to the gills, and one pumps it to the rest of the body. The three hearts work in a coordinated manner to ensure that the octopus receives a constant supply of oxygen, even during periods of intense activity. This efficient circulatory system allows the octopus to thrive in its diverse and challenging environment.

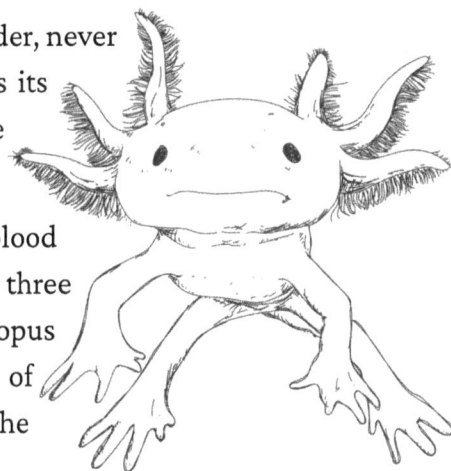

- **The Platypus's Peculiar Features:** The platypus is a bizarre mix of traits: it's a mammal that lays eggs, has a duck-like bill, webbed feet, and even produces venom! No wonder it puzzled early scientists.

- **The Narwhal's Unicorn Horn:** The narwhal, known as the "unicorn of the sea," has a long, spiral tusk that can grow up to 10 feet. This tusk is actually an elongated tooth and can sense changes in the water.

- **The Hairy Frog's Claws:** Also known as the "Wolverine frog," this species can break its own bones to produce claws that puncture through its skin for defense. It's both wild and a little creepy! But also pretty cool, wouldn't you agree?

- **Penguins' Pebble Proposals:** Penguins propose to their mates with pebbles. If the female accepts, they remain partners for life, making it one of the animal kingdom's sweetest courtships.

- **The Naked Mole Rat's Longevity:** Naked mole rats are nearly hairless, live underground, and are resistant to cancer. They can also live up to 30 years, much longer than most other rodents.

- **The Blobfish's Unusual Looks:** The blobfish, often called the world's ugliest animal, lives in deep waters off the coast of Australia. Out of water, its gelatinous body sags, giving it its famously droopy appearance.

- **The Yeti Crab's Hairy Arms:** The yeti crab, discovered near hydrothermal vents in the Pacific Ocean, has long, hairy claws covered in bacteria, which it uses to detoxify the poisonous chemicals in its habitat.

- **The Pistol Shrimp's Sonic Snap:** The pistol shrimp can snap its claw so fast that it creates a bubble that reaches temperatures as hot as the sun's surface, producing a shockwave that stuns or kills its prey. Sounds similar to the Mantis shrimp? But these two aren't really related!

- **The Aye-Aye's Long Finger:** The aye-aye, a type of lemur from Madagascar, has an extra-long middle finger that it uses to tap on trees and locate insects. Once it finds its prey, it uses this finger to fish them out.

- **The Saiga Antelope's Bizarre Nose:** The saiga antelope has a large, bulbous nose that looks like something out of a cartoon. This unique nose helps filter out dust and regulate body temperature in its harsh desert habitat.

- **The Kakapo's Noisy Nights:** The kakapo, a flightless parrot from New Zealand, is nocturnal and makes booming calls that can be heard up to four miles away during its mating season. Despite its odd habits, it's critically endangered.

- **The Slow-Moving Sloth:** Sloths move so slowly that algae grow on their fur, giving them a greenish tint that helps them blend into the trees. They can sleep up to 20 hours a day in the rainforest canopy. They also have the slowest metabolism of any mammal, allowing them to survive on a diet of leaves and conserve energy with that same slow movement!

O **The Pink Fairy Armadillo:** This tiny armadillo species, native to Argentina, is covered in pink armor and measures just 5 inches long. Its unique shell helps it burrow underground to escape predators quickly.

O **The Shoebill Stork:** With its massive beak resembling a shoe, the shoebill stork looks like a prehistoric dinosaur! Found in Africa, this bird is known for its slow, robotic movements and impressive fishing skills.

O **The Glass Frog:** Found in Central and South America, the glass frog has translucent skin, allowing you to see its organs! This bizarre feature helps it blend into its surroundings to avoid predators.

And that's a wrap on our wild adventure through the animal kingdom! From the incredible abilities of nature's most resourceful creatures to the hidden habitats that house some of the world's most unique species, we've marveled at the wonders of the natural world that remind us just how extraordinary our planet is.

Our next chapter takes us on a tour of **geographical places,** where we'll explore the breath-taking landscapes, awe-inspiring natural wonders, and culturally rich locations that define our world. From towering mountains to mysterious deserts, vibrant cities to remote islands, each place holds its own secrets and stories. So, pack your bags and let's go!

Globe-Trotting Games

Astonishing Landscapes

O **The Grand Canyon's Immense Depth:** The Grand Canyon, carved by the Colorado River, is over a mile deep, revealing nearly two billion years of Earth's geological history through its vibrant layers of rock.

O **That Wanaka Tree:** "That Wanaka Tree" in New Zealand, an internationally recognized Instagram star and symbol of resilience, actually began its life as an ordinary fence post! A willow branch, once discarded and stuck in the ground, took root and flourished, transforming into the iconic solitary figure that stands proudly in Lake Wanaka today.

O **The Breathtaking Cliffs of Moher:** The Cliffs of Moher in Ireland rise over 700 feet above the Atlantic Ocean. On a clear day, you can see the Aran Islands and even the mountains of Connemara.

O **The Enchanted Forest of Hallerbos:** Hallerbos, located in Belgium, transforms into a magical blue carpet every spring as millions of bluebells bloom, creating a stunning landscape.

O **The Colorful Danxia Landforms:** China's Zhangye Danxia Landforms are famous for their vibrant, rainbow-colored mountains. The unique hues are the result of millions of years of sandstone and mineral deposits.

O **The Otherworldly Wadi Rum:** Wadi Rum, also known as the Valley of the Moon, is a desert in Jordan with red sand dunes, towering rock formations, and ancient petroglyphs, often used as a film location for Mars.

O **The Mesmerizing Plitvice Lakes:** Plitvice Lakes National Park in Croatia features 16 interconnected lakes cascading into each other through a series of waterfalls, surrounded by lush greenery and wildlife.

O **The Danakil Depression:** Found in Ethiopia, the Danakil Depression is one of the hottest places on Earth and is home to colorful salt formations, acid pools, and bubbling lava lakes!

O **The Stunning Antelope Canyon:** Antelope Canyon in Arizona is famous for its wave-like structure and light beams that shine down into narrow openings, creating a surreal, glowing effect. The smooth, wave-like walls were carved by flash flooding over centuries.

O **The Pristine Beauty of Banff National Park:** Banff National Park in Canada is home to stunning glaciers, crystal-clear lakes like Lake Louise, and the rugged peaks of the Canadian Rockies, making it a top spot for adventurers.

O **The Mysterious Moeraki Boulders:** The Moeraki Boulders in New Zealand are unusually large and spherical rocks scattered along the coast. They formed millions of years ago from sediment and are steeped in Māori legend.

- **The Ever-Changing Badlands:** The Badlands in South Dakota feature jagged peaks, deep gorges, and layered rock formations that reveal fossils from millions of years ago. The landscape constantly changes due to erosion.

- **The Alien Landscapes of Cappadocia:** Cappadocia in Turkey is known for its "fairy chimneys," tall, cone-shaped rock formations. The region is also famous for its ancient cave dwellings and hot air balloon rides over the surreal landscape.

- **The Lush Green Terraces of Banaue:** The Banaue Rice Terraces in the Philippines, carved into the mountains over 2,000 years ago by the Ifugao people, are often called the "Eighth Wonder of the World."

- **The Socotra Archipelago:** This remote island chain off the coast of Yemen is home to a unique ecosystem with bizarre plants and animals found nowhere else on Earth, earning it the nickname "the Galapagos of the Indian Ocean."

Hidden Gems Around the Globe

- **The Fairy Pools of Skye:** Located on Scotland's Isle of Skye, the Fairy Pools are a series of crystal-clear, icy blue waterfalls and pools that look straight out of a fantasy novel.

- **Wai-O-Tapu Thermal Wonderland, New Zealand:** Wai-O-Tapu, located on New Zealand's North Island, is known for its colorful geothermal hot springs, bubbling mud pools, and geysers. The vibrant hues are created by natural minerals in the water.

- **The Hidden Beach, Mexico:** Located on the Marieta Islands off the coast of Mexico, this secluded beach is nestled inside a crater-like opening, accessible only by swimming through a short tunnel. Its pristine waters and unique setting make it a truly hidden paradise.

- **The Hidden Temples of Bagan:** Bagan, Myanmar, is an ancient city with over 2,200 temples and pagodas. The stunning architecture, set against a backdrop of lush plains, is often overlooked by travelers.

- **Underwater Waterfall:** The Denmark Strait cataract, between Greenland and Iceland, is the world's largest underwater waterfall, with a drop of about 3,505 meters (11,500 feet).

- **The Rainbow River of Colombia:** Caño Cristales in Colombia is known as the "River of Five Colors." During certain months, the riverbed blooms with vibrant red, yellow, green, and blue hues due to aquatic plants.

- **The Mysterious Waitomo Caves:** The Waitomo Caves in New Zealand are famous for their glowworms, which light up the dark caverns with a magical blue-green glow, creating a starry sky-like experience underground.

- **The Lost City of Petra:** Petra in Jordan, often called the "Rose City," is a UNESCO World Heritage Site carved into red sandstone cliffs. It was once a thriving trading hub but was forgotten for centuries.

o **The Isolated Faroe Islands:** The Faroe Islands, located between Iceland and Norway, are a remote archipelago with dramatic cliffs, picturesque villages, and a unique blend of Scandinavian and Celtic culture.

o **The Tranquil Monasteries of Meteora:** Meteora in Greece features ancient monasteries perched atop towering rock pillars. The site offers breathtaking views and a sense of peace, far removed from the modern world.

o **The Vibrant Town of Chefchaouen:** Chefchaouen, a small town in Morocco, is famous for its blue-washed buildings and winding streets. The town's unique charm and stunning backdrop make it a hidden gem for travelers.

o **The Ancient Forest of Białowieẞa:** Białowieẞa Forest, located on the border between Poland and Belarus, is one of the last and largest remaining parts of the primeval forest that once covered much of Europe. It's home to bison, wolves, and lynxes.

o **The Serene Lake Bled:** Lake Bled in Slovenia, with its emerald-green waters and a small island topped with a church, is a hidden gem nestled among the Julian Alps. The area is perfect for relaxation and exploration.

o **The Desert Oasis of Huacachina:** Huacachina, a tiny village in Peru, is built around a natural desert oasis. Surrounded by towering sand dunes, it's a popular spot for sandboarding and dune buggy rides.

o **The Mysterious Cenotes of Yucatán:** The cenotes of Mexico's Yucatán Peninsula are natural sinkholes filled with crystal-clear water. These hidden gems were sacred to the Maya and are now popular for swimming and diving.

o **The Hidden Fjords of Greenland:** Greenland's fjords, often overlooked by travelers, are stunning with their towering icebergs, jagged cliffs, and remote villages. The area offers incredible opportunities for wildlife viewing and adventure.

Majestic Mountains and Valleys

o **The Towering Mount Everest:** Mount Everest, standing at 29,032 feet, is the highest point above global mean sea level on Earth. Located in the Himalayas, it has attracted climbers from around the world.

o **Mauna Kea: The Tallest Mountain:** Mauna Kea in Hawaii is technically taller than Mount Everest when measured from its base below sea level, rising over 33,000 feet (around 10,000 meters).

o **The Enchanting Yosemite Valley:** Yosemite Valley in California is famous for its dramatic granite cliffs, including El Capitan and Half Dome, as well as its breathtaking waterfalls and giant sequoia trees.

o **The Sacred Mount Fuji:** Mount Fuji, Japan's highest peak, is an active stratovolcano and a cultural icon. Its nearly symmetrical cone is a symbol of beauty and inspiration for artists and pilgrims alike.

O **The Mysterious Drakensberg Mountains:** The Drakensberg Mountains, also known as the "Dragon's Mountains," are the highest range in Southern Africa, with dramatic peaks, ancient cave paintings, and rich biodiversity.

O **The Grandeur of the Andes:** The Andes is the longest continental mountain range in the world, stretching over 4,300 miles along the western coast of South America. It's home to diverse ecosystems and ancient civilizations.

O **The Hidden Valleys of the Dolomites:** The Dolomites in northern Italy are known for their towering limestone peaks and serene valleys. The area is a UNESCO World Heritage Site, offering stunning scenery and rich history.

O **The Iconic Swiss Alps:** The Swiss Alps are famous for their picturesque landscapes, with snow-capped peaks, green meadows, and charming villages. They are a top destination for skiing, hiking, and mountaineering.

O **The Rugged Beauty of the Rockies:** The Rocky Mountains stretch over 3,000 miles from Canada to New Mexico. They are known for their rugged beauty, diverse wildlife, and outdoor recreational opportunities, including national parks like Yellowstone and Rocky Mountain.

O **The Majestic Patagonia:** Patagonia, spanning southern Argentina and Chile, is a region of dramatic landscapes, including towering mountains, glaciers, and wind-swept plains. It's a paradise for adventurers and nature lovers.

O **The Hidden Valleys of Bhutan:** Bhutan's valleys, such as Paro and Punakha, are nestled between towering Himalayan peaks. Known for their stunning landscapes, ancient monasteries, and traditional culture, these valleys offer a glimpse into a hidden world.

O **The Lush Valley of Kashmir:** The Valley of Kashmir, often called "Paradise on Earth," is surrounded by the majestic Himalayas. It's known for its breathtaking beauty, including lakes, gardens, and snow-covered mountains.

O **The Ancient Zagros Mountains:** The Zagros Mountains in Iran and Iraq are among the oldest mountain ranges in the world. They are home to ancient civilizations and offer dramatic landscapes with deep valleys and towering peaks.

O **The Serene Blue Mountains:** Australia's Blue Mountains are named for the blue haze created by eucalyptus trees. The region is known for its deep valleys, waterfalls, and dramatic cliffs, offering stunning views and rich wildlife.

O **The Vibrant Valley of Flowers:** The Valley of Flowers in India's Uttarakhand state is a UNESCO World Heritage Site. During the summer, it has a vibrant display of wildflowers, creating a natural rainbow of colors.

O **The Isolated Rwenzori Mountains:** The Rwenzori Mountains, also known as the "Mountains of the Moon," are located on the border of Uganda and the Democratic Republic of Congo. They are famous for their glaciers, rare vegetation, and remote, mist-covered peaks.

Natural Wonders

O **Lençóis Maranhenses, Brazil:** Lençóis Maranhenses is a desert with an incredible twist: during the rainy season, it fills with freshwater lagoons, creating a stunning landscape of sand dunes and crystal-clear pools.

O **Zhangjiajie National Forest Park:** Located in China, this park's towering sandstone pillars inspired the floating mountains in the movie *Avatar*. The dramatic peaks often rise above mist-filled valleys, creating a magical and mysterious atmosphere.

O **The Blood Falls, Antarctica:** This eerie red waterfall flows from the Taylor Glacier onto the ice-covered surface of Lake Bonney. The color comes from iron oxide-rich saltwater that has been trapped beneath the glacier for millions of years.

O **The Mysterious Giant's Causeway:** The Giant's Causeway in Northern Ireland is a UNESCO World Heritage Site, famous for its 40,000 interlocking basalt columns, formed by an ancient volcanic eruption. The site is steeped in local mythology.

O **The Fingal's Cave, Scotland:** Located on the uninhabited island of Staffa, this sea cave is known for its hexagonal basalt columns and its unique acoustics. The cave's natural symphony of echoing waves inspired Mendelssohn's Hebrides Overture.

O **The Mystical Mount Kilimanjaro:** Mount Kilimanjaro in Tanzania is Africa's highest peak and the tallest free-standing mountain in the world. Its snow-capped summit rises above the surrounding savanna, making it a breathtaking sight.

O **The Crystal Ice Caves of Iceland:** Iceland's Vatnajökull Glacier hides stunning crystal ice caves beneath its surface. These temporary caves, formed by glacial meltwater, are illuminated in shades of blue and white, creating an ethereal landscape.

O **The Amazon River's Vast Network:** The Amazon River boasts over 1,100 tributaries. This vast network flows through the Amazon Rainforest, supporting an unparalleled diversity of life. The tributaries not only transport water but also distribute vital nutrients, sediments, and even fish species throughout the basin.

O **The Unique Rock Formations of Bryce Canyon:** Bryce Canyon National Park in Utah is known for its otherworldly rock formations called hoodoos. These tall, thin spires of rock create a surreal landscape, particularly striking at sunrise and sunset.

O **The Majestic Iguazu Falls:** Iguazu Falls, located on the border of Argentina and Brazil, is one of the largest waterfall systems in the world. The falls consist of around 275 individual drops!

O **The Spectacular Cliffs of Étretat:** The Cliffs of Étretat in France are famous for their stunning white chalk formations and natural arches, carved by the sea over millennia. The cliffs have inspired numerous artists, including Claude Monet.

O **Parcutin Volcano in Mexico:** Parcutin is a unique volcano because scientists witnessed its birth in 1943. Within a year, it grew 1,100 feet high and remains one of the youngest volcanoes on Earth.

O **Mount Everest's Growth:** Mount Everest grows about 4 millimeters each year due to tectonic activity pushing it higher!

O **The Colorful Aurora Australis:** The Aurora Australis, or Southern Lights, is the Southern Hemisphere's counterpart to the Northern Lights. This dazzling natural display is best seen from Antarctica, Australia, and New Zealand.

O **The Majestic Matterhorn:** The Matterhorn, located on the border of Switzerland and Italy, is one of the most iconic mountains in the Alps. Its pyramid-shaped peak has made it a symbol of the Swiss Alps and a challenging climb for mountaineers.

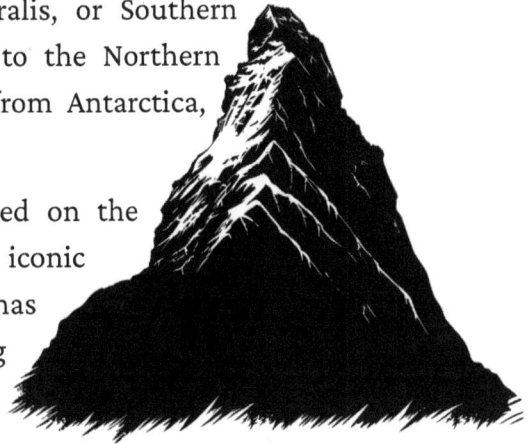

Spectacular Cities and Towns

O **Venice: The Floating City:** Venice, Italy, is famous for its canals, bridges, and historic architecture. Built on over 100 small islands, the city's intricate waterways are navigated by iconic gondolas.

O **Kyoto's Timeless Beauty:** Kyoto, Japan, is known for its well-preserved temples, shrines, and traditional wooden houses. The city's stunning cherry blossoms and vibrant autumn leaves make it a year-round destination.

O **Santorini's White-Washed Charm:** Santorini, Greece, is famous for its white-washed buildings with blue domes, perched on cliffs overlooking the Aegean Sea. The island's stunning sunsets are legendary, as are its black sand beaches.

O **Rio de Janeiro, Brazil:** Rio de Janeiro is home to the iconic Christ the Redeemer statue, which overlooks the city from Mount Corcovado. Famous for its beaches, carnival, and Sugarloaf Mountain, Rio is full of vibrant culture.

O **Prague: The City of a Hundred Spires:** Prague, Czech Republic, is renowned for its Gothic and Baroque architecture. The city's historic Old Town, stunning Charles Bridge, and Prague Castle make it a must-visit destination in Europe.

O **Reykjavik: The Northern Lights Capital:** Reykjavik, Iceland, is the world's northernmost capital. It's a charming city known for its colorful buildings, geothermal pools, and as a prime spot for viewing the Northern Lights.

O **Vancouver, Canada:** Surrounded by mountains and ocean, Vancouver offers both urban sophistication and natural beauty. Its parks, hiking trails, and vibrant neighborhoods make it one of the most livable cities in the world.

O **Dubrovnik: The Pearl of the Adriatic:** Dubrovnik, Croatia, is a medieval walled city on the Adriatic Sea. Its stunning Old Town, with limestone streets and baroque buildings, served as a filming location for *Game of Thrones*.

o **Barcelona, Spain:** Barcelona is famous for its unique architecture, especially Antoni Gaud's colorful and surreal buildings like the Sagrada Familia and Park Gell.

o **Cusco: The Gateway to Machu Picchu:** Cusco, Peru, was once the capital of the Inca Empire. Today, it's known for its mix of Incan and colonial architecture, with narrow streets that lead to bustling markets and ancient ruins.

o **Amsterdam: The City of Canals:** Amsterdam, Netherlands, is famous for its network of canals, historic homes, and vibrant cultural scene. The city's museums, such as the Van Gogh Museum and Anne Frank House, are world-renowned.

o **Havana: A Step Back in Time:** Havana, Cuba, is known for its colorful colonial architecture, vintage cars, and lively culture. The city's historic center, Old Havana, is a UNESCO World Heritage Site.

o **Fez: Morocco's Ancient Heart:** Fez, Morocco, is home to the world's oldest university, the University of Al Quaraouiyine. Its medieval medina, with narrow alleys and bustling souks, is a maze of history and culture.

o **Sydney: The Harbor City:** Sydney, Australia, is famous for its iconic Opera House, Harbor Bridge, and stunning beaches. The city's vibrant cultural scene and picturesque harbor make it one of the world's most beautiful cities.

o **Lhasa: The Spiritual Heart of Tibet:** Lhasa, Tibet, is the spiritual and administrative capital of Tibet. The city is home to the Potala Palace and Jokhang Temple, both important pilgrimage sites for Tibetan Buddhists.

Unexplored Territories

o **Siberian Permafrost:** Vast areas of Siberia's permafrost remain largely unexplored due to their remote location and harsh climate. Hidden beneath the frozen earth are preserved ancient animal remains and possibly unknown species.

o **The Remote Amazon Rainforest:** The Amazon Rainforest is so vast that many areas remain unexplored. It's home to countless undiscovered species and indigenous tribes that have had little to no contact with the outside world.

o **The Uncharted Deep Sea:** The deep sea, below 20,000 feet, is one of the least explored areas on Earth. It's a world of extreme conditions, bizarre creatures, and potential new species waiting to be discovered.

O **The Gangkhar Puensum Mountain:** Standing 24,836 feet tall, Gangkhar Puensum is the highest unclimbed mountain in the world. Located in Bhutan, the mountain remains unexplored due to religious beliefs and the country's restrictions on climbing.

O **The Isolated Kamchatka Peninsula:** The Kamchatka Peninsula in Russia is one of the most remote and unexplored regions in the world. It's a land of active volcanoes, vast wilderness, and abundant wildlife, rarely seen by humans.

O **The Unexplored Caves of Antarctica:** Antarctica's subglacial caves, formed by volcanic activity beneath the ice, are some of the least explored places on Earth. These dark, isolated environments may harbor unknown forms of life.

O **The Mysterious Skeleton Coast:** Namibia's Skeleton Coast is a remote, foggy, and harsh desert region, named for the shipwrecks and whale bones scattered along its shores. Its eerie beauty remains largely unexplored.

O **The Untouched Forests of New Guinea:** The island of New Guinea is home to some of the world's last unexplored rainforests. These dense jungles conceal isolated tribes, rare animals, and possibly even undiscovered species.

O **The Lost World of Venezuela's Tepuis:** Venezuela's tepuis are flat-topped mountains that rise abruptly from the jungle. Their isolated plateaus are home to unique ecosystems, some of which have never been fully explored.

O **The Abyssal Plains of the Ocean Floor:** The abyssal plains, located thousands of feet below the ocean's surface, cover more than 50% of the Earth's surface but remain largely unexplored due to their extreme depth and pressure.

O **The Uncharted Forests of Papua:** Papua, Indonesia, is one of the most remote regions on Earth, with vast areas of tropical rainforest that are virtually untouched by modern civilization and ripe for discovery.

O **Greenland's Ice Sheet:** Greenland's ice sheet covers 80% of the island, and underneath it lies an unexplored landscape, including mountains, valleys, and potential ancient lakes, largely concealed by ice.

O **The Dense Jungle of the Darién Gap:** The Darién Gap, a dense jungle between Panama and Colombia, is one of the most challenging regions to traverse. Its dangerous terrain and lawlessness make it a true no man's land.

O **The Harsh Desolation of the Taklamakan Desert:** China's Taklamakan Desert is one of the world's largest sandy deserts. Known as the "Sea of Death," it's largely uninhabited and unexplored due to its extreme conditions.

O **The Ice-Covered Lake Vostok:** Lake Vostok in Antarctica lies beneath 2.5 miles of ice. Despite being covered for millions of years, the lake remains liquid, and its unexplored waters may contain unknown life forms.

Alright! That's the end of our journey around the globe to some of the world's most astonishing places! These incredible locations remind us of the planet's vastness, beauty, and endless surprises.

Next, we dive into the world of human feats. Prepare to be amazed by the incredible achievements, endurance, and ingenuity of humankind. From record-breaking moments to extraordinary inventions, this chapter will celebrate the triumphs and resilience that have shaped our history and continue to inspire us today.

Superhumans Among Us

Daring Deeds

O **The First Solo Flight Across the Atlantic:** In 1927, Charles Lindbergh became the first person to fly solo nonstop across the Atlantic Ocean, from New York to Paris. It took him 33 hours!

O **Climbing the World's Tallest Building:** In 2011, Alain Robert, known as the "French Spider-Man," climbed the 2,717-feet Burj Khalifa in Dubai without ropes or safety gear. It took him over six hours to reach the top.

O **Crossing Niagara Falls on a Tightrope:** In 1859, Charles Blondin crossed Niagara Falls on a tightrope, 160 feet above the water. He performed the daring feat multiple times, even carrying a man on his back once.

O **The First Human Spacewalk:** In 1965, Soviet cosmonaut Alexei Leonov became the first person to conduct a spacewalk. He spent 12 minutes outside his spacecraft, tethered only by a 16-foot-long cable.

O **Rowing Across the Atlantic Alone:** In 1969, John Fairfax became the first person to row solo across the Atlantic Ocean. He rowed for 180 days from the Canary Islands to Florida, surviving shark attacks and storms.

O **Free Solo Climbing El Capitan:** In 2017, Alex Honnold became the first person to free solo climb El Capitan in Yosemite National Park. The 3,000-foot ascent, completed without ropes, was a feat of sheer daring and skill.

O **The World's Deepest Dive:** In 2019, Victor Vescovo became the first person to reach the deepest point of the Mariana Trench, Challenger Deep, diving nearly 36,000 feet below the ocean's surface in a submersible.

O **Biking Around the World:** In 2017, Mark Beaumont cycled around the world in just 78 days, covering 18,000 miles across 16 countries. He shattered the previous record by 44 days.

O **Crossing Antarctica on Foot:** In 2018, Colin O'Brady became the first person to cross Antarctica solo, unsupported, and unaided. His 932-mile journey took 54 days through some of the harshest conditions on Earth.

O **First Woman to Summit Everest:** In 1975, Junko Tabei from Japan became the first woman to reach the summit of Mount Everest. Her achievement paved the way for female mountaineers worldwide.

O **The Highest Balloon Flight:** In 1961, Malcolm Ross and Victor Prather set a world record by flying a helium balloon to 113,740 feet, higher than any manned balloon had gone before, in an open gondola.

- **Swimming the English Channel:** In 1875, Matthew Webb became the first person to swim across the English Channel without the aid of artificial flotation devices, completing the 21-mile swim in 21 hours and 45 minutes.

- **Circumnavigating the Globe by Boat:** In 1968, Sir Robin Knox-Johnston became the first person to sail solo nonstop around the world. His 312-day voyage aboard the *Suhaili* remains a legendary achievement in sailing history.

- **Crossing the Arctic on Foot:** In 1995, Børge Ousland became the first person to cross the Arctic Ocean solo, unsupported, and on foot, covering 1,000 miles in 58 days from Siberia to Canada.

- **The First Skydive from the Edge of Space:** In 2012, Felix Baumgartner became the first person to skydive from the edge of space, jumping from a balloon at 128,000 feet. He reached speeds of 843.6 mph during his freefall.

Extreme Endurance

- **Marathon Monks of Mount Hiei:** These Buddhist monks in Japan practice Kaihogyo, a tough training regimen that requires running and walking around Mount Hiei, over a period of 7 years!

- **The World's Longest Fast:** In 1965, Angus Barbieri of Scotland fasted for 382 days, surviving only on water, tea, coffee, and vitamins. He lost 276 pounds and holds the record for the longest medically supervised fast.

- **Rowing Across the Pacific Ocean:** In 2014, British adventurer Sarah Outen rowed solo across the Pacific Ocean, covering 4,300 miles in 150 days. Her journey from Japan to Alaska was part of a global expedition.

- **The Longest Underwater Stay:** In 2014, Fabien Cousteau and the Mission 31 team spent 31 days living underwater in the Aquarius Reef Base, breaking the record for the longest underwater mission.

- **The Longest Time Spent in a Cave:** In 1965, Michel Siffre, a French scientist, lived alone in a cave for 205 days without exposure to sunlight. His experiment studied the effects of isolation on the human body and mind.

- **Longest Time Treading Water in the Ocean:** The longest officially recognized record for treading water belongs to Albert Rizzo, who achieved the feat in 1983 by treading water for an astounding 108 hours (4 days and 12 hours). Rizzo, a Maltese mayor and auctioneer, accomplished this remarkable feat in the open sea, showcasing incredible endurance and mental fortitude.

- **Running Across the Sahara Desert:** In 2007, three ultra-marathoners, Charlie Engle, Ray Zahab, and Kevin Lin, ran 4,300 miles across the Sahara Desert in 111 days, enduring extreme heat and dehydration.

- **Climbing the Seven Summits:** In 1985, American mountaineer Richard Bass became the first person to climb the highest peak on each of the seven continents, a challenge known as the Seven Summits.

o **Swimming the Length of the Amazon River:** In 2007, Slovenian swimmer Martin Strel became the first person to swim the entire length of the Amazon River, covering 3,274 miles in 66 days, despite dangers from piranhas and parasites.

o **Cliff Young's Ultra Marathon Victory:** In 1983, 61-year-old Cliff Young won the Sydney to Melbourne Ultra Marathon. He ran non-stop for five days, beating much younger competitors.

o **The Iditarod Trail Sled Dog Race:** Mushers and their dog teams race across nearly 1,000 miles (1,609 km) of Alaskan wilderness, enduring harsh weather and challenging terrain. In 2004, Doug Swingley completed the Iditarod in a record-breaking time of 8 days, 18 hours, and 47 minutes. This feat required him to push himself and his dog team to their limits, traveling day and night through challenging conditions.

o **Climbing Mount Everest Multiple Times:** Sherpa Kami Rita holds the record for the most climbs of Mount Everest. As of 2024, he has summited the world's highest peak 30 times, showing incredible physical and mental endurance.

o **Longest Distance Cycled Non-Stop:** In 2019, ultra-cyclist Christoph Strasser rode 1,000 kilometers (621 miles) without stopping, setting the record for the longest distance cycled without sleep or rest breaks, finishing in just under 29 hours.

o **Walking Across the World:** In 1974, David Kunst became the first person verified to have walked around the Earth. His 14,450-mile journey took over four years, spanning four continents!

o **Longest Open-Water Swim:** In 1998, Croatian swimmer Veljko Rogoşić swam across the Adriatic Sea, covering 139.8 miles in 50 hours and 10 minutes, setting the world record for the longest open-water swim.

o **Completing the Triple Crown of Hiking:** The Triple Crown of Hiking consists of the Appalachian Trail, the Pacific Crest Trail, and the Continental Divide Trail. Less than 500 people have completed all three, covering over 7,900 miles.

Incredible Achievements

o **The Construction of the Eiffel Tower:** Completed in 1889, the Eiffel Tower was the tallest man-made structure in the world for 41 years. It was originally built as a temporary exhibit for the World's Fair in Paris.

o **The Launch of the First Space Station:** In 1971, the Soviet Union launched Salyut 1, the first space station. It paved the way for long-duration missions and helped establish permanent human presence in space.

o **The Building of the Hoover Dam:** Completed in 1936, the Hoover Dam in the United States was a groundbreaking engineering achievement. It generates enough hydroelectric power to serve over a million people each year.

- **First Successful Flight Around the World Without Refueling:** In 1986, the *Voyager* aircraft, piloted by Dick Rutan and Jeana Yeager, became the first plane to fly around the world non-stop without refueling. The flight lasted nine days and covered 25,000 miles.

- **The Construction of the Trans-Siberian Railway:** Completed in 1916, the Trans-Siberian Railway is the longest railway in the world, stretching over 5,700 miles across Russia. It connects Moscow with the Pacific port of Vladivostok.

- **The First Powered Flight Across the English Channel:** In 1909, Louis Blériot became the first person to fly an airplane across the English Channel. His 36-minute flight from France to England was a milestone in aviation history.

- **The First Human to Reach the North Pole:** In 1909, American explorer Robert Peary, accompanied by his team, claimed to be the first person to reach the North Pole. The expedition endured extreme weather and harsh conditions.

- **The First Transcontinental Telegraph:** In 1861, the completion of the first transcontinental telegraph line in the U.S. revolutionized communication, allowing messages to be sent across the country in a matter of minutes instead of weeks.

- **Youngest Person to Sail Solo Around the World:** In 2010, 16-year-old Australian Jessica Watson became the youngest person to sail solo, non-stop, and unassisted around the world, completing the voyage in just under 7 months.

- **The Green Revolution:** In the mid-20th century, agricultural scientist Norman Borlaug led the Green Revolution, which introduced high-yield crops and modern farming techniques, greatly increasing food production.

- **The First Photograph:** In 1826, Joseph Nicéphore Niépce took the first known photograph using a camera obscura. This historic image, titled "View from the Window at Le Gras," paved the way for modern photography.

- **First Blind Person to Climb Mount Everest:** In 2001, Erik Weihenmayer became the first blind person to reach the summit of Mount Everest, demonstrating incredible physical and mental endurance.

- **The Creation of the Periodic Table:** In 1869, Russian chemist Dmitri Mendeleev developed the first Periodic Table of Elements. This organized the known elements into groups based on their properties and remains a fundamental tool in chemistry.

- **Crossing the Atlantic by Hot Air Balloon:** In 1978, Ben Abruzzo, Maxie Anderson, and Larry Newman became the first people to cross the Atlantic Ocean by hot air balloon. The journey took 137 hours and covered 3,075 miles.

- **Developing the Polio Vaccine:** In 1955, Dr. Jonas Salk introduced the first effective polio vaccine, leading to a dramatic decline in cases worldwide and bringing the disease close to eradication.

Mind Over Matter

- **Climbing Mount Everest Without Oxygen :** In 1978, Reinhold Messner and Peter Habeler became the first climbers to reach the summit of Mount Everest without supplemental oxygen, proving that the human body can endure extreme conditions.

- **Holding the World Record for Free Diving:** In 2017, freediver Alessia Zecchini set the AIDA (Association Internationale pour le Développement de l'Apnée) world record by diving to a depth of 104 meters (341 feet) on a single breath in the constant weight category.

- **Completing the Ironman Triathlon:** The Ironman Triathlon is one of the most challenging endurance races, consisting of a 2.4-mile swim, a 112-mile bike ride, and a 26.2-mile marathon. Competitors push their minds and bodies to the limit.

- **Surviving 63 Days Lost at Sea:** In 1982, Steven Callahan survived for 63 days alone on a life raft in the Atlantic Ocean after his sailboat sank. His mental resilience and resourcefulness kept him alive.

- **The Longest Yoga Marathon:** In 2010, BKS Iyengar, a renowned yoga teacher, held a continuous yoga session for 72 hours, demonstrating the power of mental discipline and physical endurance through meditation and postures.

- **David Blaine's Breath-Holding Record:** Magician David Blaine held his breath underwater for 17 minutes and 4 seconds on live television in 2008. He used meditation and relaxation techniques to push beyond normal human limits.

- **Breaking the Plank World Record:** In 2020, George Hood set the world record for holding a plank position for 8 hours, 15 minutes, and 15 seconds at the age of 62. His focus and mental stamina were key to his success.

- **Running a Marathon on Every Continent:** In 2017, Dr. Brent Weigner set a record by running a marathon on all seven continents, completing 26 marathons in Antarctica alone. His persistence and mental toughness drove him to achieve this feat.

- **Rosie Swale-Pope's Solo Run Around the World:** Rosie Swale-Pope ran around the world after the death of her husband, covering 20,000 miles over five years. Her mental fortitude and determination helped her face freezing temperatures and loneliness.

- **Juliane Koepcke's Survival in the Amazon:** At age 17, Juliane Koepcke survived a plane crash in the Amazon Rainforest. She trekked alone for 11 days through the jungle, relying on her mental strength and knowledge of the forest to survive.

- **Hiroo Onoda's 30-Year WWII Survival:** Hiroo Onoda, a Japanese soldier, continued fighting World War II on an isolated island for nearly 30 years, refusing to believe the war was over. His mental discipline allowed him to survive for decades in the jungle.

- **Meditating for World Peace:** In 1996, 6,000 monks, nuns, and meditators gathered in the United States to meditate for world peace, demonstrating the collective power of the mind and the importance of mindfulness.

- **Nando Parrado's Survival in the Andes:** After his plane crashed in the Andes Mountains, Nando Parrado trekked 10 days over dangerous snow-capped peaks to find help. His determination and mental strength helped save the lives of 16 survivors.

- **Completing the Appalachian Trail:** In 2017, Joe McConaughy set a speed record for completing the 2,190-mile Appalachian Trail, doing so in just 45 days without any outside support. His mental resilience was key to his success.

- **The Longest Ice Bath:** In 2019, Dutch "Iceman" Wim Hof set the record for the longest full-body ice bath, staying submerged for 1 hour, 52 minutes, and 42 seconds. His techniques highlight the power of mind over body.

Remarkable Resilience

- **Helen Keller's Triumph Over Disability:** Despite being deaf and blind, Helen Keller learned to communicate through sign language, graduated from college, and became a renowned author and advocate for people with disabilities.

- **The Survival of Ernest Shackleton's Crew:** In 1915, after their ship *Endurance* was trapped and crushed by Antarctic ice, Ernest Shackleton led his crew on a two-year journey to safety.

- **The 33 Chilean Miners' Rescue:** In 2010, 33 miners were trapped underground for 69 days after a cave-in. They survived on minimal food and water before a miraculous rescue, demonstrating incredible mental and physical resilience.

- **Malala Yousafzai's Fight for Education:** After surviving an assassination attempt by the Taliban in 2012, Malala Yousafzai continued her advocacy for girls' education, becoming the youngest-ever Nobel Prize laureate at 17.

- **The Recovery of Aron Ralston:** In 2003, mountaineer Aron Ralston was trapped by a boulder in a Utah canyon. After six days, he amputated his own arm to free himself and survived, demonstrating extraordinary resilience and determination.

- **Louis Zamperini's Survival Story:** During World War II, Louis Zamperini survived 47 days on a raft in the Pacific Ocean and two years as a prisoner of war. His story of survival and forgiveness is a testament to human resilience.

- **The Rebuilding of Hiroshima:** After the atomic bombing of Hiroshima in 1945, the city was left in ruins. Through incredible resilience, the people of Hiroshima rebuilt their city into a symbol of peace and recovery.

o **Viktor Frankl's Survival in a Concentration Camp:** Psychiatrist Viktor Frankl survived the horrors of Nazi concentration camps and later wrote *Man's Search for Meaning*, where he described how finding purpose and mental resilience helped him endure unimaginable suffering.

o **The Survival of the Donner Party:** In 1846, the Donner Party, a group of pioneers, became trapped in the Sierra Nevada mountains during winter. Despite unimaginable hardships, some members survived, displaying remarkable endurance and resilience.

o **The Endurance of Anne Frank:** During World War II, Anne Frank and her family hid from the Nazis for two years in a secret annex. Her diary, written during this time, remains a powerful testament to resilience and hope.

o **The Reconstruction After the 2004 Tsunami:** The 2004 Indian Ocean tsunami devastated coastal communities across 14 countries. Through global cooperation and the resilience of the survivors, many communities were rebuilt stronger than before.

o **The Grit of Harriet Tubman:** Escaping slavery in 1849, Harriet Tubman returned to the South 13 times to lead approximately 300 enslaved people to freedom via the Underground Railroad, showing extraordinary courage and resilience.

o **The Endurance of Terry Fox:** In 1980, after losing a leg to cancer, Canadian athlete Terry Fox embarked on a cross-country run to raise awareness for cancer research. Though he couldn't finish, his Marathon of Hope continues to inspire millions.

o **The Courage of Irena Sendler:** During World War II, Polish social worker Irena Sendler smuggled 2,500 Jewish children out of the Warsaw Ghetto, risking her life and demonstrating incredible resilience against Nazi oppression.

o **The Phoenix of London After the Great Fire:** In 1666, the Great Fire of London destroyed much of the city. Through determination and resilience, London was rebuilt, leading to the creation of iconic structures like St. Paul's Cathedral.

Superhuman Strength

o **The Incredible Strength of Bruce Lee:** Martial arts legend Bruce Lee was known for his lightning-fast reflexes and powerful strikes. His famous one-inch punch could send an opponent flying backward, showcasing his extraordinary physical power.

o **The Remarkable Feat of Aaron Fotheringham:** Aaron "Wheelz" Fotheringham, a wheelchair athlete, became the first person to land a backflip in a wheelchair. His strength and determination redefine what's possible for adaptive sports.

o **The Unyielding Strength of Wim Hof:** Known as "The Iceman," Wim Hof has set records for withstanding extreme cold, including climbing Mount Kilimanjaro in shorts and running a marathon in the Arctic Circle barefoot.

- **The Enduring Strength of Dachhiri Sherpa:** Dachhiri Sherpa, a Nepalese ultra-marathon runner, ran the grueling Ultra-Trail du Mont-Blanc—a 106-mile race across the Alps—several times. His incredible endurance and mental toughness are legendary.

- **Paul Anderson's Backlift Record:** In 1957, Paul Anderson, an American weightlifter, lifted a staggering 6,270 pounds in a backlift. His feat is still considered one of the greatest displays of human strength.

- **The Heroic Strength of Tilly Smith:** In 2004, 10-year-old Tilly Smith saved over 100 people from a tsunami in Thailand by recognizing warning signs she had learned in school. Her quick thinking and courage were spectacular.

- **The Impressive Strength of Julianna Peña:** MMA fighter Julianna Peña stunned the world by defeating the seemingly unbeatable Amanda Nunes in 2021. Her victory was a testament to her incredible mental and physical strength.

- **The Superhuman Resilience of Reshma Begum:** In 2013, Reshma Begum survived 17 days trapped under rubble after a factory collapse in Bangladesh!

- **The Mental Strength of Helen Thayer:** Helen Thayer, at age 50, became the first woman to trek solo to the magnetic North Pole without support!

- **Tommy Kono: Olympic Champion:** Tommy Kono, a weightlifting legend, overcame asthma to win two Olympic gold medals and set 26 world records in various weight classes. His strength and resilience earned him global respect.

- **The Endurance of Kilian Jornet:** Kilian Jornet, a Spanish ultra-runner, set a record by ascending and descending Mount Everest twice in a week without supplemental oxygen.

- **Kevin Fast – Heaviest Plane Pulled:** Canadian pastor Kevin Fast set a world record in 2009 by pulling a 416,299-pound CC-177 Globemaster III military aircraft in a Canadian Forces Base in Ontario, Canada.

- **The Strength of Becca Meyers:** Paralympic swimmer Becca Meyers, who is deaf and blind, won six medals in the 2016 Rio Paralympics, proving that strength comes in many forms, including overcoming incredible odds.

- **The Stamina of Marshall Ulrich:** Marshall Ulrich ran across the United States at age 57, covering 3,063 miles in 52 days. His feat is a testament to physical endurance, mental toughness, and superhuman stamina.

- **The Power of Jessica Long:** Jessica Long, born without fibulas, underwent 25 surgeries before age 10 and went on to become a multi-gold medal-winning Paralympic swimmer.

Throughout this chapter we've witnessed the boundless strength, resilience, and determination of people who have pushed the limits of what's possible. Whether it's climbing the highest peaks, surviving against all odds, or changing the world through sheer willpower, these feats inspire us to strive for greatness.

Next, prepare to embark on a vibrant journey through the kaleidoscope of human culture. We'll explore the diverse customs, traditions, and creative expressions that define societies across the globe. From ancient rituals to modern trends, from music and dance to food and festivals, this chapter will take you on a cultural celebration that highlights the beauty of human diversity.

A Small Favor

Thank you so much for purchasing our book. We really appreciate it!

Could you consider leaving a review on the platform? It would be the easiest and fastest way to support small independent brands like us.

>> Leave a review on Amazon US <<QR Code

>> Leave a review on Amazon UK <<QR Code

We would really appreciate your kind words and would love to hear what you liked about our book! Thank you once again, Onward and forward to the next chapter!

Tapestry of Time

Art and Artistry

O **The Mona Lisa's Smile:** Leonardo da Vinci's <u>Mona Lisa</u> is famous for her mysterious smile. Some believe her expression changes depending on where you stand!

O **Banksy's Shredded Artwork:** In 2018, Banksy's <u>Girl with Balloon</u> shredded itself immediately after being auctioned for over a million dollars. This act transformed it into a new artwork called <u>Love is in the Bin</u>.

O **The Sistine Chapel's Ceiling:** Michelangelo painted the Sistine Chapel's ceiling lying on his back for four years. The masterpiece includes over 300 figures, with <u>The Creation of Adam</u> being the most iconic.

O **Vincent van Gogh's Artistic Dedication:** Vincent van Gogh created over 2,100 artworks, including 860 oil paintings, despite only painting for ten years. He famously sold only one painting during his lifetime but is now one of the most celebrated artists in history.

O **The World's Oldest Known Art:** The world's oldest known art, found in Indonesian caves, consists of hand stencils and animal drawings dating back over 44,000 years!

O **The Ceiling of the Louvre's Pyramid:** The glass pyramid at the Louvre Museum in Paris was designed by architect I. M. Pei and completed in 1989. It stands 71 feet high and consists of 673 glass panels.

O **Hidden Faces in Salvador Dalí's Art:** Salvador Dalí often hid faces within his surrealist paintings. For example, a bullfighter's face is cleverly disguised in <u>The Hallucinogenic Toreador</u>.

O **The Color-Changing Egyptian Blue:** Ancient Egyptians created a blue pigment that glows under infrared light. One of the earliest synthetic colors, it is still studied for its potential modern uses.

O **Frida Kahlo's Self-Portraits:** Frida Kahlo painted 55 self-portraits out of her 143 works. Her art reflects her physical and emotional pain, making her a symbol of resilience.

O **The Great Wave's Hidden Mount Fuji:** Hokusai's <u>The Great Wave off Kanagawa</u> almost hides Mount Fuji in the background, emphasizing the wave's power over Japan's iconic mountain.

O **England's Chalk Hill Figures:** The Cerne Abbas Giant and the Uffington White Horse are among England's ancient chalk hill figures, carved into hillsides and surrounded in mystery.

O **The Sistine Chapel's Hidden Brain:** Some researchers believe Michelangelo painted a hidden anatomical brain in <u>The Creation of Adam</u>, symbolizing the connection between God and human intellect.

o **The Art of Sand Mandalas:** Tibetan monks create intricate sand mandalas using colored sand, which can take days or weeks to complete. Once finished, the mandala is destroyed, symbolizing the impermanence of life.

o **The Spiral Jetty:** In 1970, artist Robert Smithson created the *Spiral Jetty*, a massive land art installation in Utah's Great Salt Lake. Made of rock and earth, the spiral stretches 1,500 feet into the lake, visible only when water levels are low.

o **Banksy's Real Identity:** Despite being one of the most famous artists in the world, Banksy's true identity remains unknown. His street art often carries political messages, making him a mysterious figure in the art world.

Cultural Quirks

o **Japan's Love for Kit Kats:** In Japan, Kit Kats come in over 300 unique flavors, including wasabi, green tea, and soy sauce. The candy's name sounds like "kitto katsu," meaning "surely win," making it a popular good luck charm.

o **The Whistling Language of La Gomera:** In La Gomera, Spain, locals communicate using a whistling language called Silbo Gomero. This allows messages to be sent across the island's deep ravines, carrying sounds up to 3 miles away.

o **Viking Burials in Boats:** Vikings believed ships carried warriors to the afterlife. Wealthy Vikings were buried with their ships, treasures, and weapons, symbolizing their journey to the next world.

o **Thailand's National Anthem Pause:** In Thailand, the national anthem is played twice daily, at 8 a.m. and 6 p.m. Wherever they are, people pause and stand still out of respect, even in busy public places.

o **Slurping Noodles in Japan:** In Japan, slurping your noodles loudly is polite and shows you're enjoying your meal. It's also believed to enhance the flavor by cooling the noodles.

o **Italy's August Shutdown:** In August, many Italians observe "Ferragosto," a traditional holiday. Businesses close for weeks, and cities empty as people head to the beach or mountains to escape the summer heat.

o **India's Holy Cows:** In India, cows are considered sacred and are often seen wandering freely through cities. Hindus revere cows for their gentle nature and life-giving properties, like milk.

o **Norway's "Slow TV" Phenomenon:** Norway's "Slow TV" broadcasts include hours-long shows featuring mundane activities, like a train journey or knitting marathon. Surprisingly, these broadcasts attract millions of viewers seeking relaxation.

o **Mexico's Day of the Dead:** During Mexico's Day of the Dead, families build colorful altars and decorate graves with marigolds, candles, and sugar skulls to honor their deceased loved ones in a festive, joyous celebration.

o **Ethiopia's Unique Calendar: A Fascinating Time Warp:** Ethiopia's calendar, known as the Ethiopian calendar or the Ge'ez calendar, stands out as a unique and intriguing system of timekeeping. The Ethiopian calendar consists of 12 months, each with 30 days, and a 13th month called Pagume, which has 5 days in a common year and 6 days in a leap year. It was introduced in the 16th century by Emperor Ge'ez Sarsa Dengel of Abyssinia (Ethiopia).

O **Germany's Silent Sundays:** In Germany, "Ruhetag" or "Silent Sunday" laws prohibit loud activities, like mowing the lawn or playing loud music, to ensure peace and quiet. These laws reflect Germany's strong respect for rest and relaxation.

O **Japan's Bowing Etiquette:** In Japan, bowing is a common greeting and a sign of respect. The depth and duration of the bow depend on the situation and relationship, with deeper bows showing greater respect.

O **Finland's Wife-Carrying Championship:** Each year, Finland hosts the Wife-Carrying World Championship, where men race while carrying their wives. The winner's prize is the wife's weight in beer, and the event draws contestants from around the world.

O **Greece's Evil Eye Protection:** In Greece, many people wear a blue eye charm called "mati" to ward off the evil eye, a superstition believed to cause bad luck or misfortune. The charm is also common in Turkey and other Mediterranean cultures.

O **China's Lucky Red Envelopes:** In China, during Lunar New Year, people give red envelopes filled with money as gifts. The color red symbolizes good luck, and the envelopes are believed to bring good tidings and fortune.

O **Spain's Tomatina Festival:** Each August, the town of Buñol, Spain, hosts La Tomatina, a massive tomato fight. Tens of thousands of people hurl tomatoes at each other, turning the streets into a red, squishy mess.

O **Russia's Superstition About Whistling Indoors:** In Russia, whistling indoors is believed to bring bad luck, especially in terms of losing money. The saying goes, "If you whistle in the house, you will whistle away your money."

Dance and Drama

O **The Flamenco's Fiery Passion:** Flamenco, a traditional Spanish art form, combines singing, guitar playing, dance, and clapping. Originating from Andalusia, it expresses deep emotion, known as "duende," and is recognized as a UNESCO cultural heritage.

O **Japan's Noh Theatre:** Noh is one of Japan's oldest forms of theater, dating back over 600 years. Performers wear intricate masks and their slow, deliberate movements convey complex emotions and stories rooted in Japanese folklore.

O **Bollywood's Lavish Dance Sequences:** Bollywood films are famous for their elaborate dance sequences. These dances blend classical Indian styles with modern influences, creating visually stunning performances that often tell part of the movie's story.

o **The Brazilian Carnival:** Carnival in Brazil features vibrant parades filled with samba dancers, extravagant costumes, and lively music. This festival, held before Lent, is a dazzling display of Brazilian culture.

o **The Ballet Originates in Italy:** Although ballet is often associated with France, it actually originated in the Italian Renaissance courts in the 15th century. It later evolved into the form we know today in France and Russia.

o **The Kathakali of India:** Kathakali is a traditional Indian dance-drama known for its colorful costumes, detailed makeup, and elaborate gestures. Originating in Kerala, it often depicts stories from Hinduism like the Mahabharata.

o **The Haka: A Dance of Strength:** The Haka is a traditional Māori war dance from New Zealand, performed by the All Blacks rugby team before matches. It's a powerful display of strength, unity, and cultural pride.

o **Chinese Peking Opera:** Peking Opera is a traditional Chinese theater combining music, vocal performance, mime, dance, and acrobatics. It's known for its elaborate costumes and makeup, as well as its symbolic gestures and movements.

o **Kabuki: A Traditional Japanese Art Form:** Kabuki, a classical Japanese dance-drama, was first performed in the early 17th century. Known for its elaborate costumes and stylized movements, Kabuki often tells stories of historical events and legends.

o **The Viennese Waltz:** Originating in Austria, the Viennese Waltz is the oldest ballroom dance, characterized by its fast tempo and graceful, flowing movements. It's still performed at grand balls across Vienna today.

o **Ballet Folklorico: Mexico's Cultural Dance:** Ballet Folklorico is a vibrant traditional Mexican dance that showcases the country's diverse cultures and histories. The colorful costumes and energetic performances bring Mexican folk traditions to life.

o **Greece's Zorba Dance:** The Sirtaki, commonly known as the Zorba dance, became famous worldwide thanks to the 1964 film *Zorba the Greek*. It starts slow and builds in intensity, embodying Greek spirit and camaraderie.

o **The Russian Ballet Legacy:** Russian ballet is world-renowned for its technical precision and emotional depth. Legendary companies like the Bolshoi and Mariinsky have produced some of the greatest dancers and choreographers in history.

o **Ireland's Riverdance Phenomenon:** Riverdance brought Irish step dancing to global fame in the 1990s. Known for its fast-paced footwork and synchronized movements, this performance showcases Ireland's rich cultural heritage.

O **Capoeira: Brazil's Dance-Fight:** Capoeira is a unique blend of dance, acrobatics, and martial arts developed by enslaved Africans in Brazil. It's characterized by fluid movements and rhythmic music, making it both a cultural and physical art form.

Festivals and Feasts

O **Diwali: The Festival of Lights:** Diwali, celebrated in India and by millions worldwide, is known as the Festival of Lights. Families light oil lamps, decorate with rangoli, and enjoy sweets to celebrate the victory of light over darkness.

O **Glastonbury Festival in England:** Glastonbury is one of the world's largest music and performing arts festivals, held annually in the English countryside. It draws hundreds of thousands of music lovers for live performances over several days.

O **Burning Man in the Nevada Desert:** Burning Man is a week-long festival in Nevada's Black Rock Desert, where attendees create a temporary city focused on art, self-expression, and community. The festival culminates in the burning of a giant wooden effigy.

O **Thanksgiving in the United States:** Thanksgiving, celebrated on the fourth Thursday of November, is a time for feasting and giving thanks. The traditional meal includes turkey, stuffing, and pumpkin pie, enjoyed with family and friends. Canadian Thanksgiving, celebrated on the second Monday in October, is a harvest festival similar to its American counterpart.

O **Oktoberfest in Germany:** Oktoberfest, held annually in Munich, Germany, is the world's largest beer festival. Visitors enjoy traditional Bavarian food, music, and liters of beer while dressed in lederhosen and dirndls.

O **The Lantern Festival in China:** The Lantern Festival marks the end of Chinese New Year celebrations. Families release lanterns into the sky or float them on water, symbolizing the letting go of the past and embracing the future.

O **Holi: The Festival of Colors:** Holi, celebrated in India and Nepal, is a vibrant festival where people throw colored powders at each other, dance, and celebrate the arrival of spring and the victory of good over evil.

O **The Qixi Festival: China's Timeless Celebration of Love:** The Qixi Festival, also known as the Double Seventh Festival or Chinese Valentine's Day, is a cherished tradition celebrated on the 7th day of the 7th lunar month, which typically falls in August. It commemorates the legendary love story of Zhin (the Weaver Girl) and Niulang (the Cowherd), who are allowed to meet only once a year on this day. It is now seen as a Chinese equivalent to Valentine's Day, with couples celebrating their relationships and single people hoping to find love.

O **Songkran: Thailand's Water Festival:** Songkran, Thailand's New Year festival, is celebrated with massive water fights in the streets. People splash water on each other to wash away bad luck and welcome the new year with a fresh start.

- **Mardi Gras in New Orleans:** Mardi Gras, or Fat Tuesday, in New Orleans is famous for its colorful parades, masquerade balls, and festive atmosphere. The celebration marks the final day of indulgence before Lent.

- **The Mid-Autumn Festival in China:** The Mid-Autumn Festival, also known as the Moon Festival, is celebrated with mooncakes, lanterns, and family gatherings. It honors the harvest and the full moon's beauty.

- **The Edinburgh Fringe Festival:** The Edinburgh Fringe Festival is the world's largest arts festival, held every August in Scotland. It features thousands of performances, including comedy, theater, music, and dance, in venues across the city.

- **Eid al-Fitr: The Festival of Breaking the Fast:** Eid al-Fitr is a major Islamic holiday marking the end of Ramadan, a month of fasting. It's celebrated with prayers, feasting, and giving to charity, bringing families and communities together.

- **Hanami: Japan's Cherry Blossom Festival:** Hanami, the traditional Japanese custom of enjoying cherry blossoms, is celebrated with picnics under blooming cherry trees. The delicate flowers symbolize the fleeting beauty of life.

- **Inti Raymi in Peru:** Inti Raymi, or the Festival of the Sun, is an ancient Inca celebration held in Cusco, Peru. It honors the Sun God and marks the winter solstice with colorful parades, dances, and reenactments of traditional ceremonies.

Music and Melody

- **Beethoven's Deafness:** Despite losing his hearing, Ludwig van Beethoven composed some of his greatest works, including the Ninth Symphony. He continued to create masterpieces by feeling vibrations through the floor and using an ear trumpet.

- **Mozart's Childhood Genius:** Wolfgang Amadeus Mozart composed his first piece of music at just five years old and performed before European royalty by age six. He is generally considered to be one of the greatest composers in history.

- **The Birth of Rock 'n' Roll:** Rock 'n' roll emerged in the 1950s, blending elements of rhythm and blues, country, and gospel. Elvis Presley, known as the "King of Rock 'n' Roll," was one of the leading figures.

- **The World's Oldest Musical Instrument:** The world's oldest known musical instrument, a 40,000-year-old flute made from vulture bone, was discovered in a cave in Germany. This suggests that music has been a part of human culture for millennia.

- **The First Electric Guitar:** The first electric guitar, invented by George Beauchamp in 1931, revolutionized music by giving rise to rock and roll and modern music genres.

- **The World's Largest Orchestra:** In 2021, Venezuela's El Sistema won the Guinness World Record for largest orchestra, assembling 8,573 instrumentalists and singers!

O **The Mystery of the Theremin:** The theremin, an electronic instrument invented in 1920, is played without physical contact. Musicians control the pitch and volume by moving their hands near its antennas, creating eerie, otherworldly sounds.

O **The Power of Gospel Music:** Gospel music, rooted in African American spirituals, played a significant role in the civil rights movement. Songs like "We Shall Overcome" became anthems for change and unity.

O **The Influence of Jazz:** Jazz, born in the early 20th century in New Orleans, is characterized by improvisation, syncopation, and strong rhythms. Icons like Louis Armstrong and Duke Ellington helped shape this uniquely American art form.

O **The Traditional Music of the Didgeridoo:** The didgeridoo is a traditional wind instrument of the Aboriginal people of Australia. Made from hollowed-out eucalyptus, it produces deep, resonant tones used in ceremonial and folk healing practices.

O **The Guinness World Record for Longest Concert:** The world's longest concert lasted over 437 hours and was held in 2017 at the Earl of Whitchurch pub in Ontario, Canada. Hundreds of musicians took turns performing for 18 days straight!

O **The Origins of Country Music:** Country music originated in the rural southern United States in the 1920s, blending folk, blues, and Western music. Artists like Hank Williams and Dolly Parton became legends of the genre.

O **Bob Dylan Wins the Nobel Prize:** In 2016, Bob Dylan became the first musician to win the Nobel Prize in Literature for his contributions to songwriting. His lyrics have been praised for their poetic and literary qualities.

O **The Sound of the Sitar:** The sitar, a traditional Indian stringed instrument, produces a complex and resonant sound. Made famous by musicians like Ravi Shankar, it's a central instrument in Hindustani classical music.

O **The Global Reach of Reggaeton:** Reggaeton, a music genre originating in Puerto Rico, blends Latin rhythms with hip-hop and reggae. Its infectious beats and catchy lyrics have made it a worldwide sensation, with artists like Daddy Yankee leading the way.

Unique Traditions and Rituals

O **The Japanese Tea Ceremony:** The Japanese tea ceremony, known as *chanoyu* or *sado*, is a practice that involves the preparation and consumption of matcha (powdered green tea). Every gesture and movement in the ritual comes from tradition.

O **Tibetan Sky Burials:** In Tibet, sky burials are a traditional practice where the deceased's body is left on a mountaintop as it is, reflecting Buddhist beliefs in the cycle of life and its impermanence.

O **The Balinese Nyepi Day:** Nyepi, the Balinese "Day of Silence," marks the Balinese New Year. For 24 hours, the entire island shuts down—no lights, no travel, no noise—to reflect, meditate, and rest.

O **The Maasai Jumping Dance:** The Maasai people of Kenya and Tanzania perform the Adumu, or jumping dance, as a rite of passage for young warriors. The higher the jump, the more attractive they are to females.

O **The Takanakuy Festival:** Takanakuy, a Quechua word roughly translating to "to hit each other," is a unique annual fighting festival held in the Peruvian Andes, primarily in the Chumbivilcas province near Cusco. This centuries-old tradition takes place around Christmastime and serves as a form of conflict resolution and community bonding. Each fight begins and ends with a hug or handshake, symbolizing reconciliation and forgiveness.

O **The Firewalking Ceremony in Fiji:** In Fiji, the indigenous Sawau people of Beqa Island practice firewalking. Men walk barefoot over red-hot stones as a test of faith and strength, a tradition passed down through generations.

O **The Scottish First-Footing:** In Scotland, during Hogmanay (New Year's Eve), the first person to enter a home after midnight is called the "first-foot." This person is believed to bring good luck for the coming year, especially if they bring gifts like coal or whisky.

O **The Thai Loi Krathong Festival:** During Thailand's Loi Krathong festival, people release floating lanterns and small boats, called krathongs, onto rivers. This tradition symbolizes letting go of past grievances and welcoming good fortune.

O **The Sardinian Mamutones:** In Sardinia, Italy, the Mamutones are masked men who perform a traditional dance during the Carnival of Mamoiada. Dressed in black, with heavy bells on their backs, they represent ancient agricultural rituals.

O **The Japanese Omikuji Fortunes:** At Japanese temples and shrines, visitors draw *omikuji*, or fortune slips, to see their luck for the coming year. If the fortune is bad, they tie it to a tree branch, hoping to leave the bad luck behind.

O **The Spanish Calçotada Festival:** In Catalonia, Spain, the Calçotada festival celebrates the harvest of calçots, a type of green onion. People grill the onions over an open fire and eat them with a special sauce, followed by a feast.

O **The Naga Fireballs of Thailand:** Every year along the Mekong River, glowing fireballs rise from the water during the Naga Fireball Festival. Locals believe the phenomenon is caused by the mythical serpent Naga, celebrating the end of Buddhist Lent.

O **The Zulu Reed Dance:** The Zulu Reed Dance, or Umhlanga, is a South African ceremony where young women present reeds to the king as a symbol of unity and respect. The festival promotes cultural pride and community.

O **The Mexican Quinceañera:** A Quinceañera is a traditional Mexican celebration marking a girl's 15th birthday, symbolizing her transition from childhood to womanhood. The event includes a religious ceremony, dancing, and a grand feast.

O **The Indian Raksha Bandhan:** Raksha Bandhan is an Indian festival celebrating the bond between brothers and sisters. Sisters tie a protective thread, or *rakhi*, on their brothers' wrists, while brothers give gifts in return.

And it's a wrap for our vibrant journey through Culture! We've danced through the colorful world of art, explored unique traditions that span the globe, and uncovered the quirks and rituals that make each culture so wonderfully distinct.

Up next, we explore the wonders of Planet Earth. Get ready to traverse breath-taking landscapes, discover the secrets of the oceans, and learn about the forces that shape our world. Let's continue our odyssey and discover the facts, stories, and wonders that make our planet so remarkable.

Our Blue Marble

Dramatic Deserts

O **The Sahara's Size:** The Sahara Desert is the largest hot desert in the world, covering about 3.6 million square miles—almost the size of the United States! Despite its harsh conditions, it's home to many animals.

O **The Gobi's Dinosaur Fossils:** The Gobi Desert in Mongolia is famous for its dinosaur fossils. In the 1920s, paleontologists discovered the first-ever dinosaur eggs here, making it a hotbed for fossil hunters.

O **Antarctica: A Cold Desert:** Antarctica is technically the largest desert in the world due to its extremely low humidity and precipitation. It's the coldest place on Earth, with temperatures as low as -128.6 degrees Fahrenheit!

O **The Namib's Ancient Sands:** The Namib Desert in Africa is considered the world's oldest desert, with sand dunes that are over 55 million years old. Some of its dunes are taller than the Empire State Building!

O **Dasht-e Lut: Iran's Hottest Desert:** The Dasht-e Lut in Iran is one of the hottest places on Earth, with surface temperatures reaching up to 159 degrees Fahrenheit. Its salt flats and sand dunes create an alien-like landscape.

O **The Mojave's Joshua Trees:** The Mojave Desert in the United States is home to the unique Joshua tree, which isn't a tree at all, but a type of yucca plant. They can live for hundreds of years.

O **The Simpson Desert's Red Sands:** Australia's Simpson Desert is famous for its striking red sand dunes, some of which stretch over 200 kilometers (124 miles) long. The vivid color comes from iron oxide in the sand.

O **The Arabian Desert's Oil Wealth:** Beneath the vast sands of the Arabian Desert lies one of the world's largest reserves of oil, making it both a harsh and highly valuable region.

O **The Thar Desert's Camel Festival:** The Thar Desert in India hosts the annual Pushkar Camel Fair, where thousands of camels are paraded, traded, and decorated in colorful attire. It's a vibrant celebration in the desert.

O **The Painted Desert's Vibrant Colors:** The Painted Desert in Arizona, USA, is named for its stunning array of colors—red, orange, pink, and purple—caused by mineral deposits in the rock layers.

O **The Rub' al Khali's Empty Quarter:** The Rub' al Khali, or "Empty Quarter," in the Arabian Peninsula is the world's largest continuous sand desert. Its vast dunes can reach heights of up to 800 feet.

O **The Kalahari's Surprising Life:** The Kalahari Desert in southern Africa is not as barren as it seems. It supports a variety of wildlife, including meerkats, lions, and elephants, thanks to its seasonal rains.

O **The Sonoran Desert's Giant Cacti:** The Sonoran Desert in North America is home to the iconic saguaro cactus, which can grow over 40 feet tall and live for more than 150 years.

O **The Patagonian Desert's Wind:** The Patagonian Desert in Argentina is one of the windiest places on Earth. Strong winds blow constantly across its flat plains, shaping the landscape over time.

O **The Great Victoria Desert's Isolation:** The Great Victoria Desert in Australia is one of the most remote places on the planet. With vast stretches of uninhabited land, it remains largely untouched by humans.

Forests and Jungles

O **The Amazon: The Lungs of the Earth:** The Amazon Rainforest produces about 20% of the world's oxygen and is home to 10% of all known species. It's the largest rainforest on Earth, covering over 2.1 million square miles. Some areas of the Amazon rainforest receive rainfall that originated in the Atlantic Ocean, thousands of miles away. This incredible phenomenon, known as "flying rivers," occurs as massive amounts of water vapor are released by the rainforest's trees through transpiration. These airborne rivers travel vast distances across the continent, carrying moisture that eventually falls as rain in far-off regions, even reaching the Andes Mountains.

O **Disappearing Act:** It is indeed unfortunate that every year, forest regions are being lost to deforestation. And the total area lost is actually close to the size of the country Panama!

O **Amazon Rainforest Canopy:** The Amazon's tree canopy is so dense that only about 1-2% of sunlight reaches the forest floor. Can you imagine how a plant would feel?

O **Borneo's Orangutans:** Borneo's rainforests are home to the endangered orangutan, whose name means "person of the forest" in Malay.

O **The Daintree Rainforest's Age:** Australia's Daintree Rainforest is one of the oldest rainforests in the world, dating back 180 million years. It's home to unique species found nowhere else on Earth.

O **The Amazon's Pink Dolphins:** The Amazon River Dolphin, also known as the pink river dolphin, swims in the Amazon Basin's freshwater rivers. These playful creatures are known for their distinctive pink color.

O **Rainforests Create Their Own Rain:** Tropical rainforests help create their own rain through a process called transpiration, where plants release water vapor into the air.

O **Trees Communicate Underground:** Trees in forests communicate with each other through underground fungal networks, sharing nutrients and information about their environment.

O **Jaguars of the Amazon:** Jaguars are top predators in the Amazon rainforest, known for their ability to swim and hunt prey in both water and on land.

- **Baobab Trees Store Water:** The iconic baobab trees of Africa's savannas can store thousands of gallons of water in their trunks to survive droughts.

- **The Amazon's Kapok Trees:** Kapok trees in the Amazon Rainforest can reach heights of over 200 feet. These towering giants are considered sacred by many indigenous peoples and provide habitat for countless species.

- **The Cloud Forests of Costa Rica:** Costa Rica's cloud forests, like the one in Monteverde, are shrouded in mist and home to incredible biodiversity, including the rare resplendent quetzal bird and colorful orchids.

- **The Great Bear Rainforest:** Located in British Columbia, Canada, the Great Bear Rainforest is one of the world's largest temperate rainforests. It's home to the rare Kermode bear, also known as the "spirit bear."

- **The Amazon's "Walking Trees":** Some trees in the Amazon are known as "walking trees" because their roots move slowly over time, allowing the tree to "walk" a few feet each year to find sunlight.

- **The Tapanuli Orangutan Discovery:** In 2017, scientists identified a new species of orangutan in the Batang Toru Forest of Sumatra, Indonesia. The Tapanuli orangutan is now one of the world's most endangered great apes. You might want to call them endangered "people of the forest." Putting what you just learnt from an earlier fact to immediate use!

Mystical Mountains

- **Machu Picchu's Mountain Setting:** The ancient Incan city of Machu Picchu was built on a mountain ridge at 7,970 feet, making it one of the world's most mystical archaeological sites.

- **K2: The Savage Mountain:** K2, the second-highest mountain in the world, is known as the "Savage Mountain" due to its extreme difficulty. With a peak of 28,251 feet, it has one of the highest fatality rates for climbers.

- **Mount Etna's Frequent Eruptions:** Mount Etna in Sicily is one of the most active volcanoes in the world, frequently erupting and reshaping its landscape.

- **Mount Elbrus: Europe's Highest Peak:** Mount Elbrus, located in Russia's Caucasus Mountains, is the highest peak in Europe at 18,510 feet.

- **The Carpathians' Mysterious Forests:** The Carpathian Mountains in Eastern Europe are home to dense forests, ancient legends, and the largest population of brown bears in Europe.

- **Mount Vinson: Antarctica's Highest Peak:** Mount Vinson, at 16,050 feet, is the tallest mountain in Antarctica and remains one of the most remote and challenging to climb.

O **The Himalayas' Spiritual Significance:** The Himalayas are not only home to the world's tallest peaks but are also a spiritual sanctuary. Many Himalayan mountains, like Mount Kailash, are sacred to multiple religions, including Hinduism, Buddhism, and Jainism.

O **The Sacred Mount Shasta:** Mount Shasta is a potentially active stratovolcano, rising to an elevation of 14,179 feet, making it the fifth-highest peak in California and the second-highest in the Cascade Range. It is considered a sacred site by Native American tribes

O **Table Mountain's Unique Flat Top:** Table Mountain in South Africa is famous for its flat summit, which is often covered in a "tablecloth" of clouds. The mountain offers panoramic views of Cape Town and the surrounding oceans.

O **Mount Denali: The Tallest in North America:** Mount Denali, also known as Mount McKinley, is the tallest peak in North America, standing at 20,310 feet. Located in Alaska, it's known for its extreme weather and challenging climbs.

O **Mount Ararat's Biblical Legend:** Mount Ararat in Turkey is traditionally considered the resting place of Noah's Ark, making it religiously significant to Christians, Jews, and Muslims.

O **Mount Olympus: Home of the Gods:** Mount Olympus in Greece was believed by ancient Greeks to be the home of the gods, led by Zeus. The mountain stands at 9,573 feet and is a UNESCO Biosphere Reserve.

O **The Peaks of the Tien Shan:** The Tien Shan, meaning "Heavenly Mountains," stretches across Central Asia and is known for its dramatic, snow-capped peaks.

O **The Atlas Mountains' Berber Roots:** The Atlas Mountains in Morocco are home to Berber communities who have lived in these rugged landscapes for thousands of years.

O **Aoraki/Mount Cook: New Zealand's Tallest Peak:** Aoraki/Mount Cook is New Zealand's highest mountain, standing at 12,218 feet. It's revered in Māori mythology as the ancestor of the Ngāi Tahu people and is a popular destination for mountaineers.

Oceans and Oddities

O **The Pacific Ocean's Size:** The Pacific Ocean covers more than 63 million square miles, making it larger than all of Earth's landmasses combined.

O **Underwater Volcanoes:** Around 80% of the world's volcanic activity occurs underwater, with some forming entire islands after eruptions.

O **The Indian Ocean's Monsoon Effect:** The Indian Ocean is the only ocean where monsoons regularly occur, creating powerful seasonal winds that affect global weather.

O **The Atlantic's Mid-Ocean Ridge:** The Mid-Atlantic Ridge, the longest mountain range on Earth, runs along the Atlantic Ocean's floor, stretching over 10,000 miles.

- **The Sargasso Sea's Floating Forest:** The Sargasso Sea in the Atlantic Ocean is unique because it has no land boundaries. It's known for its floating mats of sargassum seaweed, which provide a habitat for marine life.

- **Sperm Whales' Deep Dives:** Sperm whales are known to dive to depths of over 7,380 feet, in order to hunt for giant squid in the dark ocean abyss.

- **The Giant Kelp Forests:** Giant kelp forests, found off the coasts of California and South America, are underwater jungles that can grow up to 2 feet per day. They provide shelter for a diverse range of marine species.

- **The Great Pacific Garbage Patch:** The Great Pacific Garbage Patch is a massive collection of plastic debris floating in the Pacific Ocean. It's twice the size of Texas and highlights the growing issue of ocean pollution.

- **The Red Sea's Coral Reefs:** The Red Sea is home to some of the most resilient coral reefs in the world. Despite rising temperatures, these reefs have managed to thrive, offering a glimmer of hope for coral survival.

- **The Baltic Sea's Shipwrecks:** The cold, low-oxygen waters of the Baltic Sea have preserved thousands of shipwrecks, some dating back to the Middle Ages. These shipwrecks provide valuable insights into maritime history.

- **The Gulf Stream's Oceanic Conveyor Belt:** The Gulf Stream, a powerful ocean current, carries warm water from the Gulf of Mexico up the eastern coast of the United States and across the Atlantic. It plays a crucial role in regulating the climate.

- **The Ocean's Midnight Zone:** The "Midnight Zone" begins at about 3,300 feet underwater, where no sunlight penetrates, and bizarre creatures like anglerfish thrive.

- **The Ross Sea: Last Ocean Frontier:** The Ross Sea in Antarctica is often called the "Last Ocean" because it's one of the most pristine marine ecosystems left on Earth, largely untouched by human activity.

- **The Bay of Fundy's Extreme Tides:** The Bay of Fundy, located between New Brunswick and Nova Scotia, Canada, experiences the highest tides in the world, with a difference of up to 53 feet between high and low tide.

- **The Mariana Snailfish's Record Depth:** The Mariana Snailfish holds the record for the deepest living fish, found at depths of 26,000 feet in the Mariana Trench. It survives under crushing pressure where no sunlight reaches.

Raging Rivers and Majestic Lakes

O **The Amazon River's Endless Flow:** The Amazon River in South America is the world's largest river by volume, discharging about 7.7 million cubic feet of water per second into the Atlantic Ocean.

O **Lake Baikal: The World's Deepest Lake:** Lake Baikal in Siberia, Russia, is the world's deepest and oldest freshwater lake, plunging to a depth of over 5,300 feet. It holds 20% of the world's unfrozen freshwater.

O **The Nile: The Lifeblood of Egypt:** The Nile River, stretching over 4,100 miles, is the longest river in the world. It has been a vital source of water, food, and transportation for Egyptian civilization for thousands of years.

O **Lake Titicaca: Sacred Waters:** Lake Titicaca, located on the border of Peru and Bolivia, is the highest navigable lake in the world, sitting at 12,507 feet above sea level. It's also considered sacred by the Inca civilization.

O **The Mississippi River's Mighty Flow:** The Mississippi River is the second-longest river in North America, flowing over 2,300 miles from Minnesota to the Gulf of Mexico. It's a vital waterway for transportation and agriculture in the United States.

O **Crater Lake's Clear Waters:** Oregon's Crater Lake is the clearest lake in the world, formed in a volcanic crater and with visibility down to 100 feet below the surface.

O **The Yangtze River: China's Lifeline:** The Yangtze River is the longest river in Asia, stretching 3,915 miles. It's crucial for China's economy, providing water for agriculture, industry, and transportation.

O **Lake Superior's Vastness:** Lake Superior, the largest of North America's Great Lakes, holds enough water to cover the entire landmass of North and South America in one foot of water. It's also the coldest and deepest of the Great Lakes.

O **The Congo River's Untamed Rapids:** The Congo River in Africa is the world's deepest river, with depths reaching over 720 feet. It's also home to Inga Falls, one of the most powerful waterfalls by flow rate.

O **Lake Victoria's Vital Role:** Lake Victoria, located in East Africa, is the world's largest tropical lake. It's a vital resource for millions of people, providing fish, water, and transportation. However, it's also facing environmental challenges.

O **The Colorado River's Grand Carving:** The Colorado River is responsible for carving out the Grand Canyon, one of the most iconic natural wonders of the world. It stretches 1,450 miles from the Rocky Mountains to the Gulf of California.

O **The Mekong River's Biodiversity:** The Mekong River flows through six countries in Southeast Asia and is one of the most biodiverse rivers in the world, home to rare species like the giant catfish and Irrawaddy dolphin.

- **The Caspian Sea: World's Largest Lake:** The Caspian Sea is the world's largest enclosed inland body of water, and technically should be called a lake. It's bordered by five countries and is rich in oil and natural gas resources.

- **Lake Malawi's Cichlids:** Lake Malawi in East Africa is home to more species of fish than any other lake in the world, particularly cichlids, which are famous for their bright colors and unique behaviors.

- **The Volga River's Cultural Significance:** The Volga River is the longest river in Europe, flowing through central Russia. It's often called "Mother Volga" and has been a vital cultural and economic lifeline for centuries.

Weather Wonders

- **Tropical Cyclone Intensity:** Typhoon Tip, which formed in 1979, is the most intense tropical cyclone ever recorded, with a central pressure of 870 mb and a diameter of 1,380 miles. It circulated the Western Pacific for 20 days.

- **The Eye of a Hurricane:** The eye of a hurricane is surprisingly calm compared to the surrounding storm. While the outer edges have powerful winds and rain, the center can be eerily peaceful with clear skies.

- **The Sahara's Dust Travels:** Every year, over 180 million tons of dust from the Sahara Desert blow across the Atlantic Ocean to the Amazon Rainforest, helping to fertilize its rich ecosystem.

- **Lightning Strikes the Same Place:** Despite the saying lightning never strikes the same place twice, lightning can and does strike the same spot more than once. The Empire State Building in New York City is struck by lightning about 25 times per year.

- **The Hottest Temperature on Earth:** The hottest temperature ever recorded on Earth was 134 degrees Fahrenheit (56.7 degrees Celsius) in Furnace Creek, Death Valley, California, on July 10, 1913. It's one of the driest places on the planet.

- **The Coldest Temperature on Earth:** The coldest temperature ever recorded on Earth was -128.6 degrees Fahrenheit (-89.2 degrees Celsius) at the Soviet Union's Vostok Station in Antarctica on July 21, 1983.

- **The Longest Drought in History:** The Atacama Desert in Chile holds the record for the longest drought in history. Some parts of the desert haven't seen rainfall for over 500 years!

- **Rain in the World's Wettest Place:** Mawsynram in India holds the title for the world's wettest place, receiving an average of 467 inches of rain per year, enough to fill a 39-story building!

O **The Snowiest Place on Earth:** Aomori City in Japan is the snowiest place on Earth, receiving an average of 312 inches of snow each year. The city is famous for its snow-covered landscapes and winter festivals.

O **Hailstones the Size of Softballs:** In 2010, Vivian, South Dakota, experienced the largest hailstone ever recorded, measuring 8 inches in diameter—about the size of a volleyball—and weighing nearly 2 pounds!

O **The Everlasting Lightning Storm:** In the Democratic Republic of Congo, the town of Kifuka sees the second highest frequency of lightning strikes, with an average of 158 flashes per square kilometer each year.

O **The Foggy City:** San Francisco, California, is famous for its thick fog, nicknamed "Karl." This weather phenomenon occurs regularly, rolling in from the Pacific Ocean and blanketing the city.

O **Tornado Alley:** Tornado Alley in the central United States is prone to tornadoes, with over 1,000 twisters touching down each year. The area's flat terrain and warm, moist air create ideal tornado conditions.

O **The World's Most Active Volcano:** Mount Kilauea in Hawaii is one of the most active volcanoes on Earth, continuously erupting since 1983. Its lava flows have created new land, adding over 500 acres to the island.

O **The Sirocco Wind's Sahara Journey:** The Sirocco is a hot, dry wind that blows from the Sahara Desert across the Mediterranean, often bringing dust storms to Southern Europe.

And so, our exhilarating expedition across Planet Earth draws to a close! From the calm eye of a hurricane to the magical glow of bioluminescent bays, Earth's wonders have shown us just how extraordinary our planet truly is.

Now, let's turn our attention to a different kind of feast – one for the senses!. Get ready to discover mouth-watering delicacies, bizarre foods, and the fascinating history behind your favorite snacks. Let's dig in!

Sip, Slurp, & Savor

Bizarre Bites

O **Casu Marzu: Maggot Cheese:** Casu Marzu, a Sardinian delicacy, is a cheese infested with live maggots. The larvae help ferment the cheese, which is considered a delicacy but banned in many places due to health concerns.

O **Balut: Fertilized Duck Egg:** In the Philippines, Balut is a popular street food made from fertilized duck eggs, where the embryo is partially developed. It's enjoyed boiled, often with a pinch of salt.

O **Hákarl: Iceland's Fermented Shark:** Hákarl is an Icelandic dish made from Greenland shark, which is buried and fermented for months before being eaten. It's known for its strong ammonia smell and is often an acquired taste.

O **Stink Bugs as Snacks:** In parts of Africa, stink bugs are roasted or boiled and eaten as a crunchy snack. They're packed with protein, despite their strong odor, which surprisingly disappears when cooked.

O **Escamoles: Ant Larvae:** In Mexico, escamoles, also known as "insect caviar," are ant larvae harvested from agave plants. These buttery, nutty-tasting larvae are often served with tortillas or eggs.

O **Century Eggs: Preserved Delicacies:** Century eggs, a Chinese delicacy, are preserved in clay, ash, and salt for several weeks to months. Despite their appearance, with a dark green yolk, they have a rich, creamy flavor.

O **Fugu: Poisonous Pufferfish:** In Japan, fugu, or pufferfish, is a risky delicacy because its liver contains deadly toxins. Only licensed chefs are allowed to prepare it, and it's considered a culinary adventure.

O **Sannakji: Live Octopus:** Sannakji is a Korean dish made from live octopus, served while it's still wriggling. Diners must chew it carefully to avoid the suction cups sticking to the throat.

O **Jellied Moose Nose:** A delicacy in parts of Canada, jellied moose nose is exactly what it sounds like—boiled and then cooled to create a jelly-like texture. It's a traditional dish in some indigenous communities.

O **Tarantula Snacks:** Fried tarantulas are a popular street food in Cambodia, served crispy with a hint of salt and garlic. They've been eaten since times of food scarcity.

O **Tuna Eyeballs:** In Japan, tuna eyeballs are considered a delicacy. They're typically boiled or steamed and taste similar to squid. The dish is said to be rich in nutrients like omega-3 fatty acids.

O **Cuy: Roasted Guinea Pig:** In Peru, cuy (roasted guinea pig) is a traditional dish that dates back to the Inca Empire. It's usually served whole, often with potatoes and corn.

- **Huitlacoche: Corn Fungus:** Huitlacoche, known as "Mexican truffle," is a fungus that grows on corn. It's considered a delicacy in Mexico, often used in tacos, quesadillas, and soups.

- **Witchetty Grub's Protein Punch:** The witchetty grub is a traditional Aboriginal food in Australia, eaten raw or cooked. It's rich in protein and has a nutty taste when roasted.

- **Blood Pudding:** Popular in the UK and Ireland, blood pudding is made from pork blood, fat, and oatmeal, formed into sausages. Despite its unusual ingredients, it's a breakfast staple.

Exotic Eats

- **Durian: The King of Fruits:** Durian is a tropical fruit known for its strong, pungent odor. While some find the smell unbearable, others love its creamy, custard-like texture and sweet, savory taste. It can be an acquired taste. We are speaking from personal experience!

- **Kangaroo Meat in Australia:** In Australia, kangaroo meat is a popular and sustainable choice. It's lean, high in protein, and often served as steaks, sausages, or even burgers.

- **Ackee and Saltfish: Jamaica's National Dish:** Ackee, a fruit native to West Africa, is cooked with saltfish (salted cod) to create Jamaica's national dish. Despite its fruit origins, ackee has a savory, scrambled egg-like texture.

- **Tagine: Morocco's Flavorful Stew:** Tagine is a North African dish slow-cooked in a clay pot of the same name. It's typically made with meat, vegetables, and a blend of spices like cumin, cinnamon, and saffron.

- **Escargot: French Snails:** Escargot, a delicacy in France, consists of snails cooked in garlic butter, parsley, and wine. Despite their unusual origin, they are prized for their rich, buttery flavor.

- **Balinese Babi Guling:** Babi Guling is a traditional Balinese dish of roasted suckling pig, seasoned with turmeric, lemongrass, and chilies. It's a centerpiece at many ceremonies and feasts.

- **Chakalaka: A South African Staple:** Chakalaka is a spicy South African vegetable relish made from tomatoes, onions, and beans. It's often served with bread or pap, a type of porridge, and pairs well with grilled meats.

- **Pho: Vietnam's Famous Noodle Soup:** Pho is a Vietnamese soup consisting of broth, rice noodles, herbs, and meat, usually beef or chicken. It's a beloved street food, known for its aromatic flavors and comforting warmth.

- **Ceviche: A Peruvian Delight:** Ceviche is a popular dish in Peru made from fresh raw fish cured in citrus juices, often accompanied by onions, cilantro, and chili peppers. It's a refreshing and tangy delicacy.

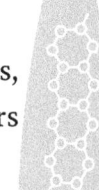

O **Peking Duck: A Chinese Classic:** Peking Duck is a famous dish from Beijing, China, known for its crispy skin and tender meat. The duck is typically served with pancakes, hoisin sauce, and scallions.

O **Feijoada: Brazil's Hearty Stew:** Feijoada is a traditional Brazilian stew made with black beans and various cuts of pork. It's slow-cooked and served with rice, collard greens, and orange slices for a perfect balance of flavors.

O **Haggis: Scotland's Savory Pudding:** Haggis is Scotland's national dish, made from sheep's heart, liver, and lungs, mixed with oatmeal and spices, and traditionally encased in the animal's stomach.

O **Jollof Rice: West Africa's Favorite:** Jollof rice is a beloved dish across West Africa, especially in Nigeria and Ghana. It's a one-pot meal made with tomatoes, onions, and spices, often served with chicken or fish.

O **Bibimbap: Korea's Mixed Rice:** Bibimbap is a Korean dish that means "mixed rice." It's typically served as a bowl of white rice topped with sautéed vegetables, kimchi, gochujang (chili paste), and a fried egg.

O **Sushi: Japan's Iconic Cuisine:** Sushi, a Japanese dish, combines vinegared rice with seafood, vegetables, and sometimes tropical fruits. The variety of ingredients and flavors makes sushi a global favorite.

Famous Feasts

O **Feast of San Gennaro:** The Feast of San Gennaro is an annual 11-day event in Little Italy, New York City, celebrating Italian-American culture with food, music, and parades.

O **Diwali's Sweet Delights:** During Diwali, the Hindu Festival of Lights, families exchange sweets and snacks like ladoos, jalebi, and barfi. The feast symbolizes the victory of light over darkness and good over evil.

O **Chinese New Year Reunion Dinner:** The Chinese New Year Reunion Dinner is the most important meal of the year for many Chinese families. Dishes like dumplings, fish, and noodles symbolize prosperity, longevity, and happiness.

O **The Indian Thali:** A thali is a traditional Indian feast served on a large platter, featuring a variety of dishes like curries, rice, bread, and chutneys to represent balance and abundance.

O **Le Grand Aioli in Provence:** Le Grand Aioli is a famous Provencal feast featuring boiled vegetables, seafood, and garlic aioli, traditionally enjoyed outdoors during summer gatherings in France.

O **Christmas Dinner in the UK:** In the UK, Christmas dinner often includes roast turkey, stuffing, roast potatoes, Brussels sprouts, and gravy, followed by Christmas pudding and mince pies. Crackers with silly hats and jokes are a must!

O **Matariki Harvest Feasts in New Zealand:** Matariki is the Māori New Year, celebrated with feasts featuring traditional foods like kumara (sweet potato), seafood, and hangi-cooked meats. It's a time to honor ancestors and welcome new beginnings.

O **Las Fallas in Spain:** Las Fallas in Valencia, Spain, is a festival of fire, but it also features massive feasts. Paella, the city's signature dish, takes center stage, along with other regional specialties.

O **Lunar New Year's Feasts in Vietnam:** In Vietnam, the Lunar New Year, or Tết, is celebrated with special foods like bánh chng (square sticky rice cakes) and thịt kho (caramelized pork), symbolizing prosperity and family unity.

O **Passover Seder:** The Passover Seder is a Jewish ritual feast marking the beginning of Passover. The meal includes symbolic foods like matzo, bitter herbs, and charoset, each representing parts of the Exodus story.

O **Greek Easter Feasts:** Greek Easter is celebrated with a grand feast, including spit-roasted lamb, red-dyed eggs, and tsoureki (a sweet bread). The meal follows a midnight service and the greeting "Christos Anesti!" (Christ is risen!).

O **Dia de los Muertos Offerings:** During Mexico's Da de los Muertos (Day of the Dead), families prepare feasts with their ancestors' favorite foods, including tamales, pan de muerto (bread of the dead), and sugar skulls, to honor their spirits.

O **The Iftar Meal During Ramadan:** Iftar is the meal Muslims eat to break their fast during Ramadan, often starting with dates and water, followed by a variety of savory dishes, soups, and sweets to replenish energy.

O **Chuseok: Korean Harvest Festival:** Chuseok, Korea's autumn harvest festival, includes a feast of traditional foods like songpyeon (rice cakes), japchae (stir-fried noodles), and galbi (marinated short ribs). It's a time for honoring ancestors.

O **Italian Christmas Eve Feast:** The Feast of the Seven Fishes is an Italian-American Christmas Eve tradition, where seven different types of seafood are served in honor of the holiday.

Global Gastronomy

O **French Cuisine: The Art of Cooking:** French cuisine is renowned for its refinement and technique, from buttery croissants to rich coq au vin. It's so influential that UNESCO recognized it as an intangible cultural heritage.

O **Italian Pasta Perfection:** Italy is famous for its pasta, with over 350 different shapes! Each region has its specialty, like spaghetti from Naples, tagliatelle from Bologna, and orecchiette from Puglia.

O **Japanese Kaiseki: A Culinary Art Form:** Kaiseki is a traditional multi-course Japanese meal that emphasizes seasonality, presentation, and balance. Each dish is a work of art, highlighting the chef's skill and the natural flavors of the ingredients.

O **Indian Spices: The Heart of Flavor:** India is the world's largest producer of spices, including turmeric, cumin, and cardamom. These spices are the foundation of Indian cuisine, creating the complex flavors in dishes like curry and biryani.

O **Mexican Street Food: A Taste Explosion:** Mexican street food is vibrant and varied, with popular dishes like tacos, tamales, and elote (grilled corn). Each bite offers a burst of flavor, from tangy lime to spicy chili.

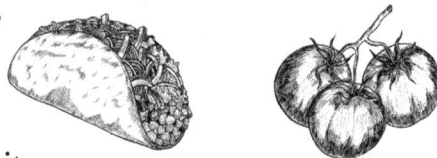

O **Thai Cuisine: A Balance of Flavors:** Thai food is known for its balance of sweet, sour, salty, and spicy flavors. Signature dishes like pad thai, green curry, and tom yum soup showcase this harmonious blend.

O **Ethiopian Injera: A Unique Dining Experience:** Injera is a spongy, sourdough flatbread that's a staple of Ethiopian cuisine. It's used as both a plate and utensil, with diners scooping up stews and vegetables with pieces of the bread.

O **Spanish Tapas: Small Plates, Big Flavors:** Tapas are small plates of food served in Spain, perfect for sharing. From patatas bravas to jamón ibérico, tapas offer a wide variety of flavors in one meal, encouraging social dining.

O **Switzerland's Fondue Tradition:** Swiss fondue, a dish of melted cheese served with bread, became a national dish in the 1930s. It was originally a way to use up stale bread and old cheese.

O **Lebanese Mezze: A Feast of Flavors:** Mezze is a collection of small dishes served in Lebanon and the Middle East, often including hummus, baba ghanoush, tabbouleh, and falafel. It's a social meal, enjoyed with family and friends.

O **Argentinian Asado: A Grilling Tradition:** Asado is Argentina's traditional barbecue, where large cuts of beef, sausages, and other meats are grilled slowly over an open flame. It's a cultural celebration as much as it is a meal.

O **Korean Kimchi: A Fermented Favorite:** Kimchi is a staple in Korean cuisine, made from fermented vegetables, typically napa cabbage and radishes, seasoned with chili pepper, garlic, and ginger. It's enjoyed as a side dish with nearly every meal.

O **Turkish Delight: A Sweet Tradition:** Turkish Delight, or lokum, is a chewy candy flavored with rosewater, lemon, or pistachios. This centuries-old treat is often dusted with powdered sugar and is a beloved part of Turkish culture.

O **Italy's Truffle Delicacy:** Italy is known for its rare and highly-prized truffles, especially white truffles from the Piedmont region, which can fetch thousands of dollars per kilogram.

O **Greek Moussaka: A Comfort Food Classic:** Moussaka is a layered casserole dish from Greece, typically made with eggplant, ground meat, and béchamel sauce. It's a hearty meal that's perfect for family gatherings and special occasions.

Sweet & Salty Treats

O **French Macarons: Colorful Confections:** Macarons are delicate French cookies made from almond flour, sugar, and egg whites, filled with ganache, buttercream, or jam. These colorful treats are a favorite in Parisian patisseries.

O **Italian Gelato: A Creamy Delight:** Gelato, Italy's answer to ice cream, is denser and more flavorful due to its lower fat content and slower churning process. It's a must-try treat when strolling through Italy's streets.

O **Belgian Waffles: A Breakfast Classic:** Belgian waffles are known for their deep pockets and crispy exterior. They're often served with powdered sugar, whipped cream, and fresh fruit, making them a popular breakfast or dessert.

O **Japanese Mochi: Chewy and Sweet:** Mochi is a Japanese rice cake made from glutinous rice, pounded into a sticky dough. It's often filled with sweet red bean paste or ice cream, offering a unique texture and taste.

O **Greek Baklava: A Honeyed Treat:** Baklava is a sweet pastry made of layers of filo dough, filled with chopped nuts, and sweetened with honey or syrup. This treat is a staple in Greek and Middle Eastern cuisine.

O **American Apple Pie: A National Icon:** Apple pie, often served with a scoop of vanilla ice cream, is an iconic American dessert. The combination of buttery crust, sweet-tart apples, and cinnamon makes it a comforting classic.

O **Dulce de Leche's Caramel Charm:** Dulce de leche, a sweet caramel-like spread made from slowly heating sweetened milk, is a beloved dessert in Argentina and other Latin American countries.

O **Indian Samosas: Spiced and Savory:** Samosas are popular Indian snacks made from a thin pastry filled with spiced potatoes, peas, and sometimes meat. They're deep-fried to a golden crisp and enjoyed with chutney.

O **British Scones: Afternoon Tea Essential:** Scones are a quintessential part of British afternoon tea. These lightly sweetened baked goods are often served with clotted cream and jam, creating a perfect balance of flavors.

O **German Pretzels: Soft and Salty:** German pretzels, or "brezels," are soft, chewy, and have a distinctive knotted shape. Traditionally topped with coarse salt, they're enjoyed with mustard, cheese, or on their own.

O **Brazilian Brigadeiros: Chocolate Bliss:** Brigadeiros are a popular Brazilian sweet made from condensed milk, cocoa powder, butter, and chocolate sprinkles. These bite-sized treats are often served at birthday parties and celebrations.

- **Mexican Churros: Cinnamon Perfection:** Churros are a beloved Mexican street food, made from fried dough coated in cinnamon sugar. They're often served with a thick chocolate sauce for dipping, creating a perfect sweet treat.

- **Austrian Sachertorte: Chocolate Elegance:** Sachertorte is a famous Viennese chocolate cake, known for its dense texture and rich flavor. It's layered with apricot jam and covered in dark chocolate glaze, often enjoyed with whipped cream.

- **Italian Cannoli: Cream-Filled Delights:** Cannoli are Italian pastries from Sicily, consisting of crispy, tube-shaped shells filled with a sweet, creamy ricotta filling. They're often topped with chocolate chips or candied fruit.

- **Gulab Jamun's Sweet Syrup:** Gulab jamun, an Indian dessert, consists of fried dough balls soaked in a sweet syrup flavored with cardamom and rosewater, served during festivals and celebrations.

Tasty Traditions

- **Ethiopian Coffee Ceremony:** In Ethiopia, the coffee ceremony is a revered tradition where beans are roasted, ground, and brewed by hand, and it's a symbol of friendship and hospitality.

- **Russian Blini for Maslenitsa:** Blini, thin Russian pancakes, are traditionally served with sour cream, caviar, or jam during Maslenitsa, the week-long celebration before Lent.

- **Haggis on Burns Night in Scotland:** On Burns Night, Scots celebrate the poet Robert Burns with a traditional meal of haggis, neeps (turnips), and tatties (potatoes). The haggis is often paraded in with bagpipes and served with a dram of whisky.

- **Tamales for Christmas in Mexico:** In Mexico, tamales are a Christmas tradition. These steamed corn dough pockets are filled with meats, cheeses, or chilies, wrapped in corn husks, and served as part of the holiday feast.

- **Hot Cross Buns for Easter in the UK:** Hot cross buns are a staple in the UK during Easter. These spiced, sweet buns are marked with a cross on top and traditionally eaten on Good Friday to commemorate the crucifixion of Jesus.

- **Sushi for New Year's in Japan:** On New Year's Day in Japan, many families enjoy a traditional meal called osechi-ryori, which often includes sushi. Each dish has symbolic meanings, such as health, happiness, and long life.

- **Pierogi for Wigilia in Poland:** In Poland, Christmas Eve dinner, known as Wigilia, features a meal of 12 dishes, including pierogi. These dumplings are filled with potatoes, cheese, or mushrooms and are a beloved holiday tradition.

- **King Cake for Mardi Gras in New Orleans:** During Mardi Gras in New Orleans, it's tradition to enjoy a King Cake, a colorful, ring-shaped cake often decorated in purple, green, and gold. A small figurine is hidden inside, and whoever finds it hosts the next party.

O **American Barbecue for Independence Day:** Barbecues are a staple of American Fourth of July celebrations, with families grilling burgers, hot dogs, and ribs while watching fireworks.

O **Stollen for Christmas in Germany:** Stollen is a traditional German Christmas bread filled with dried fruits, nuts, and marzipan, dusted with powdered sugar. It's enjoyed during Advent and symbolizes the baby Jesus wrapped in a blanket.

O **Borscht for Christmas in Ukraine:** In Ukraine, Christmas Eve dinner includes borscht, a beet soup served with garlic, mushrooms, and sour cream. This dish is part of a 12-course meal, each representing an apostle of Jesus.

O **Korean Kimjang Tradition:** Kimjang is the traditional Korean practice of making large quantities of kimchi in late autumn, a community activity that prepares families for the winter months.

O **Matzo for Passover in Jewish Culture:** During Passover, Jews eat matzo, an unleavened bread that symbolizes the haste with which the Israelites left Egypt, without time for their bread to rise. The tradition honors freedom and deliverance.

O **Italian Sunday Lunch:** In Italy, Sunday lunch is a cherished tradition where families gather to enjoy multi-course meals, often featuring pasta, meats, and dessert, like tiramisu.

O **Jewish Shabbat Dinner:** Shabbat dinner is a weekly tradition in Jewish households, where challah bread, wine, and a special meal are enjoyed with family to mark the beginning of the Sabbath.

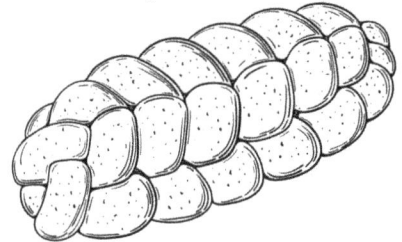

From bizarre bites to sweet treats, we've explored the incredible diversity of global cuisine and the cultural traditions that make each dish special. Whether it's a festive feast or a quick snack, food connects us all in ways that go far beyond taste.

Next up - languages! From ancient scripts to modern slang, you'll learn how language shapes our identities. So, put on your curious cap, and let's dive in!

Literal Lexicon Lingua

Amazing Accents

O **The Beatles' Scouse Accent:** The Liverpool (or Scouse) accent became world-famous thanks to The Beatles. Characterized by its unique rhythm and slang, it's one of the most easily recognized accents in the UK.

O **Australian Accent Evolution:** The unique Australian twang has barely changed since the country was colonized in the late 18th century. It's thought to have developed as a blend of various British and Irish accents.

O **Newfoundland English:** In Canada, the Newfoundland accent is a mix of Irish, English, and Scottish influences. It's so distinctive that some words and phrases are unique to the island, like "scoff" for a meal.

O **The Texan Drawl:** The Texan accent is famous for its slow drawl and elongated vowels. It's part of the Southern American English dialect family and reflects Texas' diverse history and cultural influences.

O **The French R Sound:** The French accent is known for its guttural "R" sound, produced in the back of the throat. This feature gives the French language its distinctive and elegant sound.

O **The Unique Boston Accent:** The Boston accent is famous for dropping the "r" sound, making words like "car" sound like "cah." It's a remnant of early English settlers' speech patterns.

O **South African English:** South African English has a unique blend of influences from Dutch, Afrikaans, and local African languages. This mix gives it distinctive sounds, such as the rolled "r" and clipped vowels.

O **Cockney Rhyming Slang:** The Cockney accent from East London is famous for its rhyming slang, where phrases like "apples and pears" mean "stairs." This playful language is still in use today.

O **The Scottish "Glaswegian" Accent:** Glaswegian, the accent of Glasgow, Scotland, is known for its fast pace and strong consonants. It's often considered one of the hardest accents for outsiders to understand.

O **The New York Accent:** The New York accent is famous for its dropped "r" sounds and the pronunciation of "aw" sounds, like in "coffee" and "talk." It's influenced by waves of immigrants from Italy, Ireland, and Eastern Europe.

O **Geordie: The Newcastle Accent:** The Geordie accent, from Newcastle in the UK, is one of the oldest in England, with roots in Old English. It's known for its sing-song intonation and unique vocabulary.

O **The Irish Brogue:** The Irish accent, or brogue, varies widely across the island but is characterized by a lyrical, musical quality. Irish English also retains many features of Gaelic pronunciation.

O **The Kiwi Accent:** New Zealanders, or Kiwis, have an accent that blends British and Australian influences but is distinctive for its vowel sounds, where "fish and chips" can sound like "fush and chups."

O **The Jamaican Patois:** Jamaican Patois, often heard in reggae music, is an English-based creole language with West African influences. Its accent is rhythmic, with a unique cadence that sets it apart.

O **The Welsh Lilt:** The Welsh accent is known for its musicality, influenced by the Welsh language's emphasis on intonation and vowel sounds. It's often described as lyrical and melodic.

Dialects and Dialogues

O **Mandarin Chinese: The World's Most Spoken Dialect:** Mandarin is the most spoken dialect in the world, with over 900 million native speakers. Despite being a dialect of Chinese, its influence spans across many regions. More importantly, it also formed much of the basis for Standard Chinese, the official language of China.

O **Sicilian: More Than Just Italian:** Sicilian is a distinct Romance language spoken in Sicily, Italy. Although it shares some similarities with standard Italian, it has its own vocabulary, grammar, and rich history influenced by Greek, Arabic, and Norman cultures.

O **The Longest Word in The World:** The longest word in the world is the chemical name for Titin, a protein. The word is also in English by the way. It's 189,819 letters long and would take over three hours to pronounce!

O **Quechua: The Language of the Incas:** Quechua, once the language of the Inca Empire, is still spoken by around 8 million people across the Andes. It has many regional variations and remains a vital part of South American culture.

O **Mandarin's Tones (Standard Chinese):** Mandarin Chinese (Standard Chinese) uses four different tones to distinguish meaning in words, where the same syllable can have entirely different meanings depending on the tone used.

O **Yiddish: A Fusion Language:** Yiddish, spoken by Jewish communities around the world, is a blend of German, Hebrew, and Slavic languages. It's famous for its rich expressions and has influenced English words like "schlep" and "kvetch."

O **Basque: A Language Isolate:** Basque, spoken in the Basque Country between Spain and France, is one of the few language isolates in the world, meaning it has no known relatives. Its origins remain a mystery.

O **Appalachian English: A Regional Dialect:** Appalachian English, spoken in the Appalachian region of the United States, is known for its unique grammar and vocabulary, like using "y'all" for "you all" and "ain't" as a contraction for "am not."

o **Singlish: Singapore's Unique Blend:** Singlish is a creole language spoken in Singapore that combines English with Malay, Chinese, and Tamil influences. It also has smatterings of Chinese dialects mixed in. It's known for its informal tone and phrases like "lah" to emphasize a point.

o **Hokkien: A Southern Chinese Dialect:** Hokkien, spoken in southern China, Taiwan, and Southeast Asia, is one of the oldest Chinese dialects. It has a rich history and has heavily influenced the languages of the Chinese migration.

o **AAVE: African American Vernacular English:** African American Vernacular English (AAVE) is a dialect spoken primarily by African Americans. It has its own unique grammar, pronunciation, and vocabulary, and has had a significant impact on American culture.

o **Irish Gaelic's Survival:** Irish Gaelic, one of the oldest languages in Europe, is still spoken in parts of Ireland, and the government actively promotes its use through education and media.

o **Hawaiian Pidgin: A Creole Language:** Hawaiian Pidgin, also known as Hawaii Creole English, is a creole language spoken in Hawaii. It developed as a way for people from different linguistic backgrounds to communicate, blending English with Hawaiian, Japanese, and Portuguese.

o **Arabic's Varied Dialects:** Arabic has many dialects, and while Modern Standard Arabic is used in formal settings, spoken dialects can vary greatly between regions, like Egyptian, Levantine, and Gulf Arabic.

o **Scots: Scotland's Other Language:** Scots, spoken in Scotland, is closely related to English but is considered a separate language. It has a rich literary tradition, with writers like Robert Burns and contemporary poets keeping it alive.

o **Tamil: A Classical Language:** Tamil, spoken primarily in Tamil Nadu, India, and Sri Lanka, is one of the oldest living languages. It has a rich literary history spanning over 2,000 years and is known for its classical poetry and epics.

Language Lores

o **The Tower of Babel:** The story of the Tower of Babel in the Bible explains why humans speak different languages. According to the tale, God confused the languages to prevent humans from completing the tower to heaven.

o **Morse Code for SOS:** The Morse code signal for SOS (three dots, three dashes, three dots) was chosen because it's easy to transmit and distinguish, not because it stands for any words.

o **The Origin of the Word "Alphabet":** The word "alphabet" comes from the first two letters of the Greek alphabet, "alpha" and "beta." The Greek alphabet, in turn, was derived from the Phoenician script.

o **The Legend of King Sejong and Hangul:** King Sejong of Korea created Hangul, the Korean alphabet, in the 15th century to promote literacy among commoners. Hangul is now celebrated for its simplicity and scientific design.

o **The Only Wordless Language:** The Taa language spoken in parts of Botswana has more than 160 distinct click sounds, making it one of the most complex phonetic systems in the world.

o **"Girl" Once Referred to All Youths:** In Middle English, "girl" referred to a young person of either gender. It wasn't until the 16th century that it came to refer exclusively to females.

o **Cyril and Methodius: The Fathers of Slavic Writing:** Saints Cyril and Methodius developed the Glagolitic script, which later evolved into Cyrillic, used by many Slavic languages today. They are celebrated as the "Apostles of the Slavs."

o **The Epic of Gilgamesh:** The Epic of Gilgamesh, written in cuneiform on clay tablets, is one of the earliest known works of literature. It tells the adventures of Gilgamesh, a legendary Sumerian king.

o **The Enigma Machine:** The Enigma Machine was used by Nazi Germany during World War II to encrypt secret messages. The British team at Bletchley Park, led by Alan Turing, famously cracked the code, helping to end the war.

o **Runes: The Script of the Vikings:** Runes were the letters of the ancient Germanic alphabet, used by the Vikings for writing. They believed runes held magical powers, and the script was often carved on stones and weapons.

o **The Etruscan Language Mystery:** The Etruscan language, spoken in ancient Italy, has never been fully deciphered. Though many inscriptions exist, the language remains a puzzle, with only a few words clearly understood.

o **Mayan Glyphs: A Lost Language Rediscovered:** For centuries, Mayan glyphs were a mystery. It wasn't until the 20th century that scholars cracked the code, revealing the rich history and culture of the ancient Maya civilization.

o **The Phoenix: A Symbol of Rebirth in Language:** In many cultures, the phoenix symbolizes rebirth and immortality. The word itself comes from the Greek "phoinix," meaning "purple-red," referencing the bird's vibrant plumage.

o **Hieroglyphs: Sacred Carvings of Ancient Egypt:** The word "hieroglyph" means "sacred carving" in Greek. Ancient Egyptians used hieroglyphs for religious texts and monumental inscriptions, considering them a divine form of communication.

o **The Oracle Bones of Ancient China:** Oracle bones, used during the Shang dynasty in ancient China, bear the earliest known Chinese writing. Questions were inscribed on bones and tortoiseshells, then heated until they cracked, revealing answers from the gods.

o **Linear B: The Script of the Mycenaeans:** Linear B, an ancient script used by the Mycenaeans in Greece, was deciphered in the 1950s. It revealed early records of Greek culture and is considered the oldest Greek writing system.

Linguistic Legends

- **Noam Chomsky: The Father of Modern Linguistics:** Noam Chomsky revolutionized the study of linguistics with his theory of Universal Grammar, suggesting that the ability to learn language is innate to humans. His work transformed our understanding of language acquisition.

- **Shakespeare's Lasting Impact on English:** William Shakespeare invented over 1,700 words and phrases that are still used today, including "eyeball," "bedazzled," and "break the ice." His creative use of language has had a lasting influence on English.

- **The Legend of La Malinche:** La Malinche, a Nahua woman, was the interpreter for Hernán Cortés during the Spanish conquest of Mexico. She is both vilified and revered in Mexican history for her linguistic role.

- **Homer: The Epic Poet:** Homer, the ancient Greek poet, is credited with composing "The Iliad" and "The Odyssey," two of the greatest epic poems of all time. His works laid the foundation for Western literature and language.

- **The Brothers Grimm: Collectors of Folktales:** Jacob and Wilhelm Grimm, known as the Brothers Grimm, collected and published German folktales that have become classics. Their work also helped preserve the German language during a time of cultural change.

- **Cicero: The Master of Latin Rhetoric:** Cicero was a Roman statesman and orator whose speeches and writings greatly influenced the Latin language. His works on rhetoric and philosophy became foundational texts for Western education.

- **Beowulf: The Old English Epic:** "Beowulf" is the oldest surviving epic poem in Old English, dating back to around the 8th century. Its hero's battles with monsters and dragons are central to Anglo-Saxon literature and culture.

- **Confucius: The Sage of Language and Ethics:** Confucius, the Chinese philosopher, emphasized the importance of proper language use and communication in his teachings. His ideas on morality, education, and language have shaped Chinese culture across different countries for over two millennia.

- **Johann Wolfgang von Goethe: A Literary Giant:** Goethe, one of Germany's greatest writers, was a master of both poetry and prose. His works, including "Faust," explored deep philosophical themes and expanded the possibilities of the German language.

- **Ferdinand de Saussure: The Father of Structural Linguistics:** Ferdinand de Saussure is known as the father of structural linguistics. His ideas about the structure of language, especially the concept of the signifier and signified, laid the groundwork for modern linguistics.

- **Sappho: The Lyric Poetess:** Sappho, an ancient Greek poetess from the island of Lesbos, wrote lyrical poetry that was deeply personal and emotional. Although much of her work is lost, her influence on Western literature is undeniable.

- **Vladimir Nabokov: Master of Prose:** Vladimir Nabokov, author of "Lolita," was a linguistic virtuoso, writing in both Russian and English. His intricate wordplay, storytelling, and themes made him one of the most celebrated novelists of the 20th century.

- **Dante Alighieri: The Father of the Italian Language:** Dante's epic poem "The Divine Comedy" is credited with establishing the Tuscan dialect as the standard Italian language. His work remains a cornerstone of Italian literature and language.

- **The Oldest Written Language:** Sumerian, used by the ancient Sumerians in Mesopotamia around 3,200 BCE, is considered the oldest known written language. It was written using cuneiform script on clay tablets

- **Tolstoy: The Russian Literary Titan:** Leo Tolstoy, author of "War and Peace" and "Anna Karenina," is considered one of the greatest novelists of all time. His deep exploration of human nature and society set a high standard for literary excellence in the Russian language.

Talking Traditions

- **The Navajo Code Talkers:** During World War II, Navajo Code Talkers used their language to create an unbreakable code that was instrumental in secure communications for the U.S. military.

- **Irish Blarney: The Gift of Gab:** The Blarney Stone, located in Blarney Castle in Ireland, is said to give the "gift of gab" (eloquence) to those who kiss it. The tradition has been a part of Irish culture for centuries.

- **Greetings in Tuvalu:** In Tuvalu, an island nation in the Pacific, traditional greetings involve gently pressing cheeks together while taking a deep breath—symbolizing a shared life force.

- **The Native American Talking Stick:** In many Native American tribes, a talking stick is used during council meetings. The person holding the stick has the right to speak, ensuring everyone has a turn and is listened to with respect.

- **India's Oral Tradition of Storytelling:** India has a rich oral tradition where stories, epics, and teachings are passed down through generations. The Mahabharata and Ramayana were originally transmitted orally, long before being written down.

- **Morris Dancing in England:** Morris dancing is a traditional English folk dance involving rhythmic stepping and the wielding of sticks, swords, or handkerchiefs. The dances often accompany songs and are performed at festivals and fairs.

- **The Scandinavian Art of Hygge:** In Denmark and Norway, "hygge" is a tradition of creating cozy, warm, and comfortable atmospheres, often shared with friends and family. Conversation over candlelight and good food is key to this cultural practice.

- **The Inuit Throat Singing:** Inuit throat singing, practiced by women in Arctic regions, is a form of musical duet that mimics the sounds of nature. The tradition was nearly lost but has seen a revival in recent years.

- **Chinese New Year Greetings:** During Chinese New Year, it's traditional to greet others with phrases like "Gong Xi Fa Cai," meaning "wishing you great happiness and prosperity."

- **The Spanish 'Sobremesa' Tradition:** In Spain, "sobremesa" refers to the time spent lingering around the table after a meal, enjoying conversation with friends and family. It's a cherished tradition that can last for hours.

- **The African Griot: Keepers of Oral History:** Griots in West Africa are traditional storytellers, poets, and musicians who preserve and transmit oral history. They play a vital role in maintaining the cultural heritage of their communities.

- **The Irish Wake: A Celebration of Life:** Irish wakes are gatherings held after a person's death, where stories and memories are shared over food and drink. The tradition emphasizes celebrating the deceased's life rather than mourning their loss.

- **Japan's Keigo Honorific Language:** In Japanese culture, *keigo* (honorific language) is used to show respect based on social hierarchy. There are different levels of politeness depending on the speaker's relationship with the listener.

- **Scottish Ceilidh: Dance and Music:** A ceilidh is a traditional Scottish gathering featuring folk music, dancing, and storytelling. The word "ceilidh" means "visit" in Gaelic, reflecting the event's focus on social interaction and fun.

- **Yodeling in the Alps:** Yodeling, a singing style involving rapid changes in pitch, originated in the Swiss Alps as a way for herders to communicate over long distances and through mountainous regions.

Word Wonders

- **The Longest English Word:** The longest word in the English dictionary is "pneumonoultramicroscopicsilicovolcanoconiosis," a lung disease caused by inhaling very fine silica dust. It has 45 letters!

- **Palindrome Perfection:** A palindrome is a word, phrase, or number that reads the same forward and backward, like "racecar" or "madam." The longest single-word palindrome in English is "detartrated," which means to remove tartar.

- **The Shortest Complete Sentence in English:** The shortest complete sentence in the English language is "I am." It consists of just two words but expresses a complete thought with a subject and a verb.

- **The Untranslatable "Schadenfreude":** "Schadenfreude" is a German word that means taking pleasure in someone else's misfortune. There's no direct translation in English, making it one of many "untranslatable" words.

- **The World's Most Translated Document:** The Universal Declaration of Human Rights, adopted by the United Nations in 1948, holds the record for the most translated document. It has been translated into over 500 languages.

- **Eunoia: A Rare and Unique Word:** "Eunoia," meaning "beautiful thinking," is the shortest English word that contains all five vowels. It's also the title of a book where each chapter uses only one vowel!

- **"Buffalo" Sentence: A Grammatical Oddity:** The word "buffalo" can be repeated eight times in a row to create a grammatically correct sentence: "Buffalo buffalo Buffalo buffalo buffalo buffalo Buffalo buffalo." It's an example of how English can be playful and puzzling.

- **The Shortest Word with All Vowels in Order:** The word "facetious" is one of the shortest words in the English language that includes all five vowels (a, e, i, o, u) in alphabetical order.

- **The Oldest Known Word:** The oldest known word in the English language is "town," derived from the Proto-Germanic word "tunaz," meaning an enclosure or settlement.

- **The Pangram: A Sentence with Every Letter:** A pangram is a sentence that contains every letter of the alphabet at least once. The most famous one is: "The quick brown fox jumps over the lazy dog."

- **English Has the Most Words:** English has the largest vocabulary of any language, with over a million words. This is due to its history of borrowing from other languages like Latin, French, and German.

- **The Word "Set" Has the Most Definitions:** The word "set" holds the record for the most meanings in the English language, with over 430 definitions. It's a small word with enormous versatility!

- **The Longest Word with One Syllable:** The longest one-syllable word in English is "screeched." It's one of only a few words with nine letters and just one syllable.

- **Ambigrams: Words That Mirror Themselves:** An ambigram is a word that reads the same upside down as it does right side up. The word "swims" is an example, reflecting perfectly in water—just like its meaning!

- **"Tsundoku": The Art of Buying Books You Don't Read:** "Tsundoku" is a Japanese term for acquiring books and letting them pile up, unread. It reflects the universal love of books, even if we don't always have time to read them!

And that's the end of our linguistic journey! We've explored the rich tapestry of languages, from ancient scripts to modern slang, uncovering the stories and traditions that connect us all through words.

Our next chapter will be plunging us into the world of the truly Bizarre! Get ready to dive into some of the strangest, most unexpected, and unbelievable trivia that will leave you scratching your head and laughing out loud. The world is a weird and wonderful place, and we're about to uncover its most peculiar secrets!

Oddball Oddities

Curious Cases

O **The Tunguska Event:** In 1908, an explosion flattened 80 million trees in Siberia. Known as the Tunguska Event, it's believed to have been caused by a meteorite, but no crater was ever found.

O **The Mary Celeste Mystery:** The Mary Celeste was found adrift in 1872 with no crew on board. The ship was in perfect condition, with the crew's belongings intact, but the sailors were never seen again.

O **The Case of Kaspar Hauser:** In 1828, a young man named Kaspar Hauser appeared in Nuremberg, Germany, claiming to have been raised in isolation. His true identity and origins remain a mystery.

O **The Giant Squid:** For centuries, sailors told stories of giant squids attacking ships. It wasn't until 2004 that the first live giant squid was photographed, proving that these elusive creatures, reaching up to 43 feet long, are real.

O **Wombats Poop Cubes:** Wombats have the unique ability to produce cube-shaped poop. This helps them mark their territory and prevents their droppings from rolling away. The final sections of the wombat's intestines have varying levels of elasticity, allowing them to contract and shape the feces into cubes.

O **The Mystery of Missing Socks:** Ever wondered why socks disappear in the laundry? Studies suggest that socks can get caught in washing machine mechanisms or hidden in the folds of clothes. There's even a mathematical equation to estimate sock loss during laundry!

O **Bald Eagles' Recovery from Near Extinction:** The bald eagle, once near extinction due to pesticide use and habitat loss, made an extraordinary comeback after the U.S. banned DDT (a type of pesticide) in the 1970s.

O **The Wow! Signal:** In 1977, a strong radio signal from space was detected by SETI researchers, dubbed the "Wow! Signal." Despite extensive searches, its origin has never been identified, sparking speculation about extraterrestrial life.

O **The Man in the Iron Mask:** A mysterious prisoner known as "The Man in the Iron Mask" was held in France for 34 years. His identity remains unknown, inspiring countless books, movies, and theories.

O **The Disappearance of D.B. Cooper:** In 1971, a man known as D.B. Cooper hijacked a plane, parachuted out with $200,000, and was never seen again. The case is still the only unsolved skyjacking in U.S. history.

O **The Disappearing Lake:** Lake Peigneur in Louisiana mysteriously drained in 1980 after an oil rig punctured a salt mine beneath it. The lake's water and surrounding land were swallowed up in a massive whirlpool.

O **The Disappearance of Flight MH370:** In 2014, Malaysia Airlines Flight MH370 vanished with 239 people on board. Despite extensive searches, the plane's exact location and the cause of its disappearance remain unsolved.

O **Mushrooms That Glow in the Dark:** Bioluminescent fungi, like *Mycena chlorophos*, glow in the dark. Scientists believe that this light helps attract insects to spread the mushroom's spores, but the exact mechanism behind the glow is still being studied. Admire it from afar. Not safe for human consumption!

O **The Great Molasses Flood:** In 1919, a giant tank of molasses burst in Boston, causing a wave that killed 21 people and destroyed buildings. Known as the Great Molasses Flood, it's one of the strangest disasters in history.

O **The Phantom Barber of Pascagoula:** During World War II, residents of Pascagoula, Mississippi, were terrorized by a mysterious intruder who cut locks of hair from people while they slept. The Phantom Barber was never caught.

Strange Sports

O **Extreme Ironing in the UK:** Extreme ironing combines the mundane activity of ironing clothes with extreme outdoor sports like rock climbing, skydiving, and even underwater diving.

O **Chess Boxing:** A hybrid sport combining rounds of boxing and chess, chess boxing requires participants to be both mentally sharp and physically fit, alternating between moves on the board and punches in the ring.

O **Toe Wrestling:** In this odd sport, two competitors lock big toes and try to pin their opponent's toe to the ground. It's similar to arm wrestling, but for toes!

O **Bog Snorkeling in Wales:** In this quirky event, participants must swim two lengths of a water-filled trench in a peat bog, using only flippers and a snorkel. Swimming strokes are not allowed!

O **Ferret Legging in the UK:** In this bizarre endurance competition, participants put live ferrets down their trousers and see who can last the longest without releasing the ferrets!

O **Ostrich Racing in South Africa/USA:** Ostrich racing, where jockeys ride on the backs of these large birds, is a popular event in some parts of South Africa and the U.S., particularly in Arizona.

O **Quidditch:** Inspired by the fictional game from *Harry Potter*, real-life quidditch is played on foot by teams who run around with broomsticks between their legs, mixing elements of rugby, dodgeball, and tag.

O **Bossaball in Spain/Belgium:** Bossaball is a mix of volleyball, soccer, and gymnastics, played on an inflatable court with trampolines, allowing players to spike or kick the ball in acrobatic ways.

O **Unicycle Polo:** Similar to traditional polo but played on unicycles, this unusual sport involves two teams trying to score goals by hitting a ball with mallets while riding one-wheeled cycles.

O **Shin Kicking in the UK:** Dating back to the 17th century, shin kicking involves two competitors trying to kick each other's shins until one falls to the ground. It's part of the annual Cotswold Olimpick Games in England.

O **Sepak Takraw in Southeast Asia:** Sepak takraw is a sport where players use their feet, head, knees, and chest to hit a rattan ball over a net, similar to volleyball but without using hands. You can witness high-flying feats of acrobatics during these games!

O **Gurning in the UK:** Gurning is a face-pulling competition where participants contort their faces in the most exaggerated and grotesque ways possible. The most famous gurning contest is held in Egremont, England.

O **Man vs. Horse Marathon in Wales:** This race, held annually in Wales, pits runners against horses over a 22-mile course. The idea started from a pub argument, and humans have won only a few times.

O **Swamp Soccer in Finland:** In this sport, teams of players battle it out on a muddy, swampy field, with traditional soccer rules but far more challenging conditions due to the thick mud.

O **Bathtub Racing in Canada:** Bathtub racing involves competitors racing modified motorized bathtubs across water. The sport originated in Nanaimo, Canada, where participants annually race their tubs in a famous competition.

Odd Occurrences

O **The Raining Fish Phenomenon:** In Yoro, Honduras, residents experienced a "rain of fish". Scientists believe it's caused by waterspouts that lift fish from rivers and drop them inland during heavy storms.

O **The Great Emu War:** In 1932, Australia declared "war" on emus that were damaging crops. Armed soldiers fought the birds, but the emus won, proving too fast and resilient for the military's efforts.

O **Yet Another Disappearing Lake:** In 2007, a lake in Chile's Patagonia region mysteriously disappeared overnight. Investigations revealed that an earthquake may have caused a large crack in the ground, draining the lake.

O **The London Beer Flood:** In 1814, a giant vat of beer burst in London, releasing a 15-foot wave of beer that destroyed homes and killed eight people. This bizarre disaster is remembered as the London Beer Flood.

O **The Kerala Red Rain of India:** In 2001, residents of Kerala, India, reported a rain shower of tiny red "blood" droplets. Later, scientists discovered the droplets contained red algae, a bizarre but natural phenomenon.

O **The Exploding Toads of Germany:** In 2005, thousands of toads in Hamburg, Germany, mysteriously swelled up and exploded. Researchers eventually linked this odd event to hungry crows targeting the toads' livers.

- **The Never-Melting Ice Cave:** In Siberia, there is an ice cave where temperatures inside remain cold enough to prevent the ice from melting, even during the summer, due to cold air being trapped within.

- **Balloonfest of 1986:** In Cleveland, Ohio, a charity event released 1.5 million helium balloons into the sky. The colorful spectacle turned chaotic when weather conditions caused the balloons to fall back to the ground, creating a huge mess and even traffic accidents!

- **The Double Sunset of Leek:** In Leek, Staffordshire in the UK, people can witness a phenomenon where the sun sets twice. This happens when the sun dips behind a hill, then briefly reappears before fully setting again. This occurs around the summer solstice (typically around June 21st) due to the specific alignment of the landscape in relation to the setting sun.

- **The Exploding Pants of New Zealand:** In the 1930s, New Zealand farmers used a chemical to kill weeds that unexpectedly made their pants highly flammable. Several incidents of pants spontaneously combusting were reported, leading to the ban of the chemical.

- **The Baltic Sea Anomaly:** In 2011, divers discovered a strange, sunken object in the Baltic Sea resembling a spaceship. Its origins remain unclear, with theories ranging from a natural formation to a crashed UFO. However, subsequent geological surveys revealed that it is most likely a glacial deposit, formed during the last ice age.

- **The Mysterious Siberian Craters:** In 2014, giant craters suddenly appeared in Siberia, Russia. Scientists later found they were caused by methane gas eruptions due to thawing permafrost, a bizarre and alarming natural phenomenon.

- **The Aurora Event:** In 1859, a powerful geomagnetic storm caused auroras to be seen as far south as the Caribbean. Telegraph systems were disrupted, and some operators reported receiving electric shocks.

- **Tree That Grows Through a Car:** In Washington State, USA, a tree grows through the middle of an old, abandoned car. The car was left under the tree in the 1950s, and the tree has grown around it ever since.

- **The South Atlantic Anomaly:** The South Atlantic Anomaly is an area where Earth's magnetic field is unusually weak. Satellites passing through experience strange malfunctions, leading to theories about what lies beneath the Earth's surface there.

Strange and Unusual

- **The Woman Who Lived Without a Heartbeat:** In 2011, doctors implanted a device in a woman that kept her alive without a pulse. Instead of a heartbeat, the device created a constant flow of blood, making her one of the first people to live without a heartbeat.

- **The Upside-Down Waterfall:** In Hawaii, there's a waterfall where the water appears to flow upward. High winds blowing against the falls cause the water to be blown back, creating an optical illusion of an upside-down waterfall.

o **The Moberly–Jourdain Incident:** In 1901, two women visiting the Palace of Versailles reported seeing people dressed in 18th-century clothing and believed they had experienced a time slip, catching a glimpse of the past.

o **Honey Never Spoils:** Honey is so naturally preserved that archaeologists have found pots of honey in ancient Egyptian tombs over 3,000 years old, and they're still edible!

o **The Man Who Hiccuped for 68 Years:** Charles Osborne from the U.S. holds the record for the longest bout of hiccups, lasting from 1922 to 1990—a total of 68 years! Despite trying various cures, nothing could stop his hiccups until they mysteriously stopped on their own.

o **The Phantom Island of Bermeja:** Bermeja, a phantom island in the Gulf of Mexico, appeared on maps for centuries before disappearing without a trace. Some believe it was never there, while others think it was submerged due to natural causes.

o **The Man Who Survived Both Atomic Bombs:** Tsutomu Yamaguchi was in Hiroshima when the atomic bomb was dropped and survived. He then traveled to Nagasaki, where he survived the second bombing three days later.

o **The Floating Islands of Lake Titicaca:** Lake Titicaca in Peru and Bolivia is home to floating islands made entirely of reeds. The Uros people live on these islands, continually adding layers of reeds to keep them afloat.

o **The Devil's Kettle Waterfall:** Minnesota's Devil's Kettle Waterfall has baffled scientists for years. Half the water falls into a hole and seemingly disappears underground, with no clearly visible exit point identified.

o **The Blue People of Kentucky:** The Fugate family of Kentucky had a genetic condition that caused their skin to appear blue. Known as methemoglobinemia, this rare disorder made them a medical curiosity in the 19th century.

o **The Tree That Owns Itself:** In Athens, Georgia, there's a white oak tree that legally owns itself. According to local legend, the tree's owner deeded it the land surrounding it, making it the only tree with property rights.

o **The London Fog of 1952:** A thick fog covered London in December 1952, causing thousands of deaths due to severe air pollution. The "Great Smog" was so dense that visibility was reduced to just a few feet.

o **The Mummified Monk in Mongolia:** In 2015, a 200-year-old mummified monk was found in Mongolia, still in the lotus position. Remarkably well-preserved, some believe he's in a deep meditative state rather than dead.

o **The Town That Reflects The Sun:** Residents of the town of Viganella in Italy placed a giant mirror on a nearby mountain to reflect sunlight into their valley during the winter months when the sun doesn't reach them.

O **Bubble Rings Created by Dolphins:** Dolphins in captivity have been observed creating underwater bubble rings for play. They release air through their blowholes, then spin the bubbles with their fins, showing their playful intelligence.

O **The Town That Moved:** Kiruna, Sweden's northernmost town, is being relocated building by building to avoid sinking due to mining operations. The entire town is being moved 3 kilometers east, a feat of engineering and planning.

Unbelievable But True

O **Bananas Are Radioactive:** Bananas contain potassium-40, a radioactive isotope. But don't worry—you'd need to eat 10 million bananas at once to get radiation poisoning!

O **The Human Magnet Syndrome:** Certain individuals, known as "human magnets," claim to have the ability to stick metal objects to their bodies. The scientific cause behind this phenomenon is still debated.

O **The Great Stink of London:** In 1858, a heatwave caused the River Thames to smell so bad it forced Parliament to suspend sessions. The "Great Stink" led to the modernization of London's sewer system.

O **The Woman Who Couldn't Forget:** Jill Price, an American woman, has a condition called hyperthymesia, allowing her to remember every day of her life in vivid detail. Her condition is so rare that only a few people in the world have it.

O **The Village That Celebrates Snake Worship:** In India, the village of Shetpal has a unique tradition: cobras freely roam the village and are worshipped as protectors. Despite the deadly snakes, there are no recorded snakebite fatalities.

O **The World's Shortest War:** The Anglo-Zanzibar War of 1896 lasted only 38 minutes, making it the shortest war in history. The conflict ended when the Sultan's palace was bombarded by British forces.

O **The Island of Cats:** Aoshima, Japan, is known as "Cat Island" because its feline population outnumbers humans by six to one. The cats were originally brought to control the rodent population but now rule the island.

O **The Boy Who Was Raised by Wolves:** In 1872, a boy named Dina Sanichar was found living among wolves in India. He was raised by the animals and exhibited wolf-like behavior, becoming an inspiration for Rudyard Kipling's "The Jungle Book."

O **The Rain That Tasted Like Grape Soda:** In 2001, grape soda-flavored rain reportedly fell in Chester, South Carolina. The phenomenon baffled scientists, who could find no explanation for the strange occurrence.

O **The Man Who Survived a Lightning Strike 7 Times:** Roy Sullivan, a park ranger, was struck by lightning seven times between 1942 and 1977 and survived each strike. He holds the record for most lightning strikes survived.

- **The City That Disappeared Overnight:** In 1930, an entire Inuit village near Lake Anjikuni in Canada vanished without a trace. The huts were intact, but the people were gone, leaving behind their belongings and even food.

- **The House That Sinks:** The Winchester Mystery House in California was continuously built and remodeled for 38 years by Sarah Winchester. The result was a labyrinth of staircases, doors to nowhere, and a house that's slowly sinking.

- **The Bridge That's Too Scary to Cross:** In 1940, the Tacoma Narrows Bridge collapsed in Washington due to wind-induced vibrations. The collapse was so dramatic that the bridge earned the nickname "Galloping Gertie."

- **The World's Largest Snowflake:** In 1887, a snowflake measuring 15 inches wide and 8 inches thick was reportedly observed in Montana, making it the largest snowflake ever recorded.

- **The One Who Was Allergic to Water:** Aquagenic urticaria is a rare condition where a person is allergic to water. Even their own tears could cause painful hives, making it one of the most unusual allergies known.

- **The Day the Sun Went Dark:** On May 19, 1780, New England experienced a mysterious "dark day" when the sky turned black in the middle of the day. The cause remains debated, with theories ranging from forest fires to volcanic ash.

Weird and Wonderful

- **Tree of 40 Fruit:** An artist in the U.S. created a single tree that grows 40 different types of fruit by grafting branches from different species. It produces cherries, plums, apricots, and more!

- **The Okapi: A Zebra-Giraffe Hybrid:** The okapi, a native of the Congo rainforest, looks like a bizarre mix of a zebra and a giraffe. It has striped legs like a zebra but is closely related to giraffes, showcasing the wonders of evolution.

- **The Eternal Flame Falls:** In a small waterfall in New York, there's a natural gas leak that creates a small, flickering flame right beneath the water. This "Eternal Flame" is both a geological and visual wonder.

- **The Singing Sands of Dunhuang:** In the Gobi Desert near Dunhuang, China, the sand dunes produce a musical hum when the wind blows. Known as the "Singing Sands," the sound can range from a gentle hum to a loud roar.

- **The Flower That Smells Like Rotting Flesh:** The corpse flower, or Titan arum, blooms only once every few years and emits a foul odor similar to rotting meat. Despite the smell, it attracts crowds due to its enormous size and rarity.

- **The Rainforest That Gets Flooded:** In Brazil's Amazon rainforest, parts of the forest are completely submerged during the wet season. Known as "Várzea" and "Igapó," these flooded forests are home to unique species that have adapted to the aquatic environment.

O **The Lake That Turns Animals to Stone:** Lake Natron in Tanzania has such high alkalinity that animals who touch its water are calcified, appearing as if they've turned to stone. The eerie phenomenon is caused by the lake's extreme conditions.

O **The Underwater River in Mexico:** Cenote Angelita in Mexico has an underwater river, where a layer of hydrogen sulfide separates fresh water from salt water, creating the illusion of a river flowing beneath the sea.

O **The Blue Lava of Kawah Ijen:** In Indonesia, the Kawah Ijen volcano emits blue flames due to sulfuric gases igniting as they escape through cracks. This creates a spectacular "blue lava" effect during the night.

O **The Rainbow Eucalyptus Tree:** The Rainbow Eucalyptus, found in the Philippines, has bark that peels away to reveal vibrant stripes of green, blue, purple, and orange. This natural rainbow is one of nature's most colorful wonders.

O **The Pink Lake of Australia:** Lake Hillier in Australia is a bubblegum-pink lake, caused by algae that produce carotenoids. The lake's color remains vibrant year-round, making it a unique and stunning natural feature.

O **The Tree That Grows on Another Tree:** In Panama, the "Strangler Fig" starts its life on a host tree, eventually enveloping and "strangling" it as it grows. Over time, the host tree dies, leaving the hollow fig standing alone.

O **The House of Black and White:** The House of Black and White in Bahia, Brazil, is a centuries-old building that was split between two feuding brothers. They painted their respective halves in starkly contrasting colors, and it remains divided to this day.

O **Venus Flytrap's Quick Snaps:** The Venus flytrap can snap its trap shut in less than a second when its sensitive hairs detect prey. It digests its catch with enzymes, feeding on insects and spiders.

O **The Ocean That Glows:** The "Sea of Stars" on Vaadhoo Island in the Maldives glows blue at night due to bioluminescent plankton. The glowing effect creates the illusion that the ocean's surface is sparkling with stars.

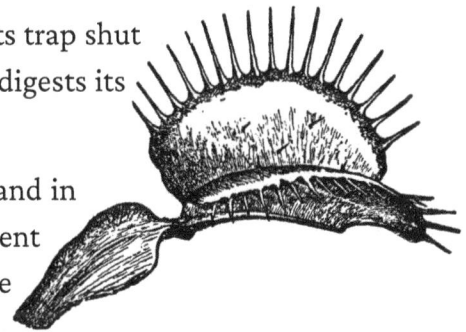

Give yourselves a pat on the back! We've just navigated some of the world's most bizarre phenomena, puzzling mysteries, and mind-bending oddities that truly make you wonder about the world we live in. These strange tales remind us that just when you think you've seen it all, something completely unexpected comes along!

But hold onto your hats, because our journey is far from over! Get ready to have your mind blown WIDE open as we dive into a universe of COOL FACTS! Whether it's cutting-edge technology, awe-inspiring nature, or unbelievable records, this chapter is packed with information that will leave you saying, "Wow!" So, let's go!

Radical Coolness

Amazing Adventures

O **Climbing Mount Everest:** Mount Everest, the world's highest peak, has been summited over 10,000 times. The first successful climbers were Sir Edmund Hillary and Tenzing Norgay in 1953, starting an adventure legacy.

O **Kayaking Norway's Fjords:** Norway's fjords, with their towering cliffs and serene waters, offer stunning kayaking adventures, with opportunities to explore secluded coves and waterfalls.

O **Ziplining Through Costa Rican Rainforests:** Costa Rica offers some of the world's most thrilling ziplining adventures, allowing adventurers to soar above lush rainforests and spot wildlife like monkeys and toucans.

O **Diving to the Titanic:** Only a few people have dived down to the Titanic wreck, located 12,500 feet below the North Atlantic Ocean. The first successful dive was in 1986, over 70 years after it sank.

O **Caving in Vietnam's Son Doong Cave:** Son Doong Cave in Vietnam is the largest known cave in the world. Adventurers can explore its enormous chambers, underground rivers, and towering stalagmites.

O **Swimming the English Channel:** The English Channel swim is one of the world's most famous long-distance swims. Swimmers brave cold water, strong currents, and jellyfish to complete the 21-mile journey between England and France.

O **Cycling the Death Road in Bolivia:** Bolivia's Death Road, known as one of the world's most dangerous roads, offers a heart-pounding mountain biking experience with narrow paths and steep drops.

O **Driving the Pan-American Highway:** The Pan-American Highway stretches from Alaska to Argentina, covering over 19,000 miles. It's the world's longest road, taking drivers through deserts, jungles, and mountains across two continents.

O **Skydiving Over Dubai:** Skydiving over Dubai offers a breathtaking view of the Palm Jumeirah islands and the futuristic skyline, combining urban landscapes with the thrill of freefalling.

O **Whitewater Rafting the Zambezi River:** The Zambezi River, below Victoria Falls, is famous for its wild rapids, offering adrenaline-pumping whitewater rafting adventures through gorges and rocky terrain.

O **Diving the SS Yongala Shipwreck:** Off the coast of Queensland, Australia, the SS Yongala shipwreck is one of the world's best dive sites, with marine life like turtles, sharks, and colorful corals surrounding the sunken vessel.

- **Exploring the Arctic by Dog Sled:** Dog sledding across the Arctic is an exhilarating adventure, with teams of huskies pulling sleds over frozen landscapes. Explorers endure freezing temperatures and long days in the harsh, beautiful wilderness.

- **Hiking the Pacific Crest Trail:** The Pacific Crest Trail stretches 2,650 miles from Mexico to Canada. Hikers traverse deserts, forests, and snowy mountains, taking months to complete the journey.

- **Base Jumping off Angel Falls:** Angel Falls in Venezuela is the world's highest waterfall, with a drop of 3,212 feet. Brave base jumpers leap from the top, free-falling before opening their parachutes.

- **Bungee Jumping at the Verzasca Dam:** The Verzasca Dam in Switzerland is one of the highest bungee jumping spots in the world, offering a thrilling freefall of 720 feet, famously featured in the James Bond movie *GoldenEye*.

Awesome Achievements

- **Crossing Antarctica:** In 1911, Norwegian explorer Roald Amundsen became the first person to reach the South Pole, marking an incredible achievement in polar exploration.

- **The Largest Human Gathering:** The Kumbh Mela pilgrimage in India holds the record for the largest human gathering, with over 30 million people attending in 2013.

- **The Creation of the Suez Canal:** The Suez Canal, completed in 1869, is one of the most important waterways in the world, linking the Mediterranean Sea to the Red Sea and shortening the journey between Europe and Asia.

- **Building the International Space Station:** The International Space Station (ISS) is a collaborative effort involving 15 nations. It's the largest human-made structure in space, orbiting Earth and serving as a hub for scientific research.

- **The Apollo 13 Rescue Mission:** In 1970, NASA successfully brought home the Apollo 13 astronauts after an oxygen tank explosion threatened their lives. Their return was hailed as one of the greatest rescue missions in space history.

- **The First Circumnavigation of the Globe:** In 1522, Ferdinand Magellan's expedition became the first to circumnavigate the globe, proving that the Earth is round and establishing crucial maritime routes.

- **The Construction of the Channel Tunnel:** Completed in 1994, the Channel Tunnel, or "Chunnel," is a 31-mile rail tunnel beneath the English Channel, connecting England and France and revolutionizing travel between the two countries.

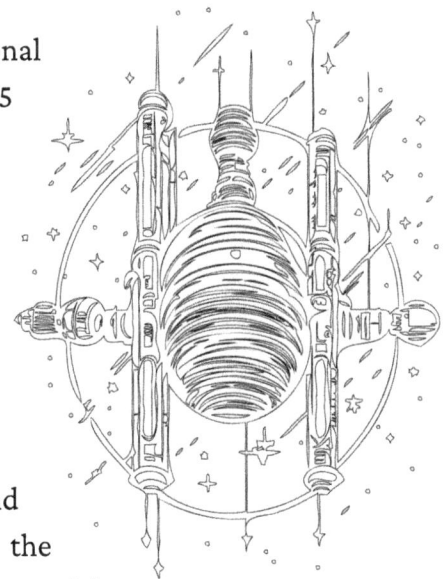

O **Building the Empire State Building:** Completed in 1931, the Empire State Building in New York City stood as the world's tallest building for nearly 40 years and remains an icon of American engineering.

O **The Construction of the Three Gorges Dam:** Completed in 2012, the Three Gorges Dam in China is the largest hydroelectric power station in the world, stretching over 1.4 miles across the Yangtze River.

O **The First Organism to Be Genetically Modified:** In 1973, scientists created the first genetically modified organism (GMO), using bacteria to produce insulin, a breakthrough that led to advancements in medicine and agriculture.

O **The Mars Rover Landing:** In 2012, NASA's *Curiosity* rover successfully landed on Mars, beginning a mission to explore the planet's surface, analyze its soil, and search for signs of life.

O **The Completion of the Transcontinental Railroad:** The U.S. Transcontinental Railroad, completed in 1869, connected the East and West coasts for the first time. The achievement transformed travel and commerce in America.

O **The First Female Vice President of the United States:** In 2021, Kamala Harris made history as the first woman, the first Black woman, and the first South Asian woman to be elected Vice President of the United States.

O **The First Powered Flight by a Solar-Powered Aircraft:** In 2016, *Solar Impulse 2* completed the first solar-powered flight around the world without using any fuel, a breakthrough for renewal energy.

O **The First Human to Break the Sound Barrier:** In 1947, Chuck Yeager became the first person to fly faster than the speed of sound, piloting the Bell X-1 aircraft. His achievement marked a significant milestone in aviation history.

Cool Careers

O **Astronaut:** Astronauts train for years to explore space, conducting experiments on the International Space Station and even walking on the Moon. It's one of the most challenging and awe-inspiring careers.

O **Marine Biologist:** Marine biologists study ocean life, from tiny plankton to massive whales. They dive into the deep sea to research marine ecosystems, helping to protect the oceans and the creatures that live there.

O **Video Game Designer:** Video game designers create the worlds, characters, and stories that players love. They combine art, technology, and storytelling to develop games that entertain millions of people worldwide.

O **Foley Artist:** They create sound effects for films and television, using everyday objects to mimic sounds like footsteps or breaking glass.

o **Storm Chaser:** Storm chasers pursue extreme weather, like tornadoes and hurricanes, to study and photograph these powerful natural events. Their work helps scientists better understand and predict severe weather.

o **Odor Judge:** These nasally brave individuals assess the effectiveness of deodorants and other personal care products by smelling human armpits and feet.

o **Forensic Scientist:** Forensic scientists analyze evidence from crime scenes to help solve cases. They use chemistry, biology, and other sciences to uncover clues that can catch criminals and bring justice.

o **Astronomer:** Astronomers study the stars, planets, and galaxies, exploring the universe's mysteries. They use powerful telescopes and advanced technology to observe celestial objects far beyond our solar system.

o **Special Effects Artist:** Special effects artists create the impressive visuals seen in movies, TV shows, and video games. From realistic explosions to fantastical creatures, they bring the impossible to life on screen.

o **Snake Milker:** These fearless individuals extract venom from snakes, contributing to the production of antivenom and other medical treatments.

o **Food Scientist:** Food scientists develop new flavors, improve food safety, and create healthier options. They experiment with ingredients to innovate the foods we eat every day, making meals tastier and more nutritious.

o **Ocularist:** They create custom-made prosthetic eyes, matching the color and appearance of the patient's natural eye.

o **Robotics Engineer:** Robotics engineers design and build robots, from simple machines to advanced androids. Their work helps automate industries, explore space, and even perform surgery, pushing the boundaries of technology.

o **Forensic Entomologist:** They study insects found at crime scenes to determine time of death and other crucial details, aiding criminal investigations.

o **Dice Inspector:** They scrutinize dice used in casinos to ensure they are perfectly balanced and fair for gambling.

Incredible Innovations

o **The Integrated Circuit:** Invented in 1958 by Jack Kilby and Robert Noyce, the integrated circuit (microchip) laid the foundation for modern computers, smartphones, and nearly all electronic devices.

o **The Hovercraft:** Invented in 1955 by Christopher Cockerell, the hovercraft can travel over land, water, mud, and ice, thanks to its air cushion technology, making it useful in rescue missions and transportation.

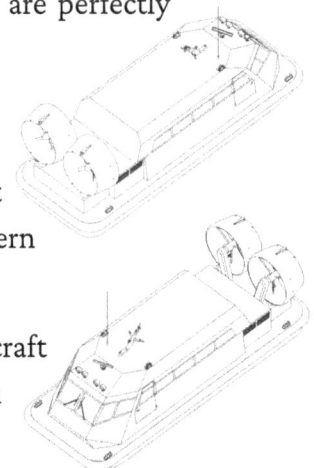

o **The Electric Car:** Electric cars, powered by batteries instead of gasoline, are a greener alternative for transportation. Innovations in this field have made electric vehicles more efficient and popular, leading the charge for sustainable travel.

o **The Contact Lens:** Invented in 1887 and improved over the 20th century, contact lenses provide an alternative to eyeglasses, helping millions of people with vision correction.

o **The Flush Toilet:** The flush toilet, invented by John Harrington in 1596 and improved in the 19th century, revolutionized sanitation and greatly improved public health.

o **The Zipper:** The modern zipper, invented by Gideon Sundback in 1913, became an essential fastening device for clothing, luggage, and countless other items.

o **The Defibrillator:** The defibrillator, developed in the 1930s, uses electrical shocks to restart the heart during cardiac arrest, saving countless lives in emergency situations.

o **The Hybrid Car:** The development of hybrid vehicles, combining internal combustion engines with electric power, has helped reduce emissions and improve fuel efficiency in transportation.

o **The Washing Machine:** The first electric washing machine, invented in 1908, revolutionized home life by automating the labor-intensive task of washing clothes, saving time and effort.

o **The Hyperloop:** The Hyperloop is a futuristic transportation system that promises to transport people and cargo at near-supersonic speeds through vacuum tubes. This innovation could revolutionize travel as we know it.

o **Drones:** Drones, or unmanned aerial vehicles, are used for everything from aerial photography to delivering packages. These versatile flying machines are revolutionizing industries like agriculture, filmmaking, and logistics.

o **The Turing Machine:** Alan Turing's theoretical "Turing machine," developed in 1936, laid the groundwork for modern computers by formalizing the concept of computation and algorithms.

o **Quantum Computing:** Quantum computers use quantum bits, or qubits, to perform complex calculations at incredible speeds. This cutting-edge technology could solve problems that are currently impossible for traditional computers.

o **Biodegradable Plastics:** Biodegradable plastics break down more quickly than traditional plastics, reducing environmental impact. Innovations in this field aim to solve the global problem of plastic waste and pollution.

o **Google Search Engine:** Launched in 1998, Google revolutionized the way people access and find information on the internet, becoming the dominant global search engine.

Remarkable Records

o **The Tallest Building:** The Burj Khalifa in Dubai stands at an astonishing 2,717 feet, making it the tallest building in the world. It's so tall that residents on the top floors can see the sunset twice: once from the ground and once from their windows.

- **The Longest Fingernails:** Lee Redmond from the USA holds the record for the longest fingernails ever, with a combined length of 28 feet 4.5 inches! She stopped cutting them in 1979 and grew them for nearly 30 years.

- **Longest Nonstop Flight:** In 2022, Singapore Airlines set a record for the longest nonstop commercial flight, covering 9,537 miles from Singapore to New York in just over 18 hours.

- **The Longest Time Spent in Space:** Russian cosmonaut Valery Polyakov holds the record for the longest continuous time spent in space, living aboard the Mir space station for 437 days from 1994 to 1995.

- **The Oldest Person Ever:** Jeanne Calment from France lived to be 122 years and 164 days old, making her the oldest person ever recorded. She met Vincent van Gogh when she was 13 and outlived her entire family.

- **Largest Diamond:** The Cullinan Diamond, discovered in South Africa in 1905, is the largest diamond ever found, weighing 3,106 carats before being cut into multiple gems.

- **The Largest Pizza:** The world's largest pizza is 13,990 square feet and was created by YouTuber Airrack (Eric Decker) and Pizza Hut in Los Angeles, California on January 19, 2023.

- **The Longest Ice Cream Sundae:** In 2018, a 1.3-mile-long ice cream sundae was created in Spirit Lake, Iowa, setting a new world record. The massive dessert used over 500 gallons of ice cream, 800 pounds of toppings, and took a team of volunteers to assemble.

- **Most T-shirts Worn at Once:** How many t shirts can you wear at one go? Well for Ted Hastings, he donned on 260 tees at once on April 24, 2019. This world record took place in Ontario, Canada.

- **The Longest Time Holding One Breath:** Spanish free diver Aleix Segura Vendrell holds the record for the longest time holding one's breath, lasting an incredible 24 minutes and 3 seconds underwater without any breathing aids in 2016.

- **The Largest Snow Maze:** In 2019, a snow maze in Canada set the world record for the largest snow maze, covering an area of 2,789.11 square meters (30,021.73 square feet). The maze was built with walls made entirely of snow and took weeks to complete.

- **The Longest Train:** In 2022, Switzerland set a new record for the longest passenger train, measuring 1.91 miles long and consisting of 100 connected coaches. The train wound through the Swiss Alps in a spectacular journey.

- **The Most Skips Over a Single Rope in One Minute:** The record for the most skips over a single rope in one minute is held by Harumitsu Takahashi from Japan, who achieved 348 skips in 60 seconds! His rapid footwork earned him this impressive title.

- **The Tallest Tree:** The world's tallest tree is a coast redwood named Hyperion, standing at an incredible 379.7 feet tall in California's Redwood National Park. It's taller than the Statue of Liberty!

O **The Largest Rubber Band Ball:** Joel Waul from the USA created the world's largest rubber band ball, weighing 9,032 pounds and measuring 6 feet 7 inches tall. The ball is made of over 700,000 rubber bands of various sizes and colors.

Super Skills

O **Speed-Reading Champion:** Howard Berg holds the title of the world's fastest reader, reportedly reading over 25,000 words per minute!

O **Memory Master:** Akira Haraguchi memorized and recited 100,000 digits of pi in 2006, a feat that took him over 16 hours to complete. His skills are the result of years of practice and dedication.

O **Incredible Human Calculator:** Shakuntala Devi, also known as the "Human Computer," could solve complex mathematical problems in her head faster than a calculator. She once multiplied two 13-digit numbers in just 28 seconds!

O **Record-Setting Typist:** Barbara Blackburn holds the record for the world's fastest typist, achieving a speed of 212 words per minute using a modified keyboard. She could maintain 150 words per minute for 50 minutes straight!

O **The World's Best Whistler:** Geert Chatrou is a world champion whistler who can produce clear, melodic tunes using just his lips. His skill has won him multiple international whistling competitions.

O **Amazing Sword Swallower:** Dan Meyer is a master sword swallower who can safely swallow swords up to 30 inches long. His daring skill is part of a long tradition dating back thousands of years.

O **Rubik's Cube Speedsolver:** Yusheng Du holds the record for solving a standard Rubik's Cube in just 3.47 seconds! His lightning-fast reflexes and spatial reasoning make him one of the world's top "speedcubers."

O **Flawless Free Diver:** Stig Severinsen holds multiple world records for free diving, including holding his breath underwater for 22 minutes. His ability to control his body is both a mental and physical superpower.

O **Juggling Genius:** Anthony Gatto is one of the world's greatest jugglers, holding several records for juggling multiple objects simultaneously. He can juggle up to 9 balls or 7 clubs with remarkable precision.

O **Mind-Blowing Beatboxer:** Tom Thum, an Australian beatboxer, can imitate an entire orchestra using only his mouth. His unique talent has taken him around the world, performing in front of thousands.

O **Remarkable Contortionist:** Russian contortionist Zlata can twist her body into seemingly impossible shapes. She holds the world record for the most backbends in a minute, demonstrating her extraordinary flexibility.

O **Super-Fast Ice Sculptor:** Junichi Nakamura is a master ice sculptor who can create intricate ice sculptures in record time. His works range from delicate flowers to towering statues, all carved with precision and speed.

O **Unbelievable Parkour Artist:** Jason Paul is a professional freerunner who uses parkour to navigate urban environments with incredible agility. His gravity-defying stunts include flips and wall runs.

O **World-Class Origami Artist:** Sipho Mabona is a renowned origami artist who can fold complex paper creations, from lifelike animals to detailed geometric designs. His giant origami elephant, made from a single sheet of paper, is a masterpiece.

O **Extreme Tree Climber:** Bernd Heinrich, a biologist and ultra-endurance athlete, is known for his extreme tree-climbing skills. He uses his ability to study wildlife in the tallest treetops, reaching heights few others can.

Hold on tight, curious minds! From remarkable records to mind-blowing skills, we've explored achievements and innovations that showcase the incredible capabilities of both humans and technology. But don't put the book down just yet—there's even more to discover!

Next up, prepare to be captivated as we dive into a world of extraordinary individuals! Get ready to meet the trailblazers, the rule-breakers, the ones who dared to dream big and changed the world in their own unique way. Their stories will inspire, amaze, and surprise you. So, let's turn the page!

Unforgettable Trailblazing Mavericks

Eccentric Personalities

O **Nikola Tesla's Pigeon Obsession:** Nikola Tesla, the famous inventor, was obsessed with pigeons. He fed them daily and even claimed to love a particular pigeon as much as a human being.

O **Howard Hughes: The Reclusive Billionaire:** Howard Hughes, an aviator and film producer, became a recluse later in life, living in dark hotel rooms and generally avoiding people due to his severe OCD.

O **Salvador Dal's Quirky Mustache:** The surrealist artist Salvador Dal was known for his eccentric mustache, which he styled into a sharp, upward curve. He once claimed it was a "most serious thing" about him.

O **The Emperor Who Tried to Rename Months:** Roman Emperor Caligula attempted to rename the month of September after himself, calling it "Germanicus." He also declared war on the sea, ordering his soldiers to attack the waves.

O **Poe's Duel Challenge:** Edgar Allan Poe, known for his dark tales, once challenged a critic to a duel after receiving a scathing review, showcasing his fierce and witty reputation.

O **Tycho Brahe's Metal Nose:** Danish astronomer Tycho Brahe lost part of his nose in a duel and wore a prosthetic nose made of brass for the rest of his life. He even had a pet elk that reportedly died after drinking too much beer.

O **Lord Byron's Pet Bear:** The poet Lord Byron had a pet bear while studying at Cambridge University. He kept it in his dorm room as a protest against the rule forbidding students from having pet dogs.

O **William Buckland's Unusual Diet:** British geologist William Buckland claimed to have eaten his way through the entire animal kingdom, including panthers, moles, and even crocodiles!

O **Hetty Green: The Miserly Millionaire:** Hetty Green, known as the "Witch of Wall Street," was one of America's richest women, but her extreme frugality was legendary. She once spent hours searching for a lost two-cent stamp.

O **Joshua Norton: Emperor of the United States:** Joshua Norton, a San Francisco resident, declared himself "Emperor of the United States" in 1859. Though not officially recognized, he issued his own currency, which was accepted by local businesses.

O **Grigori Rasputin: The Mad Monk:** Rasputin, a Russian mystic who influenced the Romanov family, was known for his wild behavior and belief in his own mystical powers. His influence and erratic actions made him a controversial figure.

- **The Great Moon Hoax:** In 1835, Richard Adams Locke published a series of articles claiming that life had been discovered on the Moon, including bat-like creatures. The "Great Moon Hoax" fooled many readers of the time.

- **Marlon Brando's Refusal of an Oscar:** Marlon Brando refused to accept his Best Actor Oscar for "The Godfather" in 1973, sending a Native American activist in his place to protest Hollywood's portrayal of Native Americans.

- **Oscar Wilde's Fashion Statement:** Oscar Wilde, the famed playwright, once delivered a lecture wearing a velvet coat, knee breeches, and a sunflower in his hand, shocking the conservative society of his time.

- **Virginia Woolf's Daring Stunt:** In 1910, author Virginia Woolf and a group of friends dressed as Abyssinian princes and tricked the British Navy into giving them a guided tour of a battleship!

- **The Minister's Treehouse:** Horace Burgess, a minister from Tennessee, built the world's largest treehouse after claiming God told him to do so. The treehouse spanned 97 feet in height and contained over 80 rooms. Unfortunately, the treehouse and its supporting trees were burnt down in 2019.

Famous Figures

- **Albert Einstein's Late Bloomer Story:** Albert Einstein didn't speak until he was four years old and was considered a slow learner. Despite this, he became one of the greatest physicists in history, revolutionizing our understanding of the universe.

- **Catherine the Great:** Catherine the Great was one of Russia's most powerful rulers, expanding the empire and promoting Enlightenment ideals, art, and education during her reign from 1762 to 1796.

- **Sigmund Freud:** Sigmund Freud, the father of psychoanalysis, developed influential theories about the unconscious mind and is known for his concepts of the id, ego, and superego.

- **Queen Elizabeth I's Defiance:** Queen Elizabeth I of England famously declared that she had "the heart and stomach of a king" when addressing her troops during the Spanish Armada invasion, proving her strength as a leader.

- **Winston Churchill's Painting Passion:** Winston Churchill, known for his leadership during World War II, was also an avid painter. He found solace in art, creating over 500 paintings during his lifetime.

- **Mahatma Gandhi's Salt March:** In 1930, Mahatma Gandhi led the Salt March, a 240-mile protest against British salt taxes in India. This peaceful act of civil disobedience inspired movements for freedom around the world.

- **Simón Bolvar:** Simón Bolvar, known as "El Libertador," played a crucial role in liberating several South American countries, including Venezuela, Colombia, Ecuador, and Peru, from Spanish rule.

- **Mark Twain:** Mark Twain, born Samuel Clemens, was a celebrated American author known for his novels *The Adventures of Tom Sawyer* and *Adventures of Huckleberry Finn*, often hailed as classics of American literature.

- **Franz Ferdinand:** Archduke Franz Ferdinand of Austria's assassination in 1914 sparked the outbreak of World War I, setting off a chain of events that reshaped global history.

- **Emmeline Pankhurst:** Emmeline Pankhurst was a leader of the British suffragette movement, advocating for women's right to vote. Her activism was crucial in women gaining suffrage in the UK in 1918.

- **Franz Kafka:** Franz Kafka was a Czech writer known for his existential, surreal works such as *The Metamorphosis* and *The Trial*, which explore themes of alienation and absurdity.

- **Sojourner Truth:** Sojourner Truth was an African American abolitionist and women's rights activist, best known for her speech "Ain't I a Woman?" delivered at the 1851 Women's Rights Convention.

- **Franklin D. Roosevelt's New Deal:** President Franklin D. Roosevelt's New Deal programs helped lift the United States out of the Great Depression. He is also the only U.S. president to serve four terms in office.

- **Che Guevara:** Che Guevara was an Argentine Marxist revolutionary who played a key role in the Cuban Revolution and became a symbol of rebellion and anti-imperialism worldwide.

- **Leon Trotsky:** Leon Trotsky was a key leader in the Russian Revolution of 1917 and founder of the Red Army. He was later exiled and assassinated under orders from Joseph Stalin.

Pioneers and Pathfinders

- **Amelia Earhart's Solo Flight:** In 1932, Amelia Earhart became the first woman to fly solo across the Atlantic Ocean. Her daring journey paved the way for future female aviators and made her an American icon.

- **Marco Polo:** Marco Polo was a Venetian explorer whose 13th-century travels to China were documented in *The Travels of Marco Polo*, inspiring generations of explorers.

- **Matthew Henson:** Matthew Henson, an African American explorer, is credited as one of the first people to reach the North Pole in 1909, alongside Robert Peary.

- **Galileo Galilei's Telescope:** Galileo Galilei was the first person to use a telescope to observe the heavens, discovering moons around Jupiter and supporting the heliocentric model of the solar system.

- **James Cook:** Captain James Cook was a British explorer who made three voyages to the Pacific Ocean, mapping many areas including Australia, New Zealand, and Hawaii.

O **Ada Lovelace: The First Computer Programmer:** In the 19th century, Ada Lovelace wrote the first algorithm intended for a machine, making her the world's first computer programmer. She foresaw the potential of computers long before they existed.

O **Jean Batten:** Jean Batten was a pioneering New Zealand aviator who became famous for her solo flights across the world, including the first direct flight from England to New Zealand in 1936.

O **Sacagawea:** Sacagawea, a Shoshone woman, was a guide and interpreter for the Lewis and Clark expedition, helping them navigate through the Western U.S. in the early 1800s.

O **Thor Heyerdahl:** Thor Heyerdahl, a Norwegian explorer, famously sailed a small raft called *Kon-Tiki* across the Pacific Ocean in 1947 to prove ancient peoples could have made long sea voyages.

O **Leif Erikson's New World Discovery:** Long before Columbus, Viking explorer Leif Erikson sailed to North America around the year 1000 AD. He established a settlement in what is now Newfoundland, Canada, marking the first known European presence in the New World.

O **Bertrand Piccard:** Bertrand Piccard co-piloted the first nonstop balloon flight around the world in 1999 and later the first solar-powered flight around the globe in 2016.

O **Ibn Battuta:** A Moroccan explorer who lived in the 14th century. He traveled over 75,000 miles, documenting his journeys in his famous book *The Rihla*. Throughout his travels, he stepped foot on most of the known Islamic world then and even beyond!

O **Dian Fossey:** Dian Fossey was an American primatologist who spent years studying and protecting endangered mountain gorillas in Rwanda, becoming a leading figure in wildlife conservation.

O **Lewis and Clark's Expedition:** In 1804, Meriwether Lewis and William Clark embarked on an expedition to explore the American West. Their journey provided valuable knowledge about the vast, uncharted territory of the United States.

O **Marie Stopes: A Pioneer of Women's Health:** Marie Stopes was a trailblazer in family planning and women's health. Her work in the early 20th century made contraception more accessible and changed societal attitudes toward women's reproductive rights.

Remarkable Lives

O **Rachel Carson:** Rachel Carson's 1962 book *Silent Spring* is credited with launching the modern environmental movement by raising awareness about the dangers of pesticide use.

O **Lech Wałsa:** Lech Wałsa, co-founder of the Solidarity movement in Poland, played a key role in ending communist rule in Poland and later became the country's first democratically elected president.

O **Desmond Tutu:** Desmond Tutu, a South African Anglican bishop, was a leading figure in the fight against apartheid and received the Nobel Peace Prize in 1984 for his nonviolent activism.

O **The Man Who Planted a Forest:** Jadav Payeng single handedly planted a 550-hectare forest over the course of 30 years in Assam, India. Talk about dogged determination!

o **Mother Teresa: A Life of Compassion:** Mother Teresa dedicated her life to helping the poor and sick in Calcutta, India. Her selfless work earned her a Nobel Peace Prize and made her a global icon of humanitarianism.

o **Winston Churchill: Wartime Leader:** Winston Churchill, Britain's Prime Minister during World War II, is celebrated for his leadership and stirring speeches. His resolve helped inspire the British people during their darkest hours.

o **Frederick Douglass: Voice of Freedom:** Frederick Douglass, an escaped slave, became a leading abolitionist, author, and speaker. His powerful words and advocacy were instrumental in the fight to end slavery in the United States.

o **Siddhartha Gautama (Buddha):** Siddhartha Gautama, known as the Buddha, founded Buddhism after attaining enlightenment, teaching principles of mindfulness, compassion, and the Middle Way.

o **Gregor Mendel:** Gregor Mendel, often called the father of modern genetics, discovered the fundamental laws of inheritance through his experiments with pea plants.

o **Albert Einstein: Theoretical Trailblazer:** Albert Einstein revolutionized our understanding of space and time with his theory of relativity. His iconic equation, $E=mc^2$, changed the course of physics and created the framework for understanding nuclear energy.

o **James Baldwin:** James Baldwin was an influential American writer and activist whose works, such as *Go Tell It on the Mountain* and *The Fire Next Time*, explored race, sexuality, and identity.

o **Martin Luther King Jr: A Dream of Equality:** Martin Luther King Jr.'s leadership in the American civil rights movement, marked by his famous "I Have a Dream" speech, helped bring about major societal changes and inspired generations to fight for justice.

o **Jane Goodall: Chimpanzee Champion:** Jane Goodall spent decades studying chimpanzees in the wild, providing unprecedented insights into their behavior. Her work has made her a leading figure in animal conservation and environmentalism.

o **Wangari Maathai:** Wangari Maathai was the first African woman to win the Nobel Peace Prize in 2004 for her environmental work, including founding the Green Belt Movement, which has planted millions of trees in Kenya.

o **Eleanor Roosevelt: First Lady of the World:** Eleanor Roosevelt redefined the role of First Lady, using her position to advocate for human rights, women's rights, and social justice. She later served as a delegate to the United Nations.

Trailblazers

O **Rosa Parks: The Spark of the Civil Rights Movement:** Rosa Parks refused to give up her seat on a bus in 1955, igniting the Montgomery Bus Boycott and becoming a symbol of the fight against racial segregation in the United States.

O **Eleanor of Aquitaine:** Queen of France and later England, Eleanor was a powerful and influential figure in medieval politics and culture. She actively participated in the Crusades, patronized troubadours and poets, and played a significant role in shaping the courts of both France and England.

O **Mary Anning:** She was a self-taught paleontologist whose fossil discoveries along the English coast in the early 19th century sparked greater understanding to the study of prehistoric life.

O **Frances Perkins:** Frances Perkins was the first female U.S. Cabinet member, serving as Secretary of Labor from 1933 to 1945, and played a key role in creating Social Security.

O **Ella Fitzgerald:** Ella Fitzgerald, known as the "First Lady of Song," broke racial barriers in the entertainment industry and won 13 Grammy Awards during her legendary jazz career.

O **Mae Jemison:** In 1992, Mae Jemison became the first African American woman to travel to space, aboard the space shuttle *Endeavour*.

O **Mahatma Gandhi: Champion of Nonviolence:** Mahatma Gandhi led India's struggle for independence through peaceful resistance and civil disobedience. His approach inspired global movements for civil rights and freedom.

O **Cesar Chavez:** Cesar Chavez co-founded the United Farm Workers and fought tirelessly for the rights of farm laborers, advocating for better wages and working conditions.

O **Kalpana Chawla:** Kalpana Chawla was the first woman of Indian origin to travel into space. She flew on two space shuttle missions before tragically losing her life in the Columbia disaster in 2003.

O **Ruth Bader Ginsburg:** Ruth Bader Ginsburg was a trailblazing Supreme Court Justice known for her work in advancing gender equality and women's rights, serving on the U.S. Supreme Court from 1993 to 2020.

O **Susan B. Anthony: Women's Suffrage Leader:** Susan B. Anthony was a key figure in the women's suffrage movement in the United States. Her tireless advocacy helped pave the way for the 19th Amendment, granting women the right to vote.

O **Shirley Chisholm:** In 1968, Shirley Chisholm became the first Black woman elected to the U.S. Congress and later the first Black woman to run for president of the United States in 1972.

O **Gerty Cori:** Gerty Cori was the first woman to win a Nobel Prize in Physiology or Medicine in 1947 for her research on carbohydrate metabolism, a key discovery in understanding diabetes.

- **I.M. Pei:** I.M. Pei, a renowned architect, designed iconic buildings such as the glass pyramid at the Louvre in Paris and the Bank of China Tower in Hong Kong, reshaping modern architecture.

- **Jacques Cousteau: Ocean Explorer:** Jacques Cousteau was a pioneering oceanographer and filmmaker who brought the wonders of the underwater world to the public. His work inspired global efforts to protect marine life.

Unsung Heroes

- **Claudette Colvin:** Nine months before Rosa Parks' famous bus protest, 15-year-old Claudette Colvin refused to give up her seat to a white passenger in Montgomery, Alabama, in 1955.

- **Clara Barton: Angel of the Battlefield:** Clara Barton, founder of the American Red Cross, was a nurse during the Civil War who tended to soldiers on the front lines. Her dedication earned her the nickname "Angel of the Battlefield."

- **Raoul Wallenberg: The Diplomat Who Defied Nazis:** Swedish diplomat Raoul Wallenberg saved tens of thousands of Hungarian Jews during the Holocaust by issuing protective passports and sheltering them in buildings designated as Swedish territory.

- **Viola Desmond: Canada's Civil Rights Pioneer:** Viola Desmond challenged racial segregation in Canada by refusing to leave a whites-only section of a theater in 1946. Her courage sparked the civil rights movement in Nova Scotia.

- **Oskar Schindler: The Man Who Saved 1,200 Lives:** Oskar Schindler, a German industrialist, saved the lives of 1,200 Jews during the Holocaust by employing them in his factories and shielding them from Nazi persecution.

- **Alice Paul: The Silent Sentinel:** Alice Paul was a key leader in the U.S. women's suffrage movement. She organized the Silent Sentinels, who picketed the White House for over two years, leading to the passage of the 19th Amendment.

- **Sybil Ludington: The Teenage Revolutionary:** At just 16 years old, Sybil Ludington rode 40 miles at night to alert colonial forces of a British attack during the American Revolution, earning her the nickname "the female Paul Revere."

- **Chiune Sugihara: The Japanese Schindler:** Chiune Sugihara, a Japanese diplomat in Lithuania, issued thousands of visas to Jewish refugees during World War II, enabling them to escape Nazi persecution whilst actively disobeying his government's orders.

- **Bessie Coleman: The First Black Female Pilot:** Bessie Coleman was the first African American woman to earn a pilot's license. She overcame racial and gender barriers to become a pioneering aviator, inspiring future generations.

- **Desmond Doss: The Hero Without a Gun:** Desmond Doss was a conscientious objector who served as a medic during World War II. He saved 75 men during the Battle of Okinawa, earning the Medal of Honor without firing a single shot.

O **Dr. Charles Drew: Pioneer of Blood Plasma:** Dr. Charles Drew developed techniques for blood storage and established blood banks during World War II. His work revolutionized medical care and saved countless lives.

O **Nellie Bly: The Investigative Journalist:** Nellie Bly was an investigative journalist who exposed abuse in a mental institution by going undercover as a patient. Her groundbreaking work led to reforms in the treatment of the mentally ill.

O **Harriet Jacobs: The Freedom Writer:** Harriet Jacobs was an enslaved woman who escaped and wrote "Incidents in the Life of a Slave Girl," one of the first autobiographical narratives by a woman about the struggle for freedom from slavery.

O **Unsinkable Molly Brown:** Margaret "Molly" Brown survived the sinking of the Titanic in 1912 and helped other passengers into lifeboats, later becoming an advocate for women's rights and worker's rights.

O **Dietrich Bonhoeffer: The Defiant Theologian:** Dietrich Bonhoeffer, a German pastor and theologian, actively opposed the Nazi regime and was involved in a plot to assassinate Hitler. He was executed for his resistance but is remembered for his moral courage.

From daring explorers to pioneering scientists, each of these individuals left a permanent mark on history, showing us the power of determination, innovation, and courage. Their stories inspire us to think big and make our own unique contributions to the world.

What's next? We're heading into a chapter filled with celebration, and festivity—Holidays! Get ready to explore the fascinating origins, customs, and fun facts about holidays from around the globe. From the joy of Christmas to the spookiness of Halloween, and from ancient festivals to modern-day celebrations, let's dive in and discover the stories behind the holidays we all love!

Merrymaking Quizmas

Celebrations Around the World

o **Christmas: A Global Celebration:** Christmas, celebrated on December 25th, is observed by Christians worldwide to mark the birth of Jesus Christ. Traditions vary, but common elements include gift-giving, Christmas trees, and festive meals.

o **Vesak (Buddhist Countries):** Vesak, also known as Buddha Day, celebrates the birth, enlightenment, and death of Buddha. It is marked by prayer, meditation, and acts of kindness.

o **Chinese New Year: A 15-Day Celebration:** Chinese New Year is the most important festival in China. It's celebrated for 15 days, with the Lantern Festival marking its end. Red decorations and dragon dances are key highlights.

o **Christmas Markets (Germany):** German Christmas markets, known as *Weihnachtsmärkte*, are a festive tradition where people gather to enjoy mulled wine, gingerbread, and handmade crafts in a magical holiday atmosphere.

o **Semana Santa (Spain):** Semana Santa, or Holy Week, is a major Catholic celebration in Spain leading up to Easter, with solemn processions, religious rituals, and reenactments of the Passion of Christ.

o **Timkat (Ethiopia):** Timkat is the Ethiopian Orthodox celebration of Epiphany, commemorating the baptism of Jesus. It is marked by colorful processions and reenactments of the baptism in the Jordan River.

o **Up Helly Aa (Scotland):** Up Helly Aa is a Viking-inspired festival held in Shetland, Scotland, featuring a torch-lit procession and the burning of a Viking longship to celebrate the region's Norse heritage.

o **Durga Puja (India):** Durga Puja is a Hindu festival celebrating the goddess Durga's victory over the demon Mahishasura. It involves elaborate statues, music, dancing, and feasting.

o **Junkanoo (Bahamas):** Junkanoo is a Bahamian street parade celebrated on Boxing Day and New Year's Day, featuring colorful costumes, music, and dancing.

o **Bastille Day in France: A Revolution Remembered:** Bastille Day, celebrated on July 14th, marks the French Revolution's beginning in 1789. It's a national holiday in France, featuring parades, fireworks, and parties.

o **Naadam (Mongolia):** Naadam is Mongolia's largest festival, featuring the "Three Manly Games" of wrestling, horse racing, and archery, celebrating Mongolian culture and traditions.

- **Tet Trung Thu (Vietnam):** The Mid-Autumn Festival, or Tet Trung Thu, is celebrated with lantern parades, mooncakes, and performances to honor the harvest and the full moon.

- **Guy Fawkes Night: Bonfires and Fireworks:** On November 5th, the UK celebrates Guy Fawkes Night with bonfires and fireworks, commemorating the failed Gunpowder Plot of 1605, when Guy Fawkes tried to blow up the Houses of Parliament.

- **Losar (Tibet):** Losar is the Tibetan New Year celebration, lasting 15 days and featuring traditional songs, dances, and rituals to welcome the new year with prosperity and happiness.

- **The Highland Games (Scotland):** The Highland Games are traditional Scottish festivals featuring events like caber tossing, tug-of-war, and Highland dancing, celebrating Scottish culture and athleticism.

- **Spain's Grape Tradition:** In Spain, people celebrate New Year's Eve by eating 12 grapes at midnight, one for each stroke of the clock, to bring good luck for the coming year.

Cultural Celebrations

- **Kwanzaa: Honoring African Heritage:** Kwanzaa is a week-long celebration of African American culture and heritage, observed from December 26 to January 1. It emphasizes unity, self-determination, and community with a focus on seven guiding principles.

- **Carnival of Venice: A Masked Extravaganza:** The Carnival of Venice is famous for its elaborate masks and costumes. Dating back to the 12th century, this Italian festival celebrates the city's rich history and artistic flair.

- **Da de los Reyes: The Three Kings Day:** In many Spanish-speaking countries, Da de los Reyes (Three Kings Day) on January 6th is more significant than Christmas. Children receive gifts in honor of the Magi who visited baby Jesus.

- **Carnaval de Barranquilla (Colombia):** Barranquilla's Carnaval is one of the largest in Latin America, featuring vibrant parades, music, and dances like cumbia, showcasing Colombia's cultural diversity.

- **Pongal: A Harvest Celebration in India:** Pongal is a four-day harvest festival celebrated in Tamil Nadu, India. It's a time to thank the Sun God and nature for the bountiful harvest, with cooking, dancing, and decorating homes.

- **Tet Nguyen Dan: Vietnamese New Year:** Tet, the Vietnamese New Year, is the most important celebration in Vietnam. Families clean their homes, prepare special foods, and honor their ancestors to ensure good fortune for the coming year.

- **San Fermin (Spain):** The San Fermin festival in Pamplona is famous for the Running of the Bulls, where participants run through the city streets ahead of a group of bulls.

- **Navratri (India):** Navratri is a nine-night Hindu festival celebrating the goddess Durga. It features traditional dances like Garba and Dandiya, especially popular in the state of Gujarat.

- **Nowruz: Persian New Year:** Nowruz, the Persian New Year, marks the first day of spring and has been celebrated for over 3,000 years. It's observed in many countries, including Iran, Afghanistan, and parts of Central Asia.

- **Obon: Honoring Ancestors in Japan:** Obon is a Japanese Buddhist festival that honors the spirits of deceased ancestors. Families visit graves, light lanterns, and perform dances to welcome and send off the spirits.

- **Gion Matsuri: Japan's Famous Festival:** Gion Matsuri, held in Kyoto, Japan, is one of the country's most famous festivals. It features elaborate floats, traditional music, and processions that have been celebrated for over a thousand years.

- **Semana Santa: Holy Week in Spain:** Semana Santa, or Holy Week, is celebrated in Spain with solemn processions, elaborate floats, and religious ceremonies. It's a significant cultural event that draws thousands of visitors each year.

- **Midsummer: The Longest Day Celebration:** In Sweden, Midsummer is celebrated with dancing around a maypole, feasting, and enjoying the long daylight hours. It's one of the most important holidays in Swedish culture.

- **Powwow (North America):** Powwows are Native American cultural gatherings where tribes come together to celebrate their heritage with traditional dances, drumming, singing, and crafts.

- **Eid al-Adha: The Festival of Sacrifice:** Eid al-Adha is one of the holiest Islamic holidays, commemorating the willingness of Ibrahim to sacrifice his son in obedience to God. It's marked by prayers, feasts, and charity.

Festive Facts

- **Jingle Bells: A Thanksgiving Tune?:** The song "Jingle Bells" was originally written for Thanksgiving, not Christmas! Composed in 1857 by James Lord Pierpont, it became one of the most popular Christmas songs of all time.

- **The Tallest Christmas Tree Ever:** The world's tallest Christmas tree was a 221-foot Douglas fir erected in Seattle, Washington, in 1950. It was so tall that it required the use of multiple cranes to decorate.

- **New Year's Eve in Times Square:** The Times Square Ball Drop has been a New Year's Eve tradition in New York City since 1907. The ball is made of Waterford crystal and weighs nearly 12,000 pounds!

- **Easter Eggs: A Symbol of New Life:** Easter eggs symbolize new life and resurrection. The tradition of decorating eggs dates back to ancient times and has become a central part of Easter celebrations worldwide.

- **Why We Kiss Under the Mistletoe:** Kissing under the mistletoe during Christmas has roots in ancient Norse mythology, where the plant was a symbol of love and peace. The tradition became popular in Victorian England.

O **The Origin of Jack-O'-Lanterns:** Jack-o'-lanterns originated in Ireland, where people carved turnips to ward off evil spirits. When Irish immigrants came to America, they discovered that pumpkins were easier to carve.

O **The World's Largest Hanukkah Menorah:** The world's largest Hanukkah menorah stands 32 feet tall and is lit each year in New York City. It symbolizes the miracle of the oil that lasted eight days in the Jewish temple.

O **The First Halloween Parade:** The first Halloween parade in the U.S. was held in Anoka, Minnesota, in 1920. The town calls itself the "Halloween Capital of the World" and hosts an annual parade to this day.

O **The Longest Yule Log Cake:** The longest Yule log cake ever made was 1,068 feet long! This French Christmas dessert, also known as "bche de Nol," is traditionally shaped like a log to represent the warmth of the holiday season.

O **St. Patrick's Day:** St. Patrick's Day, celebrated on March 17, honors the patron saint of Ireland. People wear green and enjoy parades, music, and traditional Irish foods to celebrate Irish culture.

O **The World's Largest Pumpkin Pie:** The world's largest pumpkin pie, baked in 2010, weighed over 3,700 pounds and measured 20 feet in diameter. It was made with 1,212 pounds of pumpkin and 525 pounds of sugar.

O **Groundhog Day: Predicting Spring:** Groundhog Day is celebrated on February 2nd in the U.S. and Canada. According to folklore, if a groundhog sees its shadow, there will be six more weeks of winter; if not, spring will arrive early.

O **The Longest Lunar New Year Celebration:** The Lunar New Year is celebrated for 15 days in many Asian countries, with each day having its own customs and traditions. It's the longest and most important festival in the Chinese calendar. In some parts of China, it lasts for a whole month!

O **Piñatas: A Symbol of Hope:** Piñatas, often seen at Mexican celebrations, were originally clay pots filled with sweets. The act of breaking them symbolizes the triumph of good over evil and the rewards of hope.

O **The World's Largest Easter Egg:** The largest Easter egg ever made was over 25 feet tall and weighed 8,968 pounds. This giant chocolate egg was created in Italy in 2011 and broke a world record.

Fun Festivities

O **Pancake Day (UK):** Shrove Tuesday, or Pancake Day, is celebrated in the UK with pancake flipping races and feasts of pancakes before the Christian season of Lent.

O **Lantern Festivals Light Up the Sky:** In Taiwan, the Pingxi Sky Lantern Festival is a magical event where thousands of glowing lanterns are released into the night sky, symbolizing hopes and dreams for the future.

- **The Running of the Bulls in Spain:** Every July, the streets of Pamplona, Spain, come alive with the Running of the Bulls during the San Fermn festival. Brave participants run ahead of a group of charging bulls.

- **Snow & Ice Festival (China):** The Harbin International Snow and Ice Festival in China is the largest of its kind, showcasing giant ice sculptures, ice castles, and intricate snow carvings.

- **Albuquerque Balloon Fiesta:** The Albuquerque International Balloon Fiesta in New Mexico is the largest hot air balloon festival in the world. Hundreds of colorful balloons take to the skies, creating a breathtaking sight.

- **Boryeong Mud Festival in South Korea:** The Boryeong Mud Festival, held on Daecheon Beach in South Korea, is a messy, fun event where visitors enjoy mud wrestling, mudslides, and even mud swimming. It's a celebration of health and wellness.

- **Cheese Rolling at Cooper's Hill:** In Gloucestershire, England, people race down a steep hill chasing a round of cheese during the annual Cooper's Hill Cheese-Rolling event. The first to reach the bottom wins the cheese!

- **Krampusnacht (Austria):** On Krampusnacht, December 5th, Austrians celebrate a quirky tradition where Krampus, a scary creature, roams the streets to "punish" naughty children before St. Nicholas Day.

- **Up Helly Aa: A Viking Fire Festival:** Up Helly Aa is a fire festival in Scotland that celebrates the Viking heritage of the Shetland Islands. The highlight is the burning of a replica Viking ship by torchlight.

- **Monkey Buffet Festival in Thailand:** The Monkey Buffet Festival in Lopburi, Thailand, is held annually to honor the local monkey population. Bananas, fruits, and treats are laid out in a feast for the macaques.

- **Sinulog Festival (Philippines):** Sinulog Festival in Cebu is a lively event filled with street dancing, parades, and traditional rituals in honor of the Santo Niño (Child Jesus).

- **Pillow Fight Day:** International Pillow Fight Day is celebrated in cities around the world, where people gather in public spaces for a massive pillow fight. It's all about fun and letting off some steam!

- **Battle of the Oranges in Italy:** The Battle of the Oranges is an annual carnival in Ivrea, Italy, where teams of participants throw oranges at each other in a re-enactment of a historic battle. It's a juicy showdown!

- **Fte de la Musique (France):** Fte de la Musique is a global music celebration that started in France, where musicians of all levels take to the streets on June 21st to perform for free.

- **Elfstedentocht: The Ultimate Ice Skating Challenge:** The Elfstedentocht, or Eleven Cities Tour, is a 200-kilometer ice skating race held in the Netherlands whenever the canals freeze solid enough. It's the world's largest and longest ice skating event.

Holiday Histories

O **The Origins of Halloween:** Halloween's roots trace back over 2,000 years to the ancient Celtic festival of Samhain. The Celts believed that on October 31st, the boundary between the living and the dead blurred.

O **Lohri (India):** Lohri is a Punjabi festival celebrated in January to mark the end of winter and the arrival of longer days. It involves bonfires, singing, and dancing around the flames.

O **The Real St. Valentine:** Valentine's Day is named after St. Valentine, a Roman priest who secretly married couples when Emperor Claudius II banned marriage. He was martyred on February 14th, 269 AD.

O **Hanukkah's Eight Days of Light:** Hanukkah, the Jewish Festival of Lights, commemorates the rededication of the Second Temple in Jerusalem. The menorah is lit for eight days, symbolizing the miracle of oil that lasted eight nights.

O **Christmas Trees: A German Tradition:** The Christmas tree tradition began in 16th-century Germany when devout Christians brought decorated trees into their homes. The custom was popularized in England by Prince Albert, Queen Victoria's husband.

O **Easter's Connection to Pagan Rituals:** Many Easter traditions, like the Easter Bunny and eggs, have roots in pre-Christian pagan festivals celebrating spring and renewal. The holiday later became associated with the resurrection of Jesus Christ.

O **The First Earth Day:** Earth Day was first celebrated on April 22, 1970, in response to growing environmental concerns. It sparked the modern environmental movement, leading to significant policy changes in the United States.

O **Purim:** Purim celebrates the salvation of the Jewish people in ancient Persia from the plot of Haman, as told in the Book of Esther. It is celebrated with costumes, feasts, and giving to the poor.

O **King's Day (Netherlands):** King's Day, celebrated on April 27th, marks the birthday of King Willem-Alexander of the Netherlands. It is celebrated with street parties, flea markets, and everyone wearing orange.

O **The Evolution of New Year's Resolutions:** The tradition of making New Year's resolutions dates back to ancient Babylon, where people made promises to the gods to repay debts and return borrowed items at the start of each year.

O **The Origins of April Fool's Day:** April Fool's Day dates back to 16th-century France when the calendar was changed. People who continued to celebrate the New Year in April were called "April fools" and became the target of pranks.

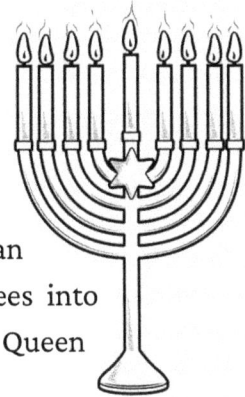

- **The First International Women's Day:** International Women's Day, celebrated on March 8th, was first observed in 1911. It began as a movement for women's rights, including suffrage and labor rights, and is now a global celebration of women's achievements.

- **Boxing Day: A Gift-Giving Tradition:** Boxing Day, celebrated on December 26th in the UK and Commonwealth countries, originated in the Middle Ages. It was a day when the wealthy gave gifts and money to their servants and the poor.

- **The Birth of Labor Day:** Labor Day in the United States was first celebrated in 1882 in New York City. It honors the contributions of American workers and the labor movement, and it became a national holiday in 1894.

- **Sinterklaas (Netherlands/Belgium):** Sinterklaas, celebrated on December 5th, is a Dutch and Belgian holiday where children receive gifts from St. Nicholas, who arrives by boat from Spain.

Unique Traditions

- **Las Posadas:** Las Posadas is a nine-day Christmas festival in Mexico that re-enacts the journey of Mary and Joseph searching for a place to stay. Celebrations include processions, songs, and traditional foods.

- **The Japanese Tradition of Eating KFC on Christmas:** In Japan, a popular Christmas tradition is to enjoy a meal from KFC. The practice began in the 1970s due to a successful marketing campaign, and now millions of Japanese families participate every year.

- **The Radish Festival in Mexico:** In Oaxaca, Mexico, the Night of the Radishes (Noche de Rábanos) is celebrated on December 23rd. People carve radishes into elaborate scenes, competing for prizes in this unique Christmas event.

- **Breaking Plates for Good Luck in Denmark:** On New Year's Eve, Danes throw old plates and dishes at the doors of friends and family. The bigger the pile of broken dishes, the more luck the person will have in the coming year.

- **The Philippines' Giant Lantern Festival:** The Giant Lantern Festival in San Fernando, Philippines, showcases enormous, intricate lanterns illuminated in dazzling displays. This annual event is known as the "Christmas Capital of the Philippines."

- **Finland's Christmas Sauna:** In Finland, it's traditional to take a sauna on Christmas Eve. Families relax and cleanse themselves before the holiday, believing it helps them start Christmas fresh and renewed.

- **Australia's Christmas on the Beach:** In Australia, where Christmas falls in the summer, many families celebrate the holiday with a barbecue on the beach. It's common to see Santa Claus in swimwear rather than his traditional suit.

- **Scotland's Hogmanay Fireball Ceremony:** In Stonehaven, Scotland, Hogmanay (New Year's Eve) is celebrated with a fireball ceremony. Participants swing blazing balls of fire around their heads as they parade through the streets.

O **The Italian Befana:** In Italy, the Befana, a friendly witch, delivers gifts to children on the night of January 5th. According to legend, she missed seeing baby Jesus and has been searching for him ever since.

O **Hatsumode (Japan):** Hatsumode is the Japanese tradition of visiting a Shinto shrine or Buddhist temple on New Year's Day to pray for good fortune in the coming year.

O **The Caga Tió in Catalonia:** In Catalonia, Spain, children feed a wooden log called "Caga Tió" (the pooping log) throughout December. On Christmas Eve, they hit it with sticks to make it "poop" out presents.

O **Gävle Goat: Sweden's Giant Straw Figure:** In Gävle, Sweden, a giant straw goat is erected every Christmas. Unfortunately, it's often targeted by vandals and has been burned down more than 30 times since its first appearance in 1966.

O **Colombia's Day of the Little Candles:** Da de las Velitas, or Day of the Little Candles, marks the start of the Christmas season in Colombia. On December 7th, people place candles and lanterns in their windows and streets to honor the Virgin Mary.

O **Polterabend (Germany):** In this pre-wedding tradition, German couples' friends and family gather to break porcelain, believing that the noise wards off evil spirits and brings good fortune to the marriage.

O **Germany's St. Nicholas Day:** On December 6th, German children leave their shoes out in hopes that St. Nicholas will fill them with treats. This tradition celebrates the feast day of the saint who inspired the modern-day Santa Claus.

Every tradition, every festive occasion, carries within it a vibrant story, a thread that weaves us into the grand tapestry of human history and shared joy. Whether it's the heartwarming glow of a Christmas hearth or the exuberant energy of a local festival, holidays remind us of the beautiful connections we share.

Coming right up! - from bizarre old laws that are still on the books to the legal decisions that changed history, this chapter goes into the justice system that govern our lives. So let's discover the intriguing, and sometimes surprising, world of law and order!

Justice, Laws & Legalese

Famous Court Cases

O **Brown v. Board of Education (1954):** In this important case, the U.S. Supreme Court decided that separating Black and white students in different schools was unfair and wrong. This helped to end school segregation in America.

O **Roe v. Wade (1973):** This case allowed women in the United States to make their own decisions about whether or not to have a baby, giving them more control over their own bodies.

O **The Trial of Socrates (399 BC):** Socrates, a wise teacher from ancient Greece, was put on trial because people thought he was teaching bad ideas. He had to drink poison as punishment, making him a symbol of standing up for what you believe.

O **The Scopes "Monkey" Trial (1925):** In this case, a teacher named John Scopes was taken to court for teaching evolution, the idea that humans came from animals. That violated a Tennessee state law at the time The trial made people talk about science and religion.

O **Nuremberg Trials (1945-1946):** After World War II, leaders of Nazi Germany were put on trial for their terrible actions. These trials showed that even powerful people can be punished for doing wrong.

O **Miranda v. Arizona (1966):** This case led to the creation of "Miranda Rights," which means that police must tell people they have the right to remain silent and have a lawyer if they're arrested.

O **United States v. Nixon (1974):** The Supreme Court ruled that President Nixon had to share secret tapes related to a scandal. This showed that even the president has to follow the law, leading to his resignation.

O **Simpson Trial (1995):** O.J. Simpson, a famous football player, was on trial for the deaths of two people. The trial was watched by millions, and he was found not guilty, which surprised many people.

O **Loving v. Virginia (1967):** This case ended laws that said people of different races couldn't get married. It all started because a couple, one Black and one white, wanted to be together.

O **Dred Scott v. Sandford (1857):** In this case, the Supreme Court decided that Black people, whether free or enslaved, couldn't be American citizens. This decision was a big reason why the Civil War started.

O **The Trial of Galileo (1633):** Galileo, a scientist, was put on trial by the church for saying that the Earth revolves around the Sun. He was forced to say he was wrong, but later, people realized he was right.

- **Marbury v. Madison (1803):** This case helped establish that the Supreme Court could decide if laws were fair. It gave the court the power to say when something is against the rules.

- **The Trial of Joan of Arc (1431):** Joan of Arc, a young French hero, was put on trial for being a witch because of her bravery in battle. She was burned at the stake, but later, people saw her as a saint.

- **Plessy v. Ferguson (1896):** This case said it was okay to keep Black and white people separate, as long as things were "equal." But it wasn't fair, and this idea was later overturned by other cases.

- **Gideon v. Wainwright (1963):** This case decided that everyone, no matter how rich or poor, has the right to a lawyer in court. It made sure people would be treated more fairly in the justice system.

Funny Laws

- **No Chewing Gum in Singapore:** In Singapore, it's illegal to chew gum, except for medical purposes. The law was introduced to keep the city clean after people kept sticking gum on public property.

- **No Selfies with Monkeys in Indonesia:** Taking selfies with monkeys is banned in Bali, Indonesia, to protect the animals from stress and being harassed by tourists.

- **No Sleeping in Cheese Factories in South Dakota:** In South Dakota, it's against the law to sleep in a cheese factory. This unusual law may have been created to keep workers alert and productive.

- **No Wearing High Heels in Ancient Sites in Greece:** In Greece, visitors aren't allowed to wear high heels at ancient sites like the Acropolis. This law helps protect the delicate ruins from damage.

- **No Flushing Toilets After 10 PM in Switzerland:** In Switzerland, it's illegal to flush the toilet after 10 PM in some apartment buildings. This is to avoid disturbing neighbors with noise.

- **No Exploding Nuclear Bombs in California:** In California, it's illegal to detonate a nuclear device within the city limits. The fine? Just $500. Thankfully, no one's tried it!

- **No Moose on the Sidewalks in Alaska:** In Fairbanks, Alaska, it's illegal to let a moose walk on the sidewalks. This law was created to prevent traffic jams and accidents caused by large animals.

- **No Wearing a Fake Mustache in Church in Alabama:** In Alabama, it's against the law to wear a fake mustache that causes laughter in church. This law was likely meant to keep services respectful and free from distractions.

- **No Whistling Underwater in Vermont:** In Vermont, it's technically illegal to whistle underwater. This is more of a joke than an actual law, but it's still on the books!

- **No Holding Salmon Suspiciously in the UK:** In the UK, it's illegal to handle salmon in suspicious circumstances under the Salmon Act of 1986. This law helps prevent illegal fishing and trade.

- **No Winnie the Pooh in Polish Playgrounds:** In Poland, Winnie the Pooh is banned from playgrounds because he's seen as "inappropriate" for not wearing pants. This was debated in the town of Tuszyn.

- **No Eating of Ice Cream in Prohibited Areas in Canada:** In Canada, it's illegal to have ice cream on Bank Street in Ottawa on Sundays. This quirky law dates back to the 1800s.

- **No Running Out of Fuel on The Autobahn:** It is technically illegal to stop unnecessarily whilst traveling on the autobahn, and stopping due to a fuel shortage is considered avoidable. Hence if you run out of fuel, you may be subject to a fine

- **No Camouflage Clothing in the Caribbean:** In many Caribbean countries, it's illegal for civilians to wear camouflage clothing. This law is to prevent confusion with military personnel.

- **Guinea Pig Companionship Law:** In Switzerland, it's illegal to own just one guinea pig. The law ensures they have companionship, as guinea pigs are social animals prone to loneliness.

- **No Sharing Your Netflix Password in Tennessee:** In Tennessee, it's illegal to share your Netflix password. The law aims to stop people from accessing services they haven't paid for.

Historic Law Moments

- **Magna Carta (1215):** The Magna Carta, signed in 1215 by King John of England, was the first document to limit the power of the king and establish that everyone, including the ruler, is subject to the law.

- **The Emancipation Proclamation (1863):** Issued by President Abraham Lincoln during the American Civil War, the Emancipation Proclamation declared that all slaves in the Confederate states were free, paving the way for the abolition of slavery in the U.S.

- **The Code of Hammurabi (circa 1754 BCE):** The Code of Hammurabi, one of the oldest written legal codes, was created by the Babylonian king Hammurabi. It included laws like "an eye for an eye," establishing early principles of justice.

- **The Civil Rights Act (1964):** The U.S. Civil Rights Act of 1964 was a landmark law that banned discrimination based on race, color, religion, sex, or national origin, making it illegal to segregate schools, workplaces, and public places.

- **The Nineteenth Amendment (1920):** The Nineteenth Amendment to the U.S. Constitution granted women the right to vote, marking a major victory for the women's suffrage movement and expanding democracy in America.

- **The Declaration of Independence (1776):** The Declaration of Independence, adopted on July 4, 1776, declared the thirteen American colonies free from British rule and laid the foundation for the United States' laws and government.

- **The Universal Declaration of Human Rights (1948):** Adopted by the United Nations in 1948, this declaration set out fundamental human rights to be universally protected, marking a historic milestone in the fight for global justice and equality.

- **The Abolition of Slavery Act (1833):** The Slavery Abolition Act of 1833 ended slavery in most of the British Empire. This historic law freed over 800,000 enslaved people and was a significant step toward human rights.

- **The Great Charter of the Forest (1217):** Often overlooked in comparison to the Magna Carta, this charter protected the rights of common people to use royal forests for grazing, fuel, and other necessities, demonstrating early concerns for environmental justice and sustainable use of resources.

- **The Voting Rights Act (1965):** The U.S. Voting Rights Act of 1965 outlawed discriminatory voting practices, like literacy tests, that had been used to prevent African Americans from voting, strengthening democracy in America.

- **The Americans with Disabilities Act (1990):** The Americans with Disabilities Act (ADA) was passed to prohibit discrimination against individuals with disabilities in all areas of public life, including employment, education, and transportation.

- **The Bill of Rights (1791):** The first ten amendments to the U.S. Constitution, known as the Bill of Rights, were ratified in 1791. These amendments protect individual freedoms, like speech and religion, and limit government power.

- **The Establishment of the European Union (1993):** The Maastricht Treaty, signed in 1992 and effective in 1993, created the European Union, a political and economic union of European countries aimed at promoting peace and prosperity.

- **The Habeas Corpus Act (1679):** The Habeas Corpus Act, passed by the English Parliament, strengthened the right of individuals to challenge unlawful detention, becoming a cornerstone of modern legal systems.

- **The First Geneva Convention (1864):** The First Geneva Convention established rules for the humane treatment of wounded soldiers during war. It marked the beginning of international humanitarian law, protecting those not involved in the fighting.

Laws Around the World

- **No Cutting Down Cacti in Arizona:** In Arizona, it's illegal to cut down a Saguaro cactus without permission. These cacti can live for over 200 years, and harming one can lead to heavy fines or even jail time.

- **Ban on Kinder Eggs in the USA:** In the United States, the famous Kinder Surprise chocolate eggs are banned because they contain a non-food item (the toy) inside, which is against U.S. food regulations.

- **No High Fives on School Property in Massachusetts:** In some Massachusetts schools, giving high fives or engaging in "horseplay" is banned. These rules are meant to reduce distractions and ensure a focus on learning.

o **No Spitting in Public in Singapore:** In Singapore, spitting in public is illegal and can result in a hefty fine. This law is part of the city-state's efforts to maintain cleanliness and hygiene.

o **No Wearing Masks in Public in Denmark:** In Denmark, it's illegal to wear masks or face coverings in public, including during protests. The law is meant to prevent people from hiding their identities.

o **Longyearbyen's No-Burial Zone:** In Longyearbyen, Norway, it's illegal to be buried because bodies don't decompose in the permafrost. Terminally ill residents are sent to other areas to pass away.

o **No Naming Your Baby "Elvis" in Sweden:** Sweden has strict naming laws, and parents cannot name their child "Elvis." The government has to approve baby names to ensure they won't cause harm or embarrassment to the child.

o **Banning of Plastic Bags in Rwanda:** Rwanda implemented one of the strictest bans on plastic bags in the world in 2008, making it illegal to import, manufacture, or use them as part of the country's environmental conservation efforts.

o **No Littering in Japan:** In Japan, littering is not just frowned upon; it's illegal in many areas, with strict fines for those caught. This law is part of Japan's commitment to maintaining cleanliness and environmental responsibility.

o **No Driving Without Headlights in Sweden:** In Sweden, drivers must keep their headlights on at all times, even during the day. This law is intended to improve visibility and reduce accidents.

o **No Public Displays of Affection in Dubai:** In Dubai, public displays of affection, such as kissing or holding hands, are illegal and can lead to fines or imprisonment, as the city has strict decency laws.

o **No Jaywalking in Germany:** In Germany, jaywalking (crossing the street without using a crosswalk) is illegal, and pedestrians can be fined. The law is strictly enforced to maintain safety and order.

o **Child Labor Ban (Brazil, 1988):** Brazil's constitution prohibits children under the age of 16 from working, except in apprenticeships, to combat child labor and ensure access to education.

o **No Drunk Driving in South Africa:** South Africa has one of the strictest drunk driving laws in the world. Drivers can face severe penalties if caught with any alcohol in their system while driving.

o **No Drones Over Cities in France:** In France, it's illegal to fly drones over cities without special permission. This law is designed to protect people's privacy and ensure safety in urban areas.

o **No Swearing in Australia:** In Australia, swearing in public is illegal in some states and can lead to fines. This law is intended to maintain public decency and respect.

Wacky and Weird Laws

○ **No Silly String in Public in Southington, Connecticut:** In Southington, Connecticut, it's illegal to use Silly String in public spaces. The law was introduced to prevent litter and property damage during Halloween.

○ **No Making Faces at Dogs:** In Oklahoma, it's illegal to make faces at a dog. The law was designed to prevent the harassment of animals and can result in fines or even jail time.

○ **No Ice Cream Cones in Back Pockets in Alabama:** In Alabama, it's illegal to carry an ice cream cone in your back pocket. This law was originally created to prevent horse theft, as people used to lure horses away with ice cream.

○ **No Crossing the Street on a Sunday in Mexico City:** In Mexico City, it's technically illegal to cross the street on Sundays without looking both ways first. While it's not heavily enforced, the law is meant to keep pedestrians safe.

○ **No Forgetting Your Wife's Birthday in Samoa:** In Samoa, it's illegal for husbands to forget their wife's birthday. The penalty? Sleeping on the couch, along with a fine! This law is meant to encourage marital harmony.

○ **No Dying in Parliament in the UK:** In the UK, it's illegal to die in the Houses of Parliament. This strange law is based on the idea that anyone who dies in a royal palace must receive a state funeral.

○ **No Public Flatulence on Thursdays After 6 PM in Florida:** In Florida, there's an old law that supposedly makes it illegal to pass gas in public places after 6 PM on Thursdays. While it's not enforced, it's still on the books!

○ **No Wearing Pants in Public in France:** At one time, it was illegal for women to wear pants in public in Paris without permission from the police. The law, created in the 1800s, was finally repealed in 2013.

○ **No Climbing Trees in Oshawa, Ontario:** In Oshawa, Ontario, it's illegal to climb a tree in any city park. The law is meant to protect both people and the trees themselves from harm.

○ **No Sharing Photos of Dogs Without Permission in Iran:** In Iran, it's illegal to post pictures of your pet dog on social media without permission from authorities. The law is part of the country's strict regulations on pet ownership.

○ **Don't Feed the Pigeons (Venice, Italy):** Feeding pigeons in Venice has been illegal since 2008 to reduce bird-related damage to historic buildings and prevent an overpopulation of pigeons.

○ **No Bike Riding in Swimming Pools in California:** In California, it's against the law to ride your bike in a swimming pool. This bizarre rule is aimed at preventing accidents and protecting public property.

- **No Disguising Your Cat in Florida:** In Florida, it's illegal to disguise your pet cat. This strange law may have been created to prevent people from sneaking their cats into places where pets are not allowed.

- **No Public Displays of Pastry in Quebec:** In Quebec, Canada, it was once illegal to display more than two types of pastry in a store window. This law was part of an effort to prevent food waste.

- **No Ketchup in French School Cafeterias:** In France, it's illegal to serve ketchup in school cafeterias, except when it's paired with French fries. This law was passed to preserve traditional French cuisine and eating habits.

- **No Singing While Wearing a Swimsuit in Florida:** In Florida, it's illegal to sing while wearing a swimsuit in public. This old law might have been created to keep beaches and pools more family-friendly and respectable.

Weird Legal Stories

- **The Man Who Sued Himself:** In 1995, a man from Kentucky, Robert Lee Brock, sued himself for $5 million, claiming he violated his own civil rights by getting drunk and committing crimes. The case was dismissed.

- **The Stolen Toaster Court Case:** In 1964, a man in England was fined for stealing a toaster. He defended himself by saying he only wanted to make toast for breakfast, but the judge didn't buy it.

- **The Monkey Selfie Lawsuit:** In 2011, a monkey named Naruto took a selfie with a photographer's camera. The photographer and PETA (People for the Ethical Treatment of Animals) ended up in a legal battle over who owned the rights to the photo.

- **The Haunted House Case:** In 1991, a New York court ruled that a house was legally "haunted" after the seller didn't disclose the ghostly reputation to the buyer. The case became known as the "Ghostbusters ruling."

- **The Case of the Missing Pants:** In 2005, a man in Washington, D.C., sued a dry cleaner for $67 million after they lost his pants. The lawsuit, which became famous for its outrageous demand, was eventually dismissed.

- **The Time a Dog Was Put on Trial:** In the 13th century, a pig in France was put on trial for murder after it killed a child. The pig was found guilty and was publicly executed in one of history's strangest legal cases.

- **The Case of the Flying Salmon:** In 2008, a man in Seattle was fined for throwing a salmon at a fish market. He claimed it was a joke, but the court ruled it as an assault with a fish!

- **The Case of the Burnt Coffee:** In 1992, a woman sued McDonald's after spilling hot coffee on herself and suffering third-degree burns. She was awarded nearly $3 million in damages, making it one of the most famous personal injury cases ever.

o **The Case of the Disappearing Sausage:** In 2017, a man in Germany sued his neighbor for stealing a sausage from his barbecue. The neighbor claimed it was an accident, but the court ordered him to replace the sausage.

o **The Lady Who Sued for Being Too Scared:** In 2000, a woman in California sued a theme park for scaring her too much in a haunted house attraction. She claimed emotional distress, but the court dismissed the case, saying it was "all in good fun."

o **The Man Who Sued a Casino for Letting Him Win:** In 2013, a man in New Jersey sued a casino for $500,000, claiming they let him win while he was drunk, which led to him losing it all later. The court sided with the casino.

o **The Fake Burglary:** In 2011, a man in Italy staged a fake burglary at his home to get insurance money. He accidentally called the police himself, thinking he was calling the insurance company, and was arrested.

o **It's Illegal to Wear Armor in Parliament:** In 1313, a law was passed in the UK banning the wearing of armor in Parliament. This medieval law is still in effect today!

o **The Man Who Sued for Not Being Invited to a Party:** In 2015, a man in Switzerland sued his coworkers for not inviting him to an office party. He claimed it was discrimination, but the court ruled that people are free to invite whoever they want.

o **The Woman Who Sued a TV Show for Failing to Make Her a Millionaire:** In 2006, a contestant on the game show "Deal or No Deal" sued the show for not offering her a higher amount of money, claiming it was unfair. The case was thrown out by the court.

From ancient codes to modern-day rulings, it's clear that laws have shaped societies in fascinating and unexpected ways. But we're not at the end yet – there's more to explore!

Get ready to discover the mind-blowing medical world. Explore the marvels of the human body, and meet the people who revolutionized healthcare. From ancient remedies to cutting-edge technology, this chapter promises to be both enlightening and inspiring. Let's go!

Wellness Wisdom

Breakthrough Treatments

O **Cochlear Implants: Restoring Hearing:** Cochlear implants, first approved in the 1980s, have transformed the lives of people with severe hearing loss by allowing them to hear sounds through electronic devices.

O **Proton Therapy: Targeting Tumors:** Proton therapy, a type of radiation treatment developed in the 1950s, uses protons instead of X-rays to precisely target tumors, reducing damage to surrounding healthy tissues.

O **3D Printing & Artificial Organs:** 3D bioprinting involves using a specialized printer to create three-dimensional structures layer by layer, using a "bio-ink" that contains living cells, growth factors, and other biomaterials. This breakthrough technology offers hope for overcoming the shortage of organ donors and reducing the risk of rejection, potentially saving countless lives in the future.

O **Immunotherapy: Harnessing the Immune System:** Immunotherapy, developed in the 21st century, uses the body's immune system to fight cancer. It has shown remarkable success in treating cancers that were once considered untreatable.

O **Monoclonal Antibodies: Targeted Treatments:** Monoclonal antibodies, first used in the 1980s, are lab-made proteins that can target specific cells, making them effective treatments for diseases like cancer and autoimmune disorders.

O **Bionic Limbs: Restoring Mobility:** Bionic limbs, developed with advanced robotics, have given amputees the ability to move and control artificial limbs with their minds, dramatically improving quality of life.

O **Deep Brain Stimulation: Treating Parkinson's:** Deep brain stimulation (DBS) was first used in the 1990s to treat Parkinson's disease. It involves implanting electrodes in the brain to reduce tremors and improve motor function.

O **Herceptin for Breast Cancer (1998):** Herceptin (trastuzumab) is a targeted therapy for HER2-positive breast cancer, dramatically improving survival rates for patients with this aggressive cancer subtype.

O **Artificial Pancreas: Managing Diabetes:** Approved in 2016, the artificial pancreas automatically monitors and regulates blood sugar levels in people with type 1 diabetes, mimicking the function of a healthy pancreas.

O **Targeted Cancer Therapies: Precision Medicine:** Targeted cancer therapies, developed in the 2000s, attack specific cancer cells based on their genetic makeup, offering personalized treatment with fewer side effects than traditional chemotherapy.

O **TAVR: Heart Valve Replacement Without Surgery:** Transcatheter aortic valve replacement (TAVR), first used in humans in 2002 and further developed in the 2010s, allows doctors to replace a failing heart valve without open-heart surgery, offering a safer option for patients.

O **Stem Cell Therapy: Regenerating Tissues:** Stem cell therapy, still in its experimental stages, uses stem cells to regenerate damaged tissues and treat conditions like spinal cord injuries, Parkinson's disease, and more.

O **CAR T-Cell Therapy: Engineering Immune Cells:** CAR T-cell therapy, first approved in 2017, involves genetically engineering a patient's T-cells to attack cancer cells, showing promising results in treating blood cancers.

O **Telemedicine: Virtual Healthcare:** Telemedicine, which became widespread during the COVID-19 pandemic, allows patients to receive medical care through video calls, making healthcare more accessible and convenient.

O **mRNA Vaccines: A New Approach to Immunization:** mRNA vaccines, first used widely in the COVID-19 pandemic, teach cells to produce a protein that triggers an immune response, offering a new method of preventing infectious diseases.

Health Heroes

O **Florence Nightingale: The Lady with the Lamp:** Florence Nightingale revolutionized nursing during the Crimean War by improving sanitary conditions in hospitals, reducing the death rate, and laying the foundation for modern nursing practices.

O **Dr. Ignaz Semmelweis:** Dr. Ignaz Semmelweis was an early advocate for handwashing in hospitals in the 1840s, dramatically reducing maternal deaths from infections and earning the title "savior of mothers."

O **Dr. Mary Edwards Walker:** Dr. Mary Edwards Walker was a pioneering surgeon during the American Civil War and received the U.S. Medal of Honor for her service.

O **Paul Farmer: Champion of Global Health:** Paul Farmer co-founded Partners In Health, providing healthcare to impoverished communities worldwide. His work in Haiti, Rwanda, and beyond has saved countless lives and improved global health equity.

O **The Persian Polymath:** Avicenna (Ibn Sina), a Persian physician and philosopher, authored "The Canon of Medicine," a medical encyclopedia that remained a standard text in European universities until the 17th century. His work encompassed anatomy, physiology, pharmacology, and psychology.

O **The Father of Ophthalmology:** Ibn al-Haytham, an Arab scientist and mathematician, made significant contributions to the understanding of vision and optics. His work laid the foundation for the development of eyeglasses and other optical instruments.

- **Dr. Albert Schweitzer:** Dr. Albert Schweitzer was a physician, theologian, and humanitarian who established a hospital in Gabon, Africa, and won the Nobel Peace Prize in 1952 for his medical mission work.

- **Henrietta Lacks: The Woman Behind HeLa Cells:** Henrietta Lacks unknowingly contributed to science when her cancer cells were taken without her consent in 1951. Her cells, known as HeLa, have been crucial in countless medical breakthroughs.

- **William Harvey: Discoverer of Blood Circulation:** In 1628, William Harvey published his findings on blood circulation, revolutionizing the understanding of the human body and laying the groundwork for modern cardiology.

- **Elizabeth Blackwell: First Female Doctor in the U.S.:** Elizabeth Blackwell became the first woman to receive a medical degree in the U.S. in 1849, breaking barriers for women in medicine and inspiring future generations of female doctors.

- **Joseph Lister: Pioneer of Antiseptic Surgery:** Joseph Lister introduced antiseptic techniques in surgery in the 1860s, drastically reducing infections and revolutionizing the safety of medical procedures.

- **Virginia Apgar: Inventor of the Apgar Score:** In 1952, Virginia Apgar created the Apgar Score, a quick test to assess the health of newborns, which has saved countless lives by ensuring immediate medical care for at-risk infants.

- **Andreas Vesalius: Father of Modern Anatomy:** In 1543, Andreas Vesalius published "De Humani Corporis Fabrica," a groundbreaking book on human anatomy, challenging outdated beliefs and advancing the study of medicine.

- **Dr. James McCune Smith:** Dr. James McCune Smith was the first African American to earn a medical degree (in 1837) and used his medical knowledge to advocate for the abolition of slavery and civil rights.

- **Vivien Thomas: Pioneer in Cardiac Surgery:** Vivien Thomas, an African American surgical technician, developed techniques for heart surgery in the 1940s, including the first successful open-heart surgery on a baby, despite having no formal medical education.

Medical Marvels

- **Conjoined Twins Separation Surgery:** Surgical techniques started in the 1950s have now advanced to successfully separate conjoined twins, dramatically improving survival and quality of life for both twins.

- **Face Transplants: A New Identity:** The first successful face transplant was performed in 2005 in France. Since then, this life-changing surgery has helped patients regain their appearance and confidence after severe injuries.

- **Bionic Eyes: Restoring Sight:** Bionic eyes, such as the Argus II, use a retinal implant and a special camera to restore partial vision to people with certain types of blindness, offering hope to the visually impaired.

- **Regenerative Dentistry:** Scientists are working on developing techniques to regenerate teeth using stem cells and other biomaterials. While still in its early stages, this research could potentially eliminate the need for dentures and implants, offering a more natural solution for tooth loss.

- **Prosthetic Limbs with Sensation:** Advanced prosthetics now include sensors that allow users to feel touch and pressure, making artificial limbs more lifelike and improving the quality of life for amputees.

- **Brain-Computer Interfaces: Mind Control:** Brain-computer interfaces (BCIs) allow people to control devices with their thoughts. These devices are being developed to help paralyzed individuals regain mobility and communication.

- **Artificial Intelligence in Diagnosis:** AI-powered systems are now being used to diagnose diseases, such as cancer, more accurately and quickly than traditional methods, revolutionizing medical diagnostics.

- **Exoskeletons: Walking Again:** Robotic exoskeletons, like the ReWalk, enable people with spinal cord injuries to walk again by providing motorized support and movement, offering new possibilities for rehabilitation.

- **Lab-Grown Skin: Healing Severe Burns:** Scientists have developed lab-grown skin that can be grafted onto patients with severe burns. This medical marvel speeds up healing and reduces the risk of infection.

- **Tissue Engineering: Building Body Parts:** Tissue engineering involves growing tissues and organs in the lab using a patient's cells. This technique has been used to create new bladders, blood vessels, and more.

- **First Successful Hand Transplant:** In 1998, surgeons in France performed the first successful hand transplant, and since then, several patients have regained functional use of their new limbs.

- **Gene Therapy: Fixing Faulty Genes:** Gene therapy, first approved in 2017, involves altering a person's genes to treat or cure diseases. It has shown promise in treating genetic disorders like hemophilia and muscular dystrophy.

- **Nanomedicine: Tiny Treatments:** Nanomedicine uses tiny particles to deliver drugs directly to diseased cells, improving the effectiveness of treatments while reducing side effects. It's a cutting-edge field with huge potential.

- **Smart Pills:** Smart pills, equipped with sensors, cameras, and transmitters, can track digestion and monitor internal organs, providing real-time data to doctors for diagnosing digestive issues.

- **Artificial Blood: A Life-Saving Substitute:** Artificial blood, still in development, could one day replace the need for blood donations. These blood substitutes can carry oxygen and are especially useful in emergencies.

Medical Mysteries

- **The Folks Who Cannot Feel Pain (Congenital Insensitivity):** People with congenital insensitivity to pain (CIP) cannot feel physical pain, a rare genetic disorder that can lead to unnoticed injuries and infections.

- **The Cause of Alzheimer's Disease:** Alzheimer's disease is one of the most common forms of dementia, yet its exact cause is still not fully understood. Researchers continue to investigate its links to genetics and lifestyle factors.

- **The Case of the "Sleeping Sickness":** Between 1916 and 1927, millions of people were affected by encephalitis lethargica, a mysterious disease that left victims in a "sleeping" state. The cause of this illness is still unknown.

- **Fibromyalgia:** Fibromyalgia is a chronic condition characterized by widespread pain and fatigue, but its exact cause remains unknown. It is believed to be related to how the brain processes pain signals.

- **The Spontaneous Remission of Cancer:** In rare cases, cancer has been known to disappear without treatment. This phenomenon, known as spontaneous remission, baffles scientists and offers hope for future cures.

- **The "Elephant Man" Mystery:** Joseph Merrick, known as the "Elephant Man," suffered from severe deformities. For years, his condition puzzled doctors, and the exact cause remains unclear, though some suggest Proteus syndrome.

- **The Exploding Head Syndrome:** Exploding head syndrome is a rare condition where people hear loud noises when falling asleep or waking up, without any external source. The cause of this bizarre phenomenon is still unknown.

- **The Case of Phineas Gage:** In 1848, Phineas Gage survived a severe brain injury when an iron rod pierced his skull. His personality drastically changed, leading to new insights into the brain's role in behavior.

- **The Disappearance of the Plague of Athens:** In 430 BC, a deadly plague struck Athens, killing thousands. The exact disease remains a mystery, with theories ranging from typhoid fever to Ebola-like viruses.

- **The Bloodletting Practice:** For centuries, bloodletting was a common medical practice, believed to cure various illnesses. Despite its popularity, it often did more harm than good, and its continued use during those days puzzled many.

- **The Mystery of "Sudden Unexplained Nocturnal Death Syndrome":** Sudden unexplained nocturnal death syndrome (SUNDS) affects seemingly healthy young people, mostly in Southeast Asia, who die in their sleep without any apparent cause.

- **Foreign Accent Syndrome:** After brain injuries or strokes, some individuals have suddenly developed foreign accents despite never having lived in the region. This rare condition remains largely unexplained.

- **The Ticking Time Bomb of Aneurysms:** Brain aneurysms can be present for years without symptoms before suddenly rupturing, often with fatal results. Why some aneurysms rupture while others do not is still unknown.

- **The Mystery of Fibrodysplasia Ossificans Progressiva:** Fibrodysplasia ossificans progressiva (FOP) is a rare genetic disorder that turns muscles and tendons into bone, effectively "freezing" the body in place. The condition remains poorly understood.

- **Chronic Fatigue Syndrome:** Chronic fatigue syndrome (CFS) is a debilitating condition characterized by extreme fatigue that doesn't improve with rest. The exact cause remains a mystery, with no definitive cure available.

Remarkable Remedies

- **Honey: Nature's Antibacterial:** Honey has been used for thousands of years to treat wounds and burns. Its natural antibacterial properties help prevent infection and promote healing, making it a time-tested remedy.

- **Garlic: The Ancient Antibiotic:** Garlic has been used since ancient times to treat infections. Its active compound, allicin, has powerful antimicrobial properties, earning it a reputation as a natural antibiotic.

- **Willow Bark: The Original Aspirin:** Willow bark has been used for centuries to relieve pain and reduce fever. It contains salicin, a natural compound that inspired the development of aspirin in the 19th century.

- **Ginger: Soothing Nausea:** Ginger is a popular remedy for nausea and motion sickness. Its anti-inflammatory properties make it effective for soothing stomach discomfort and improving digestion.

- **Aloe Vera: The Skin Healer:** Aloe vera has been used for thousands of years to treat skin conditions, particularly burns. Its gel contains vitamins, minerals, and antioxidants that promote healing and reduce inflammation.

- **Turmeric: The Golden Remedy:** Turmeric, a staple in Indian cuisine, has powerful anti-inflammatory and antioxidant properties. It's used to treat a variety of conditions, from arthritis to digestive issues.

O **Echinacea: The Immune Booster:** Echinacea is a popular herbal remedy used to boost the immune system and fight off colds and infections. Native Americans have used it for centuries as a natural medicine.

O **Peppermint: Cooling Relief:** Peppermint oil is commonly used to relieve headaches, muscle pain, and digestive issues. Its cooling effect and soothing aroma make it a versatile natural remedy.

O **Cinnamon: Blood Sugar Regulator:** Cinnamon is more than just a spice—it's also known for its ability to lower blood sugar levels. It's been used in traditional medicine to manage diabetes and improve heart health.

O **Lavender: The Calming Herb:** Lavender is widely used for its calming effects. It can reduce anxiety, improve sleep, and even help with mild pain relief. Lavender oil is a popular choice for aromatherapy.

O **Chamomile: Sleep and Relaxation:** Chamomile tea is a well-known remedy for promoting sleep and relaxation. It's also used to soothe upset stomachs and reduce anxiety, making it a favorite in herbal medicine.

O **Cloves: Dental Relief:** Clove oil has been used for centuries to relieve toothaches and gum pain. Its natural anesthetic properties make it a quick and effective remedy for oral discomfort.

O **St. John's Wort: Nature's Antidepressant:** St. John's Wort is an herbal remedy used to treat mild to moderate depression. It's been used in traditional medicine for centuries and remains popular for its mood-enhancing effects.

O **Licorice Root: Soothing Sore Throats:** Licorice root has long been used to soothe sore throats and coughs. It's also known for its anti-inflammatory properties, making it a common ingredient in herbal teas.

O **Milk Thistle: Liver Protector:** Milk thistle is commonly used to support liver health. Its active ingredient, silymarin, is believed to protect liver cells from damage and aid in detoxification.

Strange Cures

O **Maggot Therapy: Healing with bugs:** Maggot therapy involves placing live maggots on wounds to clean out dead tissue. Despite sounding gross, it's a highly effective treatment for chronic wounds and infections.

O **Leech Therapy: Bloodsucking Treatment:** Leeches have been used in medicine for centuries, and they're still used today for their anticoagulant properties, particularly in reconstructive surgery to improve blood flow to reattached tissues.

O **Bee Venom Therapy: Pain Relief with a Sting:** Bee venom therapy involves using bee stings to treat conditions like arthritis and multiple sclerosis. The venom is believed to reduce inflammation and improve symptoms, though it's not for the faint-hearted!

O **Mustard Plasters for Chest Congestion:** In the 19th century, people used mustard plasters (a paste of mustard seed) applied to the chest to relieve congestion. The heat from the mustard was believed to improve blood flow and clear the lungs.

O **Snake Oil: A Historical Hoax:** Snake oil, once promoted as a miracle cure for various ailments, was exposed as a fraud in the 19th century. The term now refers to any bogus medical treatment or scam.

O **Lobotomies: A Controversial "Cure":** In the mid-20th century, lobotomies were performed to treat mental illness by cutting connections in the brain's frontal lobe. The procedure often caused severe, irreversible damage and was eventually abandoned.

O **Laughter Therapy:** Laughter therapy, or *gelotology*, is used in some hospitals to help improve patients' moods and reduce pain. While many are aware of the general mood-boosting effects of laughter, gelotology explores its specific therapeutic potential in managing pain, stress, depression, and even certain physical ailments.

O **Trepanation: Drilling Holes in the Skull:** Trepanation, one of the oldest surgical procedures, involved drilling holes in the skull to treat head injuries, epilepsy, or mental illness. It's still practiced in some parts of the world today.

O **Mercury: A Toxic Treatment:** Mercury was once used to treat a variety of ailments, including syphilis. However, it's now known to be highly toxic, and its use in medicine has been largely abandoned.

O **Cigarettes for Asthma:** In the early 20th century, cigarettes were marketed as a treatment for asthma and other respiratory conditions. It wasn't until later that the dangers of smoking were fully understood.

O **Cupping Therapy:** Cupping therapy, practiced in ancient Egypt, China, and Greece, involves placing heated cups on the skin to create suction. It is still used in alternative medicine to improve blood flow and relieve pain.

O **Radium Water: A Deadly Drink:** In the early 20th century, radium-laced water was sold as a health tonic, believed to cure everything from arthritis to cancer. Many people who drank it suffered severe radiation poisoning.

O **Electroconvulsive Therapy (ECT): Shocking Treatment:** ECT, introduced in the 1930s, uses electric currents to treat severe depression and other mental illnesses. Although controversial, it's still used today in a more controlled and humane manner.

O **Goat's Liver on the Head for Headaches:** Ancient Mesopotamians believed that placing a goat's liver on a person's head could cure headaches, associating it with spiritual healing.

O **Spider Web Bandages:** In ancient Greece and Rome, spider webs were used as bandages. The silk contained natural antiseptic and antifungal properties, helping wounds heal faster.

From the lifesaving discoveries that shape modern healthcare to the mysteries that keep scientists puzzled, medicine is truly a field of endless fascination and vital importance. But hold on tight, because we're not done yet!

Our next chapter takes us into what they taught or did not teach in Schools. Explore the evolution of learning, from ancient schools to modern classrooms, discover educators who changed the world, and uncover surprising facts about how we learn and grow. So grab your thinking cap and let's dive in!

The Curiosity Chronicles

Fascinating Facts and Figures

O **Oldest University:** The University of Al Quaraouiyine in Morocco, founded in 859, is the oldest existing and continually operating educational institution in the world.

O **Largest School in the World:** City Montessori School in Lucknow, India, holds the Guinness World Record for the largest school, with over 50,000 students enrolled across its various campuses.

O **The First Public School in the U.S.:** Boston Latin School, founded in 1635, is the oldest public school in the United States. It has educated notable figures like Benjamin Franklin and John Hancock.

O **Teacher in Space:** In 1986, teacher Christa McAuliffe was set to become the first teacher in space aboard the Space Shuttle Challenger. Sadly, the shuttle tragically exploded shortly after launch.

O **Literacy Rates Soar:** Global literacy rates have risen dramatically over the past 50 years. In 1970, only 59% of people could read and write. Today, that number has jumped to over 86%.

O **World's Most Expensive Education:** Institut Le Rosey in Switzerland is often called the most expensive school in the world, with annual fees exceeding $130,000. It boasts alumni like royalty and famous artists.

O **First Public University to Admit Women:** The University of Iowa was the first public university in the United States to admit men and women on an equal basis in 1855, pioneering coeducation in higher learning.

O **Longest School Day:** In South Korea, students often attend school from 8 AM until 4 PM, followed by additional classes and study sessions, sometimes lasting until 11 PM, making it one of the longest school days.

O **Learning with LEGO:** The LEGO Group's education division develops kits that help students learn about robotics, coding, and engineering. It's a hands-on way to build both creative and technical skills.

O **Education in Finland:** Finland is known for its innovative education system, which emphasizes less homework, fewer school hours, and no standardized tests, yet consistently ranks among the top in the world.

O **Oldest Book Still in Use:** The I Ching, a Chinese classic text over 3,000 years old, is still used today for divination, philosophy, and as a textbook in some schools. It's one of the oldest books still in circulation.

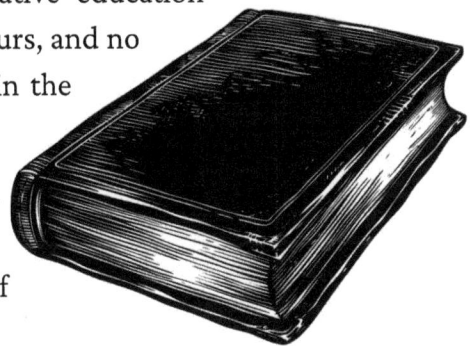

- **The One-Room Schoolhouse:** In the 19th century, many children in rural America were taught in one-room schoolhouses. These schools often served students of all ages and grades in a single classroom.

- **The "Forest Schools" Movement:** Forest schools, where children learn in outdoor environments, have become increasingly popular. Originating in Scandinavia, this approach fosters connection with nature and hands-on learning.

- **Summer Vacation Origins:** Summer vacation in the U.S. didn't originate because of farming, as commonly believed. It began in urban areas to give children a break during the hot summer months when school buildings were unbearable.

- **World's Largest Open University:** Indira Gandhi National Open University (IGNOU) in India is the largest open university in the world, with over 3 million students enrolled in distance learning courses.

Historic Educational Moments

- **The Morrill Act:** The Morrill Act, signed by President Abraham Lincoln, established land-grant colleges across the U.S. to make higher education accessible to more Americans, particularly in agriculture and engineering.

- **The First Printed Book:** In 1455, Johannes Gutenberg printed the Bible using movable type, making books more accessible and revolutionizing education by allowing knowledge to spread quickly and widely.

- **The Founding of Harvard University:** Harvard University, established in 1636, is the oldest institution of higher education in the United States. It started with just nine students and one instructor.

- **The Rise of Public Education:** In 1837, Horace Mann became the first Secretary of Education in Massachusetts, advocating for free, public education for all children, laying the groundwork for the modern public school system in the U.S.

- **The First Kindergarten:** Friedrich Froebel opened the first kindergarten in 1837 in Germany. His innovative approach focused on play-based learning, which became a cornerstone of early childhood education worldwide.

- **First Women's College in the U.S.:** Mount Holyoke College, founded in 1837, became the first institution of higher education for women in the U.S., helping pave the way for women's education.

- **The Founding of UNESCO:** The United Nations Educational, Scientific and Cultural Organization (UNESCO) was founded in 1945 to promote international collaboration in education, science, culture, and communication.

- **The First Public Library:** In 1833, the Peterborough Town Library in New Hampshire became the first tax-supported public library in the United States, offering free access to books for everyone in the community.

- **The Introduction of the SAT:** The SAT, a standardized college entrance exam, was first administered in 1926. It became a common requirement for college admissions in the U.S., shaping the educational landscape.

- **The Founding of Oxford University:** The University of Oxford, established in England around 1096, is the oldest university in the English-speaking world and has been a center of academic excellence for centuries.

- **The G.I. Bill:** In 1944, the U.S. government passed the G.I. Bill, providing educational benefits to World War II veterans, leading to a surge in college enrollments and the expansion of higher education in America.

- **The Introduction of the International Baccalaureate (IB):** The International Baccalaureate (IB) program was founded in 1968 to provide a globally recognized educational framework, focusing on critical thinking, international-mindedness, and a rigorous curriculum.

- **The Bologna Process:** Initiated in 1999, the Bologna Process created a more uniform higher education system across Europe, making it easier for students to study and work across European countries.

- **The Introduction of MOOCs:** Massive Open Online Courses (MOOCs) began in 2008, providing free access to university-level education to millions of people around the world, regardless of location.

- **The Founding of the Sorbonne:** The Sorbonne, part of the University of Paris, was founded in 1257 by Robert de Sorbon as a theological college. It became one of Europe's most important centers for learning.

Inspiring Educators

- **Maria Montessori: Pioneer of Child-Centered Learning:** Maria Montessori developed an educational method that emphasizes hands-on, child-directed learning. Her approach is used in schools worldwide, fostering independence and creativity in students.

- **Anne Sullivan: Helen Keller's Miracle Worker:** Anne Sullivan was the teacher who helped Helen Keller, a blind and deaf child, learn to communicate. Her dedication transformed Keller's life, making her a symbol of perseverance and education.

O **Jaime Escalante: The Real Stand and Deliver:** Jaime Escalante, a high school math teacher, inspired his students to excel in calculus, even when others doubted them. His story was made famous in the movie "Stand and Deliver."

O **Rafe Esquith:** Rafe Esquith, a Los Angeles teacher, became known for his innovative teaching methods in his 5th-grade classroom. He emphasized hard work, creativity, and respect, and wrote several books on education.

O **Booker T. Washington: Educator and Leader:** Booker T. Washington founded the Tuskegee Institute, providing education and vocational training for African Americans in the post-Civil War South. His work helped advance civil rights and education.

O **Socrates: The Father of Western Philosophy:** Socrates, the ancient Greek philosopher whom we mentioned a bit earlier, introduced the Socratic method, a form of teaching that uses questioning to stimulate critical thinking. His ideas laid the foundation for Western education.

O **John Dewey: The Father of Progressive Education:** John Dewey was an American philosopher and educator who promoted "learning by doing." His ideas shaped modern education, emphasizing experiential learning and the importance of democracy in schools.

O **Charlotte Mason:** Charlotte Mason was an English educator who developed a philosophy of education focused on fostering a love of learning through nature, living books, and the development of good habits.

O **Maria Gaetana Agnesi: A Mathematical Prodigy:** Maria Gaetana Agnesi was an 18th-century Italian mathematician who wrote one of the first comprehensive textbooks on calculus. Her work advanced mathematics education for generations to come.

O **Paulo Freire: Champion of Critical Pedagogy:** Paulo Freire, a Brazilian educator and philosopher, is best known for his influential work "Pedagogy of the Oppressed." He advocated for education as a tool for social justice and empowerment.

O **Rabindranath Tagore: Poet and Educator:** Rabindranath Tagore, an Indian polymath and Nobel laureate, founded Visva-Bharati University, promoting an education system that harmonizes Eastern and Western philosophies.

O **Emma Willard: Advocate for Women's Education:** Emma Willard founded the first school for women's higher education in the United States, the Troy Female Seminary. Her efforts paved the way for women's access to higher learning.

O **Salman Khan: Revolutionizing Online Learning:** Salman Khan, founder of Khan Academy, created a free, online education platform that offers lessons in a wide range of subjects, making quality education accessible to millions worldwide.

O **Montesquieu: A Founding Father of Modern Education:** Montesquieu, a French philosopher, believed that education should promote liberty and prevent tyranny. His ideas on separation of powers influenced educational systems and democratic governance.

○ **Nancie Atwell: The Teacher Who Won the "Nobel Prize" of Teaching:** Nancie Atwell, an American educator, won the first Global Teacher Prize in 2015 for her pioneering work in literacy education, including her innovative methods for teaching reading and writing.

Learning Legends

○ **Ban Zhao: One of the First Known Female Historians:** A renowned historian, writer, and philosopher, Ban Zhao completed the "Book of Han," a comprehensive history of the Han Dynasty. She also advocated for women's education and wrote influential works on female conduct and education.

○ **Marva Collins:** Marva Collins, an African American educator, founded the Westside Preparatory School in Chicago, where she taught underserved students using a rigorous curriculum, believing every child could succeed with the right support.

○ **Isaac Newton's Self-Taught Breakthroughs:** Isaac Newton's groundbreaking discoveries in physics and mathematics were largely self-taught. During a plague quarantine, he developed the theories of gravity and calculus, changing science forever.

○ **Erin Gruwell:** Erin Gruwell, an American high school teacher, inspired her at-risk students to overcome adversity through writing. Her experiences were depicted in the film *Freedom Writers*.

○ **Srinivasa Ramanujan: The Mathematical Prodigy:** Srinivasa Ramanujan, an Indian mathematician with no formal training, made significant contributions to mathematical theory. His work continues to influence modern mathematics.

○ **Hypatia of Alexandria:** A philosopher, astronomer, and mathematician who lived in Roman Egypt. She was famous for her teaching abilities and intelligence, gather many students across the Mediterranean world. She also holds the honor of being considered as one of the first women to contribute greatly in the fields of mathematics and science.

○ **Mary McLeod Bethune:** Mary McLeod Bethune founded Bethune-Cookman University, a historically Black college, and became an advocate for African American education, serving as an advisor to President Franklin D. Roosevelt.

○ **Stephen Hawking: Theoretical Physicist and Educator:** Stephen Hawking, despite being diagnosed with ALS, became one of the most influential theoretical physicists. His work on black holes and the universe's origins captivated both the scientific community and the public.

○ **Thomas Edison: The Inventor Who Never Gave Up:** Thomas Edison, who held over 1,000 patents, was known for his persistence. His learning-through-failure approach led to the invention of the phonograph, the light bulb, and much more.

○ **Plato:** Plato, a student of Socrates, founded the Academy in Athens, one of the earliest institutions of higher learning. His work in philosophy, particularly *The Republic*, remains foundational in education and ethics.

O **Malcolm X: The Power of Self-Education:** Malcolm X, a prominent civil rights leader, educated himself in prison, where he read extensively and studied languages, history, and philosophy. His transformation inspired many to value self-education.

O **Nicolaus Copernicus: Revolutionizing the Cosmos:** Nicolaus Copernicus was the first to propose that the Earth orbits the Sun, challenging the prevailing belief in a geocentric universe. His theory laid the groundwork for modern astronomy.

O **Aristotle:** Aristotle, a student of Plato, tutored Alexander the Great and established the Lyceum. His works on logic, biology, and metaphysics shaped Western educational thought for centuries.

O **Jean-Jacques Rousseau:** Rousseau's book *Emile* (1762) outlined a philosophy of education that emphasized natural learning and the development of a child's individuality, advocating for education to be child-centered.

O **John Locke:** John Locke, an English philosopher, argued that the mind is a "blank slate" at birth, with knowledge gained through experience. His ideas greatly influenced modern educational theory.

Remarkable Schools

O **Eton College: A School for Prime Ministers:** Eton College in England, founded in 1440, has educated 20 British prime ministers, including Winston Churchill. Known for its traditions, Eton remains one of the most prestigious schools in the world.

O **The School of Athens: Ancient Learning:** The School of Athens wasn't a real school but a famous painting by Raphael depicting the greatest philosophers, like Plato and Aristotle, learning together. It symbolizes the pursuit of knowledge in Ancient Greece.

O **The Harlem Children's Zone: A Model for Success:** The Harlem Children's Zone in New York offers education and community services to help children in underprivileged neighborhoods succeed. It's a groundbreaking model for combating poverty through education.

O **Phillips Exeter Academy (USA, 1781):** Phillips Exeter Academy, a prestigious U.S. preparatory school, is known for its "Harkness" teaching method, where students sit around a table to discuss topics, encouraging dialogue and critical thinking.

O **University of Timbuktu (Mali, 12th Century):** The University of Timbuktu, located in Mali, was a center of Islamic learning during the medieval period, attracting scholars from across Africa and the Middle East.

O **Green School Bali: Learning in Nature:** Green School Bali is an innovative school that teaches sustainability through hands-on learning in an entirely natural environment. The school's bamboo architecture and eco-friendly ethos set it apart.

o **Deep Springs College: Education in the Desert:** Deep Springs College in California offers a unique blend of rigorous academics and labor. Students live on a working ranch, learning practical skills alongside their studies.

o **Summerhill School: Freedom to Learn:** Summerhill School in England is one of the oldest democratic schools in the world. Founded in 1921, it allows students to decide how they spend their time, promoting independence and responsibility.

o **The Lycée Louis-le-Grand: French Excellence:** The Lycée Louis-le-Grand in Paris, founded in 1563, is renowned for producing some of France's most notable intellectuals, including philosophers, scientists, and politicians. It's considered one of the best schools in France.

o **The Waldorf Schools: Holistic Education:** Waldorf schools, based on the philosophy of Rudolf Steiner, focus on developing creativity, imagination, and practical skills. With over 1,000 schools worldwide, Waldorf education emphasizes the whole child—body, mind, and spirit.

o **The British International School of Houston: Innovation in Education:** This Texas school uses cutting-edge technology to deliver personalized learning experiences. With a focus on STEAM (Science, Technology, Engineering, Arts, and Mathematics), it prepares students for the future.

o **United World Colleges (UWC): Global Education for Peace:** United World Colleges focus on peace and sustainability. With campuses in 18 countries, UWC brings together students from diverse backgrounds to learn about global issues and foster international understanding.

o **The International School of Tanganyika: Diverse Learning:** Located in Tanzania, the International School of Tanganyika offers an International Baccalaureate (IB) curriculum in a multicultural environment. It's known for its commitment to fostering global citizenship and diverse perspectives.

o **School of the Air: Australia's Remote Classrooms:** Australia's School of the Air provides education to children in remote areas via radio and online lessons. Founded in 1951, it ensures that kids in the Outback receive quality education, no matter the distance.

o **The Maharishi School: Consciousness-Based Learning:** The Maharishi School in Iowa, USA, integrates Transcendental Meditation into its curriculum. Students practice meditation daily, which the school believes enhances creativity, intelligence, and academic performance.

o **Nalanda Mahavihara:** A renowned center of learning in ancient India, flourishing between the 5th and 12th centuries CE. Located in present-day Bihar, it's considered one of the world's first residential universities and a beacon of intellectual and cultural exchange. Nalanda was a hub for Buddhist studies, but also offered a wide range of subjects, including philosophy, logic, grammar, medicine, astronomy, and mathematics. It attracted scholars and students from across Asia, including China, Korea, Japan, Tibet, and Southeast Asia. Unfortunately, it was ransacked and abandoned around 1400.

Unusual Teaching Methods

O **The Flipped Classroom:** In a flipped classroom, students learn new content at home via videos or readings, then apply that knowledge in class through activities and discussions. This method encourages active learning and collaboration.

O **Gamification in Education:** Gamification involves using game elements like points, levels, and rewards to make learning more engaging. This method motivates students and makes complex subjects more enjoyable.

O **Inquiry-Based Learning:** Inquiry-based learning starts with a question or problem, encouraging students to research, explore, and find answers on their own. This method promotes critical thinking and independence.

O **Reggio Emilia Approach:** This Italian teaching philosophy emphasizes project-based learning and collaboration, with a strong focus on the environment as the "third teacher." Students are encouraged to explore and express themselves creatively.

O **Learning by Teaching (Lernen durch Lehren):** This method involves students teaching their peers, which reinforces their understanding of the material and fosters leadership and communication skills.

O **Project-Based Learning:** In project-based learning, students work on a project over an extended period, which requires them to investigate and respond to a complex question or challenge. This approach fosters deep understanding and real-world application.

O **Silent Classrooms (Sugata Mitra's Method):** In Sugata Mitra's method, students are left in a silent room with access to a computer to explore and learn collaboratively. This "self-organized learning" encourages independence.

O **Deschooling:** Deschooling is the process of gradually transitioning away from traditional schooling methods. It often involves a period of unstructured learning and self-discovery before adopting alternative educational approaches.

O **The Jigsaw Technique:** This cooperative learning method assigns each student a piece of the puzzle (a part of the topic) to research and teach to their peers, fostering teamwork and peer learning.

O **Unschooling:** Unschooling is a learner-driven approach where children learn through life experiences, rather than a formal curriculum. This method is based on the idea that children are naturally curious and motivated to learn.

O **Virtual Reality (VR) Learning:** VR learning uses immersive simulations to teach complex subjects like science, history, or medicine. Students can explore ancient civilizations or practice surgeries in a virtual environment.

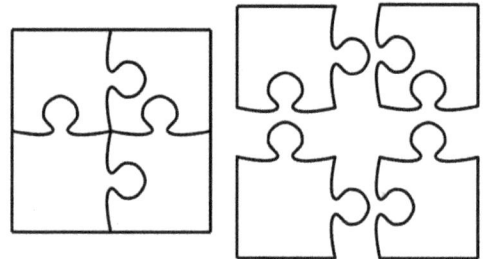

O **Mindfulness in Schools:** Some schools have introduced mindfulness exercises to help students focus, manage stress, and build emotional awareness. Activities like deep breathing and meditation are used to improve well-being.

O **Genius Hour:** Genius Hour gives students one hour a week to explore their passions and work on self-directed projects. This method encourages creativity, autonomy, and innovation.

O **Peer Teaching:** In peer teaching, students take on the role of the teacher and explain concepts to their classmates. This method reinforces their own understanding while helping others learn.

O **Flipped Faculty Meetings:** In some schools, the flipped classroom concept is applied to faculty meetings, where teachers review materials beforehand and use meeting time for discussion and planning, making meetings more efficient and productive.

Whether it's the historic milestones that paved the way for modern schooling or the innovative approaches that are transforming classrooms today, education remains a powerful force for change, growth, and discovery.

On to our final chapter - money and commerce! Get ready to explore the stories behind coins and currencies, the rise of global trade, and the minds who revolutionized the way we buy and sell. So, let's turn the page and discover the wealth of knowledge waiting for us in the world of dollars and pounds!

Haggling Bargaining Bartering

Amazing Shopping Stories

O **The World's First Department Store:** The Bon Marché in Paris, founded in 1852, is often considered the world's first department store. It revolutionized shopping by offering fixed prices and a wide range of goods under one roof.

O **Black Friday's Wild Origins:** Black Friday, the day after Thanksgiving in the U.S., got its name from the 1960s Philadelphia police, who dreaded the chaotic shopping crowds. Today, it's the biggest shopping day of the year.

O **The Multi-Million Blunt Violin:** In 2011, a rare Stradivarius violin nicknamed "The Lady Blunt" sold for nearly $16 million at auction, setting a record for the highest price ever paid for a musical instrument.

O **The Most Expensive Auction Item:** In 2017, Leonardo da Vinci's painting "Salvator Mundi" sold for $450 million at auction, making it the most expensive artwork ever sold.

O **The First Vending Machine:** The first vending machine, invented by Greek engineer Hero of Alexandria, dispensed holy water in exchange for coins. Modern vending machines now offer everything from snacks to electronics.

O **The Birth of the Shopping Mall:** The first enclosed shopping mall, Southdale Center, opened in Minnesota in 1956. Designed by architect Victor Gruen, it introduced a new way to shop and socialize.

O **Diamonds Are Forever—Thanks to Marketing:** De Beers popularized diamond engagement rings with their 1947 "A Diamond is Forever" campaign, turning diamonds into a symbol of everlasting love. Before that, diamonds weren't the go-to engagement gem.

O **The Invention of the Shopping Cart:** Sylvan Goldman, an Oklahoma grocery store owner, invented the shopping cart in 1937 to help customers buy more items. The invention revolutionized grocery shopping and boosted sales.

O **Apple Store's Genius Idea:** Apple's first retail store, opened in 2001, introduced the Genius Bar, a tech support area staffed by trained "geniuses." It redefined customer service in retail.

O **The Oldest Bookstore Still Open:** Bertrand Bookstore in Lisbon, Portugal, has been selling books since 1732, making it the world's oldest operating bookstore. It's a haven for book lovers and history buffs alike.

O **Luxury Shopping at 30,000 Feet:** Emirates Airline offers in-flight shopping, where first-class passengers can buy luxury items like watches and perfumes at 30,000 feet. It's shopping with a view!

- **Largest Mall by Gross Leasable Area:** The New South China Mall in Dongguan, China, boasts a gross leasable area of 659,612 square meters (7.1 million square feet) - making it the largest mall in the world by GLA. It features replicas of famous landmarks and a 2.1 km canal with gondolas!

- **The "One Cent" Sale:** In 1909, Woolworths introduced the "one cent sale," where customers could buy two items for the price of one plus a penny. The promotion was an instant hit and is still used today.

- **The Rise of the Dollar Store:** Dollar General, founded in 1939, started as a store where every item cost no more than a dollar. Today, it's a billion-dollar company with thousands of stores across the U.S.

- **The World's Most Expensive Handbag:** The Mouawad 1001 Nights Diamond Purse, valued at $3.8 million, holds the Guinness World Record for the most expensive handbag. It's encrusted with 4,517 diamonds!

Awesome Rich People

- **Jeff Bezos: The Billion Dollar Man:** Jeff Bezos, founder of Amazon, became the first person to reach a net worth of over $200 billion in 2020. His wealth is greater than the GDP of many small countries.

- **Charles Feeney:** Co-founder of Duty Free Shoppers, Charles Feeney secretly gave away almost his entire $8 billion fortune to education, healthcare, and human rights causes, through his foundation, Atlantic Philanthropies.

- **Warren Buffett: The Oracle of Omaha:** Warren Buffett, one of the world's wealthiest individuals, is famous for his investment strategies. Despite his immense wealth, he lives in the same modest house he bought in 1958.

- **Wealthiest Royal Family:** The Thai Royal family is widely considered to be the foremost in riches, when compared to other monarchies around the world. With a net worth of around $43 billion, that is some serious cash!

- **Richard Branson: The Adventurous Billionaire:** Richard Branson, founder of the Virgin Group, is known for his adventurous spirit. He's crossed the Atlantic Ocean in a hot air balloon and even ventured into space with his company Virgin Galactic.

- **Bill Gates: The Philanthropic Tech Titan:** Bill Gates, co-founder of Microsoft, uses much of his $100+ billion fortune for philanthropy through the Bill & Melinda Gates Foundation, which focuses on global health, education, and poverty alleviation.

- **J.K. Rowling: From Welfare to Billionaire:** J.K. Rowling, author of the Harry Potter series, went from being a struggling single mother on welfare to

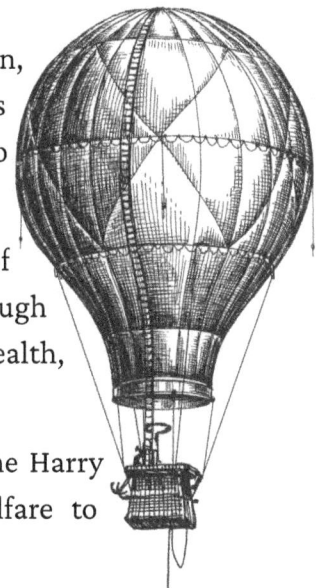

becoming the world's first billionaire author. Her books have sold over 500 million copies worldwide.

O **Carlos Slim: The Telecom Tycoon:** Carlos Slim, a Mexican businessman, was the richest person in the world from 2010 to 2013. His fortune comes primarily from his extensive holdings in telecommunications and other industries.

O **Amancio Ortega: The Fashion Giant:** Amancio Ortega, the founder of Zara, built a fashion empire that made him one of the richest men in the world. His company, Inditex, is the largest fashion retailer globally.

O **George Soros:** Investor and philanthropist George Soros is known for his Open Society Foundations, which promote democracy, human rights, and free speech around the world, particularly in former Soviet states.

O **Andrew Carnegie: The Steel Magnate:** Andrew Carnegie, a 19th-century steel tycoon, became one of the richest men of his time. He later gave away nearly all his wealth, funding libraries, education, and scientific research.

O **John D. Rockefeller: America's First Billionaire:** John D. Rockefeller, the founder of Standard Oil, became America's first billionaire in 1916. He is also known for his philanthropy, establishing foundations that supported education, science, and medicine.

O **Mackenzie Scott: Billionaire Philanthropist:** Mackenzie Scott, author and ex-wife of Jeff Bezos, is one of the world's most generous philanthropists. She's donated billions to causes ranging from racial equity to education.

O **Bernard Arnault: The Luxury King:** Bernard Arnault, CEO of LVMH, oversees brands like Louis Vuitton, Dior, and Mot & Chandon. As of 2023, he lists among the richest people globally, thanks to his luxury empire.

O **Ingvar Kamprad: The IKEA Innovator:** Ingvar Kamprad founded IKEA, the world's largest furniture retailer, in 1943 at just 17 years old. Known for his frugality, Kamprad lived modestly despite his billionaire status.

Big Business Ideas

O **The Franchise Model:** Ray Kroc popularized the franchise model with McDonald's, allowing entrepreneurs to own and operate their own locations. Today, McDonald's has over 38,000 franchises worldwide.

O **The Subscription Box Boom:** Companies like Netflix and Dollar Shave Club pioneered the subscription box model, where customers pay a recurring fee for curated products or services. This model has exploded across industries.

O **Dropshipping: A Business with No Inventory:** Dropshipping allows entrepreneurs to sell products without holding inventory. When a customer orders, the product is shipped directly from the supplier, minimizing risk and overhead costs.

O **Ride-Sharing Revolution:** Uber and Lyft revolutionized transportation by turning everyday drivers into ride-share providers. Their app-based platforms transformed the taxi industry and sparked the gig economy.

O **Freemium Model Success:** The freemium model offers basic services for free while charging for premium features. Companies like Spotify and LinkedIn have thrived using this strategy, attracting millions of users worldwide.

O **Freelance Marketplaces:** Websites like Upwork and Fiverr have created global marketplaces for freelancers, connecting them with clients across industries. This business model has transformed the way people work and earn.

O **Shared Office Space (WeWork):** WeWork introduced the concept of shared office space, where businesses could rent flexible workspaces rather than committing to long-term leases, meeting the needs of start-ups and freelancers.

O **Social Media Advertising:** Facebook and Instagram turned social media into a powerful advertising platform. Businesses can now target specific audiences with tailored ads, revolutionizing marketing and reaching billions of users.

O **Crowdfunding Innovation:** Crowdfunding platforms like Kickstarter and Indiegogo allow entrepreneurs to raise money directly from the public. This model has funded everything from innovative gadgets to creative projects.

O **Sharing Economy: Airbnb:** Airbnb disrupted the hotel industry by allowing people to rent out their homes to travelers. It transformed the way people travel and introduced the concept of the sharing economy.

O **Buy Now, Pay Later:** Services like Afterpay and Klarna offer "buy now, pay later" options, allowing consumers to split payments into installments. This idea has gained popularity among online shoppers worldwide.

O **Pop-Up Shops:** Pop-up shops are temporary retail spaces that allow businesses to create buzz and test markets. This flexible business model is popular with brands looking to create unique shopping experiences.

O **Just-In-Time Inventory:** Toyota pioneered the just-in-time inventory management system, minimizing inventory costs by receiving goods only as needed in the production process. This model became a key part of lean manufacturing.

O **Search Advertising:** Google revolutionized digital advertising with AdWords, which allows businesses to advertise based on search terms. It became a cornerstone of Google's revenue model and reshaped online marketing.

O **Green Business Initiatives:** Companies like Tesla and Patagonia focus on sustainability, turning green initiatives into profitable business strategies. They've shown that environmentally conscious practices can attract loyal customers and drive innovation.

Currency Curiosities

O **The World's Oldest Currency:** The British pound is the world's oldest currency still in use. It was first introduced in 775 AD during the reign of King Offa of Mercia, originally made of silver.

O **Playing Cards as Currency:** In the 18th century, playing cards were used as currency in French colonies in North America when official currency was scarce.

O **Giant Stone Money:** On the island of Yap in Micronesia, people used giant stone discs called Rai as currency. Some stones are so large they can't be moved, but they still count as money!

O **The Short-Lived $100,000 Bill:** The largest U.S. bill ever printed was the $100,000 bill featuring President Woodrow Wilson. Issued in 1934, it was used only for transactions between Federal Reserve Banks, not for public use.

O **The Secret Service's Original Mission:** The U.S. Secret Service was created to combat counterfeit currency. It wasn't until after Lincoln's assassination that they were also tasked with protecting the president.

O **Sweden's Cashless Society:** Sweden is leading the charge towards a cashless society, with most transactions now done digitally. By 2023, it's expected that cash will make up less than 0.5% of the value of all payments.

O **The Banana Republic Origin:** The term "banana republic" originated when the American United Fruit Company controlled much of Central America's economy and politics in the early 20th century, often paying workers in scrip (company-issued currency).

O **Hyperinflation in Zimbabwe:** In 2008, Zimbabwe experienced such extreme hyperinflation that the government issued a 100 trillion Zimbabwean dollar note, worth about $0.40 USD at the time.

O **The First Paper Money:** The first known paper money was created in China during the Tang Dynasty (618–907 AD). These early banknotes were used as a more convenient alternative to heavy metal coins.

O **Chocolate Coins: Not Just for Fun:** The ancient Aztecs used cacao beans as currency, trading them for goods and services. A turkey could cost 100 cacao beans, making chocolate quite valuable!

O **World's Heaviest/Largest Coin ever Circulated:** The world's heaviest coin is the Swedish plate coin, minted in the 17th century. Weighing up to 20 kilograms (44 pounds), these copper coins were used before paper money was introduced.

O **The Euro: A United Currency:** Introduced in 1999, the euro is the official currency of 19 of the 27 European Union countries, making it the second-most traded currency in the world after the U.S. dollar.

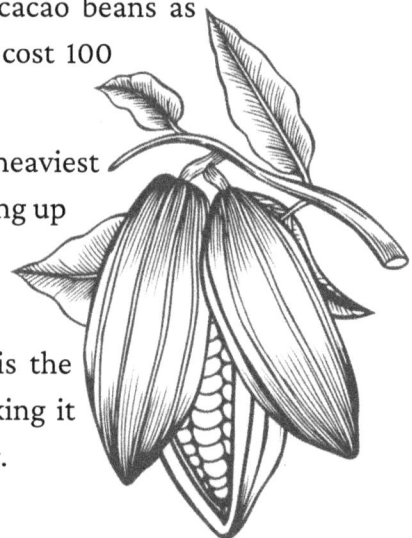

- **The Tallest Stack of Coins:** The world record for the tallest stack of coins was set in 2016, reaching 3.872 meters (12.7 feet) high. The stack consisted of 51,000 coins and took seven hours to complete.

- **Canada's Glow-in-the-Dark Coins:** In 2017, Canada issued the world's first glow-in-the-dark coin to celebrate the 150th anniversary of Confederation. The coin features two people paddling a canoe under the Northern Lights.

- **The Coinage Act of 1873:** The U.S. Coinage Act of 1873, also known as the "Crime of '73," ended the minting of silver dollars, leading to a nationwide debate over the use of gold versus silver currency.

- **Bitcoin's Pizza Purchase:** In 2010, a programmer named Laszlo Hanyecz paid 10,000 Bitcoins for two pizzas. This is considered the first real-world Bitcoin transaction, but today those Bitcoins would be worth millions!

- **Cigarettes as Currency:** During World War II, cigarettes became a form of currency in prison camps. Soldiers traded them for food, clothing, and other essentials, demonstrating how valuable everyday items can become.

Funny Money Facts

- **Money Doesn't Grow on Trees—But It's Made from Cotton!:** U.S. dollar bills are not made of paper; they're made from 75% cotton and 25% linen. This blend makes the bills more durable and able to survive a trip through the washing machine.

- **The $$$ Monopoly Set:** In 1988, jeweler Sidney Mobell created a Monopoly set worth $2 million. The board is made of 23-carat gold, with solid gold dice and houses encrusted with rubies and sapphires.

- **Bizarre Banknotes: The Animal Series:** In 2016, the Central Bank of the Bahamas released a series of colorful banknotes featuring native animals, including the flamingo, parrotfish, and blue marlin, making it one of the most eye-catching currencies.

- **Moo Money: When Cows Were Cash:** In 19th-century Africa, cows were used as a form of currency. The value of goods was often measured in cows, and wealth was determined by how many cattle a person owned.

- **The $2 Bill Conspiracy:** Some people believe the U.S. $2 bill is unlucky or rare, but it's still in circulation! Because it's used less often, many think it's no longer printed, but you can still get one at the bank.

- **Money in Space:** The first person to carry cash into space was Soviet cosmonaut Yuri Gagarin in 1961. The rubles he brought weren't needed, but it's still an interesting fact!

- **The World's Smallest Coin:** The world's smallest coin is the Croatian 1 kuna coin, which measures just 1.99 millimeters across. With a weight of 0.05 grams, it also features an image of a hummingbird!

o **Pineapple Currency:** In the Caribbean during the 17th century, pineapples were so rare and valuable that they were often used as currency among the wealthy. It was a sign of wealth to own or display one.

o **A Sticky Situation:** Canadian banknotes, made from polymer plastic, can stick together when new. This sometimes causes cashiers to accidentally hand out more money than intended. Thankfully, the issue is temporary!

o **The Million Dollar Coin:** In 2007, the Royal Canadian Mint created a $1 million gold coin that weighs 100 kilograms. Although legal tender, it's primarily a collector's item, with only a few in existence.

o **ATM Fees Are No Joke:** In 2019, the average ATM fee in the U.S. hit a record high of $4.72 per transaction. That's more than the cost of a latte, just to access your own money!

o **World's First ATM:** The first ATM was installed in London in 1967. To withdraw cash, customers used a special code and a paper voucher instead of a plastic card.

o **A Penny for Your Thoughts:** Producing a U.S. penny costs more than it's worth—about 2.1 cents per penny. Despite this, billions of pennies are minted each year, though some argue it's time to retire the coin.

o **Piggy Bank Origin:** The term "piggy bank" comes from "pygg," a type of clay used in the Middle Ages to make jars for holding money. Over time, these jars were shaped like pigs, leading to today's piggy banks.

o **The World's First Credit Card:** The first credit card was the Diners Club card, introduced in 1950. It was originally intended for use in restaurants but quickly expanded to other services, revolutionizing the way we pay.

Money Magic

o **The Magic of Compound Interest:** Albert Einstein reportedly called compound interest the "eighth wonder of the world." It's the process where money grows faster over time as you earn interest on both your initial investment and accumulated interest.

o **The Disappearing Penny:** Did you know it's possible to dissolve a penny in vinegar? The acetic acid in vinegar reacts with the copper oxide on the penny's surface, making it disappear over time.

o **Fortune Cookie Origins:** Fortune cookies, often associated with Chinese cuisine, were actually invented in the U.S. The first mass-produced fortune cookies were made in California in the early 20th century. They became a popular novelty item in restaurants.

o **The Vanishing Coin Trick:** The vanishing coin trick is one of the oldest magic tricks in history. Magicians use sleight of hand to make a coin disappear, often reappearing it in unexpected places. It's a classic example of money "magic"!

- **Invisible Ink on Banknotes:** Some countries, like the U.K., use invisible ink on their banknotes as a security feature. The ink is only visible under UV light, helping to prevent counterfeiting.

- **The Magnetic Power of Money:** U.S. paper money contains tiny amounts of iron, making it slightly magnetic. You can test this with a powerful magnet, though the effect is very weak!

- **Money in Magic: The Floating Bill:** Magicians often use invisible threads to make dollar bills float in the air. This illusion gives the appearance that money is defying gravity, delighting audiences with its mysterious movement.

- **The Secret Symbols on U.S. Currency:** The U.S. dollar is filled with mysterious symbols, like the eye on the pyramid. These designs have inspired countless conspiracy theories, though they're mostly just artistic choices.

- **Money Origami:** Origami artists use dollar bills to create intricate designs, from animals to flowers. This art form, known as "moneygami," turns cash into something far more valuable than its face value.

- **Rule of 72:** The Rule of 72 is a quick way to estimate how long it will take for an investment to double. Divide 72 by the annual rate of return, and the result is the number of years needed to double the investment.

- **The Floating Coin:** The floating coin trick involves placing a coin on the surface of the water and watching it float. It works because the surface tension of the water is stronger than the weight of the coin.

- **Money Conjurations in Ancient Times:** In ancient times, alchemists believed they could turn base metals into gold, a concept known as the Philosopher's Stone. While impossible during those times, the idea of conjuring money from nothing was captivating.

- **The Millionaire's Money Clip:** Magicians have performed tricks where a simple money clip appears to multiply dollar bills. Using sleight of hand, they create the illusion of money magically doubling in size.

- **The Maneki-neko:** This Japanese beckoning cat figurine, with its raised paw, is believed to bring good luck and fortune to businesses. It's often seen in shops and restaurants, inviting customers and prosperity.

- **The Holographic Magic of Currency:** Many modern banknotes feature holographic elements that change appearance when viewed from different angles. These high-tech designs make counterfeiting nearly impossible, adding a touch of "magic" to everyday cash.

And there you have it, intrepid adventurers of the financial world! We've scaled the dizzying heights of wealth and fortune, delved into the ingenious ideas that changed industries, and even tiptoed through the enchanting realm of money magic. It's been a wild ride, hasn't it?

Bonus

Our Gifts For You

As way of saying a **Big Thank You**! We have prepared not one, but **FOUR FREE** trivia books, each packed with 150 brain-teasing quizzes and fascinating facts!

Embark on a trivia adventure across history, nature, pop culture, and the globe with this free collection of 4 quiz books!

Free just for you!

To get instant access just go to the link or scan the QR code below:

https://thecuriosityco.com/bonustcc010

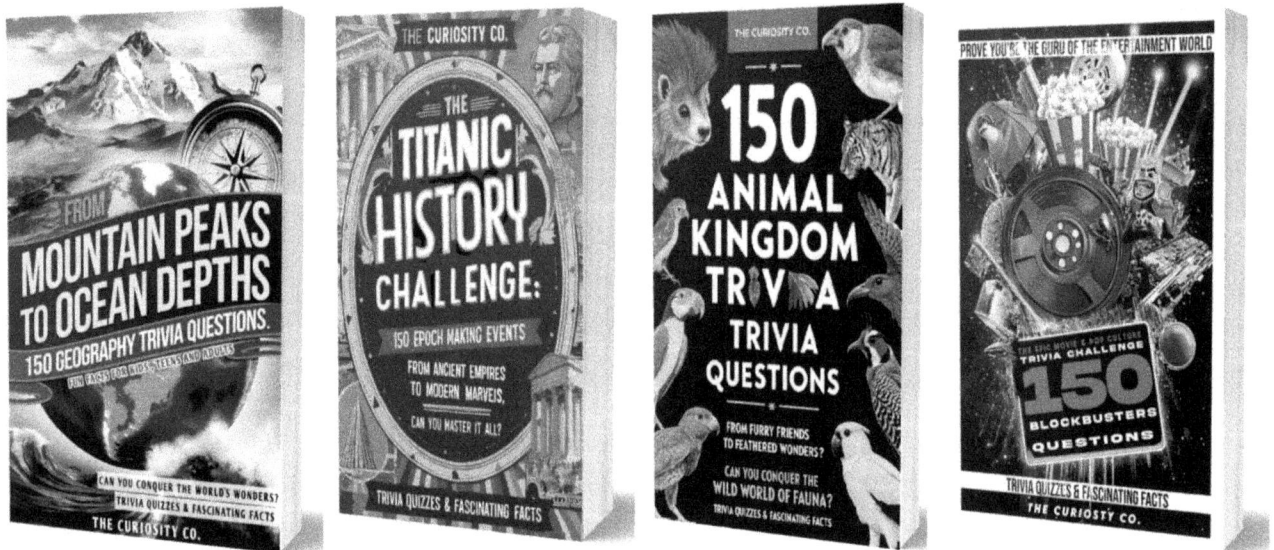

Inside these books, you will:

- **Become a Trivia Master**: Amaze your friends and family with your newfound knowledge across history, geography, pop culture, and the animal kingdom!

- **Unwind & Connect**: Enjoy hours of solo fun or spark lively conversations with friends and family over these engaging trivia challenges.

- **Sharpen Your Mind**: Give your brain a workout and boost your memory, focus, and critical thinking skills with every quiz.

Be sure to grab your Free Bonuses

Thank You

Thank you for buying this book and being a true stalwart in making it all the way to the end. (another trivia bit: Around 60-70% of books started are not finished)

You are truly a superstar and we are very grateful

Before you go, would you consider doing a favor and leave a review on the platform?

>> Leave a review on Amazon US <<

You see, posting a review is one of the easiest and best ways to support small independent brands like us over at The Curiosity Co. And it would definitely mean a lot to hear what you liked about our books

Thank you so much once again and catch you in our next book!

Thank You

Conclusion

Congratulations and take a bow, trivia champion! You've journeyed through centuries of history, ventured into the far reaches of space, explored the wonders of the human body, and uncovered the quirkiest oddities our world has to offer. From ancient civilizations to modern marvels, you've gathered an impressive collection of knowledge that's sure to entertain and enlighten. Think of all the fun conversations you can spark and the smiles you can create just by sharing what you've learned!

These facts aren't just for keeping to yourself. They're perfect for breaking the ice at parties, impressing your friends, or even enjoying some quality family time as you quiz each other on what you've discovered. Whether you're looking to bond over bizarre trivia or just want to drop some random knowledge into everyday chat, you're now fully equipped with a head full of fun, engaging facts.

So go ahead, use your newfound knowledge to connect with others, spark curiosity, and keep the fun going. And remember— There are always new discoveries to be made, new stories to uncover, and new ways to share the joy of knowledge. Keep your mind open, your curiosity kindled, and your trivia spirit alive!

Happy fact-finding!

References

Akre, K., & Rafferty, J. (2024, May 18). *Miller-Urey experiment | biochemistry*. Encyclopedia Britannica. https://www.britannica.com/science/Miller-Urey-experiment

Allchin, F. R. (2018). Indus civilization | History, Location, Map, Art, & Facts. In *Encyclopædia Britannica*. https://www.britannica.com/topic/Indus-civilization

Anand, P., Kunnumakara, A. B., Sundaram, C., Harikumar, K. B., Tharakan, S. T., Lai, O. S., Sung, B., & Aggarwal, B. B. (2008). Cancer is a Preventable Disease that Requires Major Lifestyle Changes. *Pharmaceutical Research*, *25*(9), 2097–2116. https://doi.org/10.1007/s11095-008-9661-9

Bayan, L., Koulivand, P. H., & Gorji, A. (2014). Garlic: A review of potential therapeutic effects. *Avicenna Journal of Phytomedicine*, *4*(1), 1–14.

BBC One - Planet Earth II. (n.d.). BBC. https://www.bbc.co.uk/programmes/p02544td

Becker, A. D., Masoud, H., Newbolt, J. W., Shelley, M., & Ristroph, L. (2015). Hydrodynamic schooling of flapping swimmers. *Nature Communications*, *6*(1). https://doi.org/10.1038/ncomms9514

Benda, B. (2015). Ginseng and Jet Engines. *Integrative Medicine (Encinitas, Calif.)*, *14*(2), 64. https://www.ncbi.nlm.nih.gov/pmc/articles/PMC4566475/

Biological markers for early detection and pharmacological treatment of Alzheimer's disease. (2009). *Alzheimer's Disease and Mild Cognitive Impairment*, *11*(2), 141–157. https://doi.org/10.31887/dcns.2009.11.2/hhampel

Brown, K. (2023). Alexander Fleming | Biography, Education, Discovery, & Facts. In *Encyclopædia Britannica*. https://www.britannica.com/biography/Alexander-Fleming

Cardiac resynchronization therapy - Type - Mayo Clinic. (2019). Mayoclinic.org. https://www.mayoclinic.org/tests-procedures/cardiac-resynchronization-therapy/pyc-20385014

Cartwright, F. F. (2019). Joseph Lister | British surgeon and medical scientist. In *Encyclopædia Britannica*. https://www.britannica.com/biography/Joseph-Lister-Baron-Lister-of-Lyme-Regis

CDC. (2024). *Coronavirus Disease 2019 (COVID-19)*. COVID-19. https://www.cdc.gov/covid/?CDC_AAref_Val=https://www.cdc.gov/coronavirus/2019-ncov/hcp/telehealth.html

Centers for Disease Control and Prevention. (2019). *What is ME/CFS?* CDC. https://www.cdc.gov/me-cfs/about/index.html

Chen, K.-H., Chen, I-Chu., Yang, Y.-C., & Chen, K.-T. (2019). The trends and associated factors of preterm deliveries from 2001 to 2011 in Taiwan. *Medicine*, *98*(13), e15060. https://doi.org/10.1097/md.0000000000015060

Chowdhury, C., Vinoth Kumar, N., & Khijmatgar, S. (2017). Interrelations of level of urinary cotinine and score for fagerstrom test for nicotine dependence among beedi smokers, and smokeless tobacco users in India. *Indian Journal of Psychological Medicine*, *39*(4), 392. https://doi.org/10.4103/0253-7176.211758

Cuttlefish, facts and photos. (2021, April 23). Animals. https://www.nationalgeographic.com/animals/invertebrates/facts/cuttlefish

Dream | sleep experience. (n.d.). Encyclopedia Britannica. https://www.britannica.com/topic/dream-sleep-experience

Electric Eel | National Geographic. (2010, April 11). Animals. https://www.nationalgeographic.com/animals/fish/facts/electric-eel

Erickson, H. L., & Barson, M. (2019). Charlie Chaplin | Biography, Movies, & Facts. In *Encyclopædia Britannica*. https://www.britannica.com/biography/Charlie-Chaplin

Florkin, M. (2018). Andreas Vesalius | Belgian physician. In *Encyclopædia Britannica*. https://www.britannica.com/biography/Andreas-Vesalius

Forester, S. C., & Lambert, J. D. (2011). The role of antioxidant versus pro-oxidant effects of green tea polyphenols in cancer prevention. *Molecular Nutrition & Food Research*, *55*(6), 844–854. https://doi.org/10.1002/mnfr.201000641

Gavin, M. (2002). Physician assistants. Many general practitioners would welcome having physician assistants. *BMJ (Clinical Research Ed.)*, *324*(7339), 735–736. https://www.ncbi.nlm.nih.gov/pmc/articles/PMC1122653/

Golomb, J. D., & Kanwisher, N. (2011). Higher Level Visual Cortex Represents Retinotopic, Not Spatiotopic, Object Location. *Cerebral Cortex*, *22*(12), 2794–2810. https://doi.org/10.1093/cercor/bhr357

Gregory, A. (2018). William Harvey | English physician. In *Encyclopædia Britannica*. https://www.britannica.com/biography/William-Harvey

Gupta, S. (2010). Chamomile: A herbal medicine of the past with a bright future. *Molecular Medicine Reports*, *3*(6). https://doi.org/10.3892/mmr.2010.377

Halfvarson, J., Brislawn, C. J., Lamendella, R., Vázquez-Baeza, Y., Walters, W. A., Bramer, L. M., D'Amato, M., Bonfiglio, F., McDonald, D., Gonzalez, A., McClure, E. E., Dunklebarger, M. F., Knight, R., & Jansson, J. K. (2017). Dynamics of the human gut microbiome in inflammatory bowel disease. *Nature Microbiology*, *2*(5). https://doi.org/10.1038/nmicrobiol.2017.4

Hauser, T. (2018). Muhammad Ali. In *Encyclopædia Britannica*. Britannica. https://www.britannica.com/biography/Muhammad-Ali-boxer

Hewlings, S., & Kalman, D. (2017). Curcumin: A Review of Its' Effects on Human Health. *Foods*, *6*(10), 92. https://doi.org/10.3390/foods6100092

Holmedahl, N. H., Fjeldstad, O.-M., Engan, H., Saxvig, I. W., & Grønli, J. (2019). Validation of peripheral arterial tonometry as tool for sleep assessment in chronic obstructive pulmonary disease. *Scientific Reports*, *9*(1), 19392. https://doi.org/10.1038/s41598-019-55958-2

Humphrey, J. H., & Samuel Scott Perdue. (2019). immune system | Description, Function, & Facts. In *Encyclopædia Britannica*. https://www.britannica.com/science/immune-system

In This Issue. (2017). *Proceedings of the National Academy of Sciences*, *114*(32), 8433–8434. https://doi.org/10.1073/iti3217114

Karabay, O., Tuna, N., & Yahyaoglu, M. (2012). Hepatitis B viral breakthrough associated with inappropriate preservation of entecavir. *Indian Journal of Pharmacology*, *44*(1), 136. https://doi.org/10.4103/0253-7613.91889

Kawatra, P., & Rajagopalan, R. (2015). Cinnamon: Mystic powers of a minute ingredient. *Pharmacognosy Research*, *7*(5), 1. https://doi.org/10.4103/0974-8490.157990

Keijer, J., Hoevenaars, F., Nieuwenhuizen, A., & van Schothorst, E. (2014). Nutrigenomics of Body Weight Regulation: A Rationale for Careful Dissection of Individual Contributors. *Nutrients*, *6*(10), 4531–4551. https://doi.org/10.3390/nu6104531

Koulivand, P. H., Khaleghi Ghadiri, M., & Gorji, A. (2013). Lavender and the Nervous System. *Evidence-Based Complementary and Alternative Medicine*, *2013*(681304), 1–10. https://doi.org/10.1155/2013/681304

Lai, K. N., Tang, S. C. W., Schena, F. P., Novak, J., Tomino, Y., Fogo, A. B., & Glassock, R. J. (2016). IgA nephropathy. *Nature Reviews Disease Primers*, *2*(1). https://doi.org/10.1038/nrdp.2016.1

Laidmäe, V.-I. (2013). Chronic disease: Working together. *Indian Journal of Endocrinology and Metabolism*, *17*(4), 768. https://doi.org/10.4103/2230-8210.113783

Lee, Y. S., Baek, J. S., Kim, S. Y., Seo, S. W., Kwon, B. S., Kim, G. B., Bae, E. J., Park, S. S., & Noh, C. I. (2010). Childhood Brugada Syndrome in Two Korean Families. *Korean Circulation Journal*, *40*(3), 143. https://doi.org/10.4070/kcj.2010.40.3.143

Lentz, T. L., & Erulkar, S. D. (2019). nervous system | Definition, Function, Structure, & Facts. In *Encyclopædia Britannica*. https://www.britannica.com/science/nervous-system

Mayo Clinic. (2022, May 10). *Cochlear Implants - Mayo Clinic*. Mayoclinic.org; Mayo Clinic. https://www.mayoclinic.org/tests-procedures/cochlear-implants/about/pac-20385021

Mayo Clinic. (2023, March 7). *Brain aneurysm - Symptoms and causes*. Mayo Clinic. https://www.mayoclinic.org/diseases-conditions/brain-aneurysm/symptoms-causes/syc-20361483

Minhaj Nur Alam, Thapa, D., Lim, J. I., Cao, D., & Yao, X. (2017). Quantitative characteristics of sickle cell retinopathy in optical coherence tomography angiography. *Biomedical Optics Express*, *8*(3), 1741–1741. https://doi.org/10.1364/boe.8.001741

Mirtz, T. A. (2017). A treatise for a new philosophy of chiropractic medicine. *Chiropractic & Manual Therapies, 25*(1). https://doi.org/10.1186/s12998-017-0138-y

National Geographic. (2010a, September 10). *African elephant, facts and photos*. National Geographic. https://www.nationalgeographic.com/animals/mammals/facts/african-elephant

National Geographic. (2010b, September 10). *Box Jellyfish | National Geographic*. Animals. https://www.nationalgeographic.com/animals/invertebrates/facts/box-jellyfish

National Geographic. (2010c, September 10). *Great White Sharks*. National Geographic. https://www.nationalgeographic.com/animals/fish/facts/great-white-shark

National Geographic. (2010d, September 10). *Komodo dragon, facts and photos*. National Geographic. https://www.nationalgeographic.com/animals/reptiles/facts/komodo-dragon

National Geographic. (2010e, November 11). *Saltwater Crocodile | National Geographic*. Animals. https://www.nationalgeographic.com/animals/reptiles/facts/saltwater-crocodile

National Geographic. (2011a, May 10). *African lion, facts and photos*. Animals; National Geographic. https://www.nationalgeographic.com/animals/mammals/facts/african-lion

National Geographic. (2011b, May 10). *Cheetah | National Geographic*. Animals. https://www.nationalgeographic.com/animals/mammals/facts/cheetah

National Geographic. (2011c, June 10). *Emperor Penguin | National Geographic*. Animals; National Geographic. https://www.nationalgeographic.com/animals/birds/facts/emperor-penguin

National Geographic. (2018, December 11). *Mimic Octopus Facts*. Animals. https://www.nationalgeographic.com/animals/invertebrates/facts/mimic-octopus

Nossaman, B. D., & Kadowitz, P. J. (2013). Stimulators of soluble guanylyl cyclase: future clinical indications. *Ochsner Journal, 13*(1), 147–156. https://www.ncbi.nlm.nih.gov/pmc/articles/PMC3603178/

O'Brien, L. (2019). Madonna | Biography, Songs, & Facts | Britannica. In *Encyclopædia Britannica*. https://www.britannica.com/biography/Madonna-American-singer-and-actress

Ossicle | zoology | Britannica. (n.d.). Www.britannica.com. https://www.britannica.com/science/ossicle

Paresthesia | Description, Causes, Symptoms, Diagnosis, & Treatment | Britannica. (2023, August 29). Www.britannica.com. https://www.britannica.com/science/paresthesia

Prasad, S., & Tyagi, A. K. (2015). Ginger and Its Constituents: Role in Prevention and Treatment of Gastrointestinal Cancer. *Gastroenterology Research and Practice, 2015*, 1–11. https://doi.org/10.1155/2015/142979

Raikar, S. P. (2024, January 19). *Bloodletting | medical procedure | Britannica*. Www.britannica.com. https://www.britannica.com/science/bloodletting

Rugnetta, M. (2018). neuroplasticity | Different Types, Facts, & Research. In *Encyclopædia Britannica*. https://www.britannica.com/science/neuroplasticity

Rugnetta, M. (2019). Phantom limb syndrome | neurophysiology | Britannica. In *Encyclopædia Britannica*. https://www.britannica.com/science/phantom-limb-syndrome

Salzman, D. (2023). amygdala | Definition, Function, Location, & Facts. In *Encyclopædia Britannica*. https://www.britannica.com/science/amygdala

Samarghandian, S., Farkhondeh, T., & Samini, F. (2017). Honey and Health: A Review of Recent Clinical Research. *Pharmacognosy Research, 9*(2), 121–127. https://doi.org/10.4103/0974-8490.204647

Sartore, J. (2010a, September 10). *Grizzly bear, facts and photos*. Animals. https://www.nationalgeographic.com/animals/mammals/facts/grizzly-bear

Sartore, J. (2010b, September 10). *King cobra, facts and photos*. Animals. https://www.nationalgeographic.com/animals/reptiles/facts/king-cobra

Sartore, J. (2011a, May 10). *Common Octopus | National Geographic*. Animals. https://www.nationalgeographic.com/animals/invertebrates/facts/common-octopus

Sartore, J. (2011b, May 10). *Common Octopus | National Geographic*. Animals. Interesting Facts For Curious Minds https://www.nationalgeographic.com/animals/invertebrates/facts/common-octopus

sartorius muscle | anatomy | Britannica. (n.d.). Www.britannica.com. https://www.britannica.com/science/sartorius-muscle

Schwartz, T. B., & Norris, D. O. (2019). Endocrine system | anatomy. In *Encyclopædia Britannica*. https://www.britannica.com/science/endocrine-system

Selanders, L. (2020). Florence Nightingale | Biography & Facts. In *Encyclopædia Britannica*. https://www.britannica.com/biography/Florence-Nightingale

Shang, L., Xu, T.-L., Li, F., Su, J., & Li, W.-G. (2015). Temporal Dynamics of Anxiety Phenotypes in a Dental Pulp Injury Model. *Molecular Pain*, *11*, s12990-0150040. https://doi.org/10.1186/s12990-015-0040-3

Shojaie, A., & Michailidis, G. (2010). Penalized likelihood methods for estimation of sparse high-dimensional directed acyclic graphs. *Biometrika*, *97*(3), 519–538. https://doi.org/10.1093/biomet/asq038

Solomon Asch | American psychologist. (n.d.). Encyclopedia Britannica. https://www.britannica.com/biography/Solomon-Asch

Steptoe, A. (2005). John Moore: eighteenth century physician, bearleader and social observer. *Journal of the Royal Society of Medicine*, *98*(2), 70–74. https://doi.org/10.1258/jrsm.98.2.70

Surjushe, A., Vasani, R., & Saple, D. (2008). Aloe vera: A short review. *Indian Journal of Dermatology*, *53*(4), 163. https://doi.org/10.4103/0019-5154.44785

The Day the Music Died | Description, Background, & Airplane Crash | Britannica. (2024). In *Encyclopædia Britannica*. https://www.britannica.com/event/The-Day-the-Music-Died

The Editors of Encyclopedia Britannica. (2018a). Elizabeth Blackwell | Biography & Facts. In *Encyclopædia Britannica*. https://www.britannica.com/biography/Elizabeth-Blackwell

The Editors of Encyclopedia Britannica. (2019). Hanging Gardens of Babylon | History & Pictures. In *Encyclopædia Britannica*. https://www.britannica.com/place/Hanging-Gardens-of-Babylon

The Editors of Encyclopedia Britannica. (2018b). Marie Curie | Biography & Facts. In *Encyclopedia Britannica*. https://www.britannica.com/biography/Marie-Curie

The Editors of Encyclopedia Britannica. (2019). Lucille Ball | Biography, TV Shows, Movies, & Facts. In *Encyclopædia Britannica*. https://www.britannica.com/biography/Lucille-Ball

Tjong, E., & Mohiuddin, S. S. (2020). *Biochemistry, Tetrahydrofolate*. PubMed; StatPearls Publishing. https://www.ncbi.nlm.nih.gov/books/NBK539712/

Tobias Chant Owen. (2019). Jupiter | Facts, Surface, Moons, Great Red Spot, & Rings. In *Encyclopædia Britannica*. https://www.britannica.com/place/Jupiter-planet

Toy, R., Bauer, L., Hoimes, C., Ghaghada, K. B., & Karathanasis, E. (2014). Targeted nanotechnology for cancer imaging. *Advanced Drug Delivery Reviews*, *76*, 79–97. https://doi.org/10.1016/j.addr.2014.08.002

Vargas-Mendoza, N. (2014). Hepatoprotective effect of silymarin. *World Journal of Hepatology*, *6*(3), 144. https://doi.org/10.4254/wjh.v6.i3.144

Wakeford, R. (2013). Nuclear worker studies: promise and pitfalls. *British Journal of Cancer*, *110*(1), 1–3. https://doi.org/10.1038/bjc.2013.713

Wang, L., Yang, R., Yuan, B., Liu, Y., & Liu, C. (2015). The antiviral and antimicrobial activities of licorice, a widely-used Chinese herb. *Acta Pharmaceutica Sinica B*, *5*(4), 310–315. https://doi.org/10.1016/j.apsb.2015.05.005

White, T. (2019). Bob Marley | Jamaican Musician. In *Encyclopædia Britannica*. https://www.britannica.com/biography/Bob-Marley

Zhang, H. (2009). Signaling pathways involved in phase II gene induction by □, □-unsaturated aldehydes. *Toxicology and Industrial Health*, *25*(4-5), 269–278. https://doi.org/10.1177/0748233709102209